I THOUGHT
ALL MEOWY
DAYS WOULD
BE JUST LIKE
YESTERDAY...

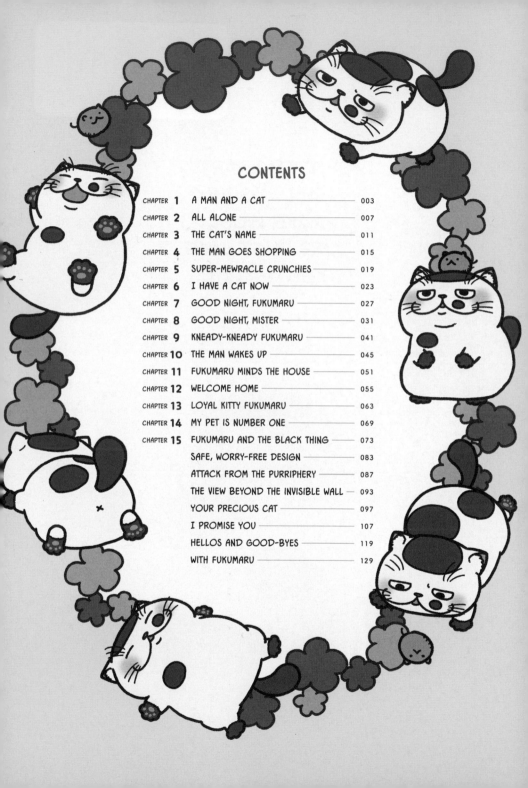

# CONTENTS

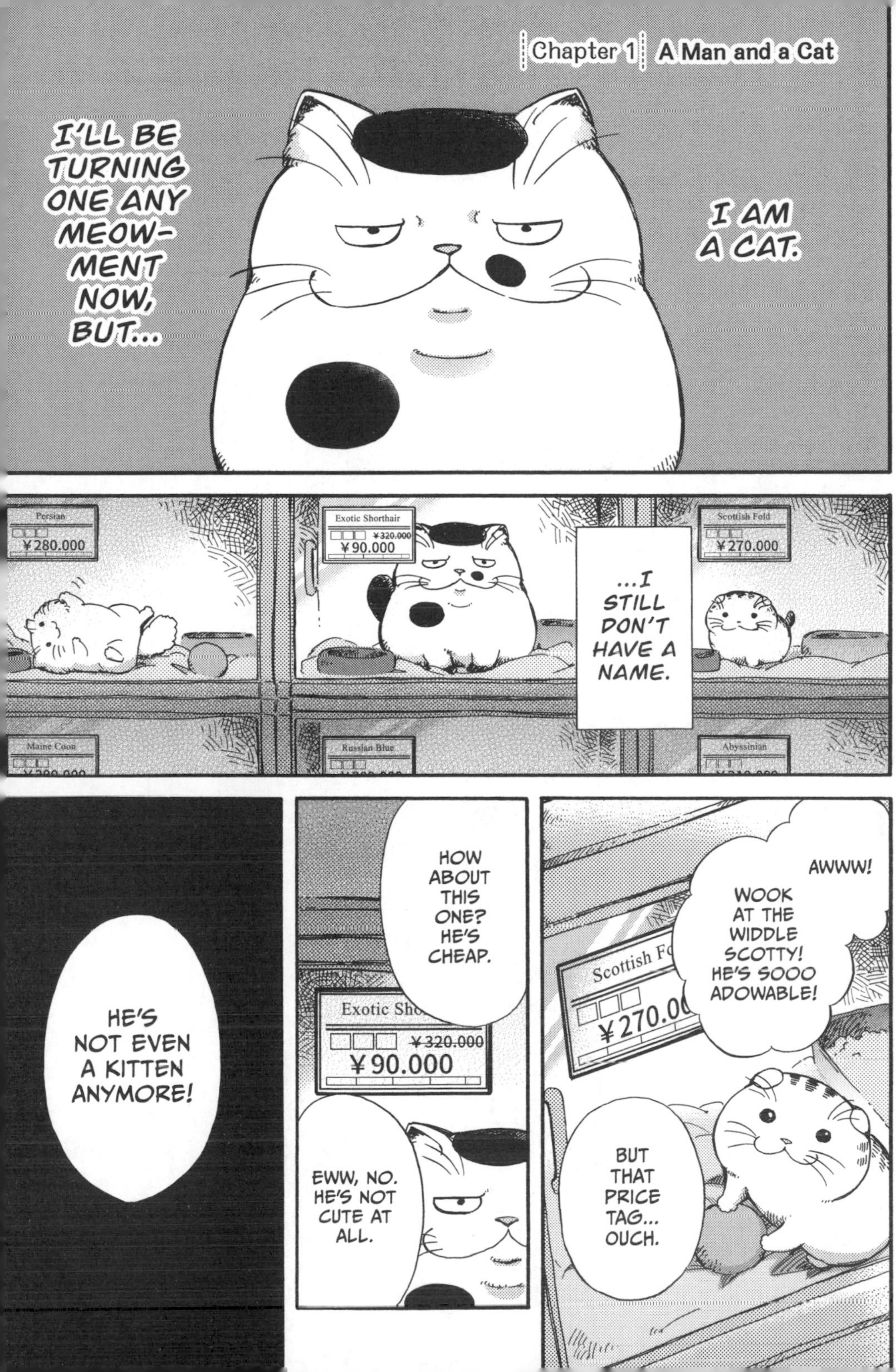
Chapter 1 A Man and a Cat
I AM A CAT.
I'LL BE TURNING ONE ANY MEOW-MENT NOW, BUT...
Scottish Fold
¥270.000
...I STILL DON'T HAVE A NAME.
Exotic Shorthair
¥320.000
¥90.000
Persian
¥280.000
Abyssinian
Russian Blue
Maine Coon
AWWW! WOOK AT THE WIDDLE SCOTTY! HE'S SOOO ADOWABLE!
BUT THAT PRICE TAG... OUCH.
HOW ABOUT THIS ONE? HE'S CHEAP.
EWW, NO. HE'S NOT CUTE AT ALL.
HE'S NOT EVEN A KITTEN ANYMORE!

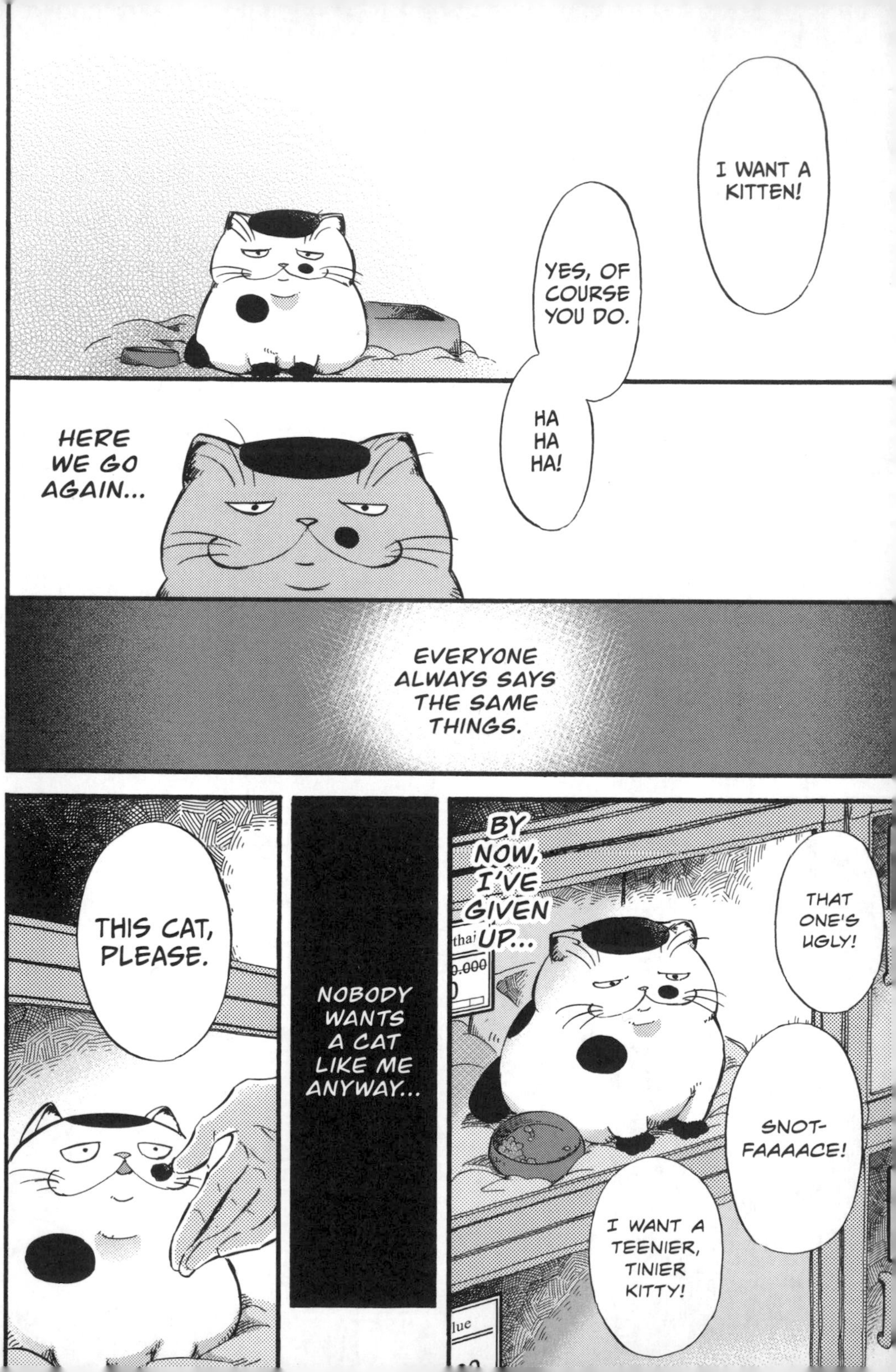
I WANT A KITTEN!
YES, OF COURSE YOU DO.
HA HA HA!
HERE WE GO AGAIN...
EVERYONE ALWAYS SAYS THE SAME THINGS.
THAT ONE'S UGLY!
BY NOW, I'VE GIVEN UP...
SNOT-FAAAACE!
I WANT A TEENIER, TINIER KITTY!
NOBODY WANTS A CAT LIKE ME ANYWAY...
THIS CAT, PLEASE.

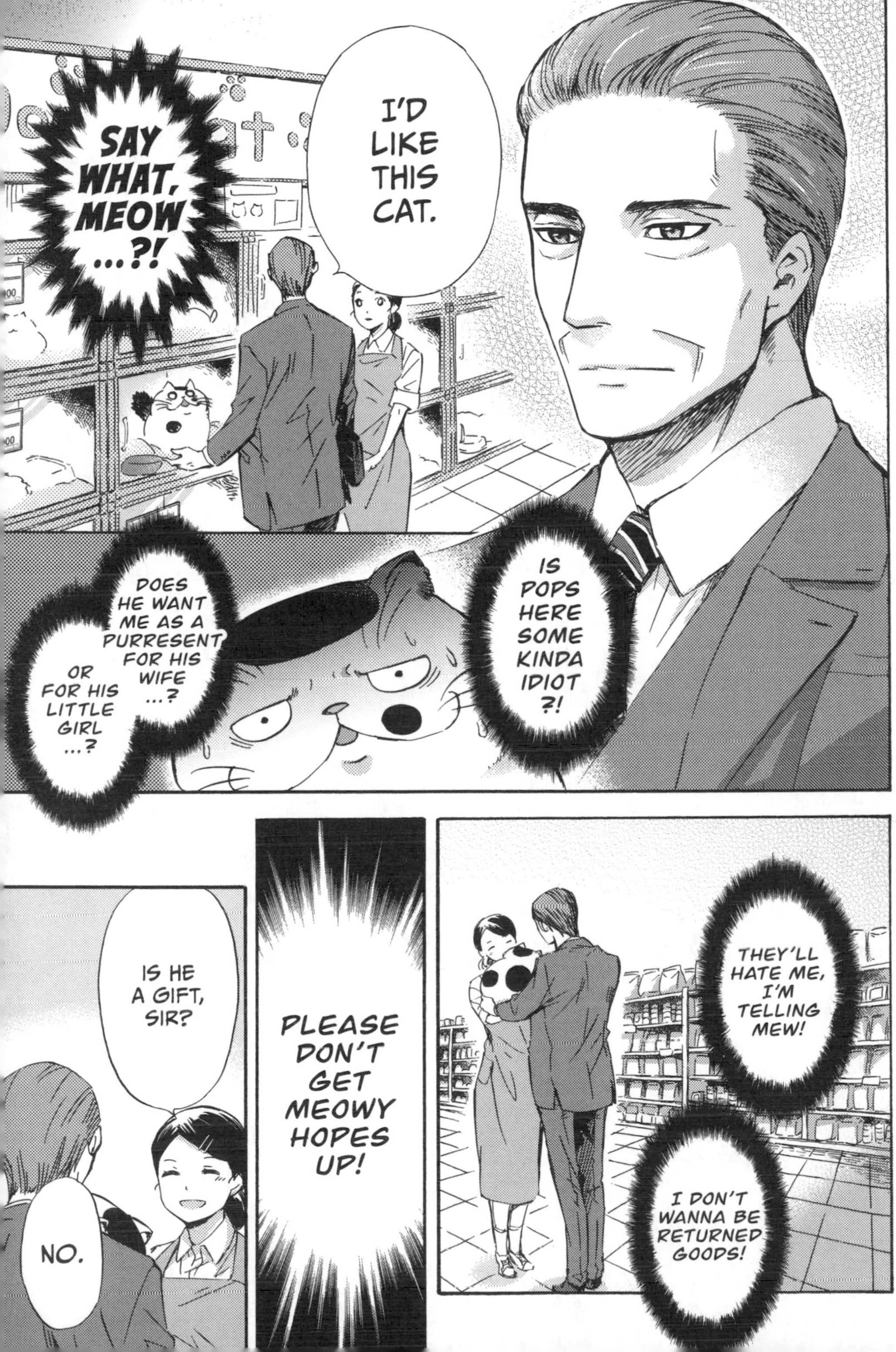
I'D LIKE THIS CAT.
SAY WHAT, MEOW ...?!
IS POPS HERE SOME KINDA IDIOT ?!
DOES HE WANT ME AS A PURRESENT FOR HIS WIFE ...?
OR FOR HIS LITTLE GIRL ...?
THEY'LL HATE ME, I'M TELLING MEW!
I DON'T WANNA BE RETURNED GOODS!
PLEASE DON'T GET MEOWY HOPES UP!
IS HE A GIFT, SIR?
NO.

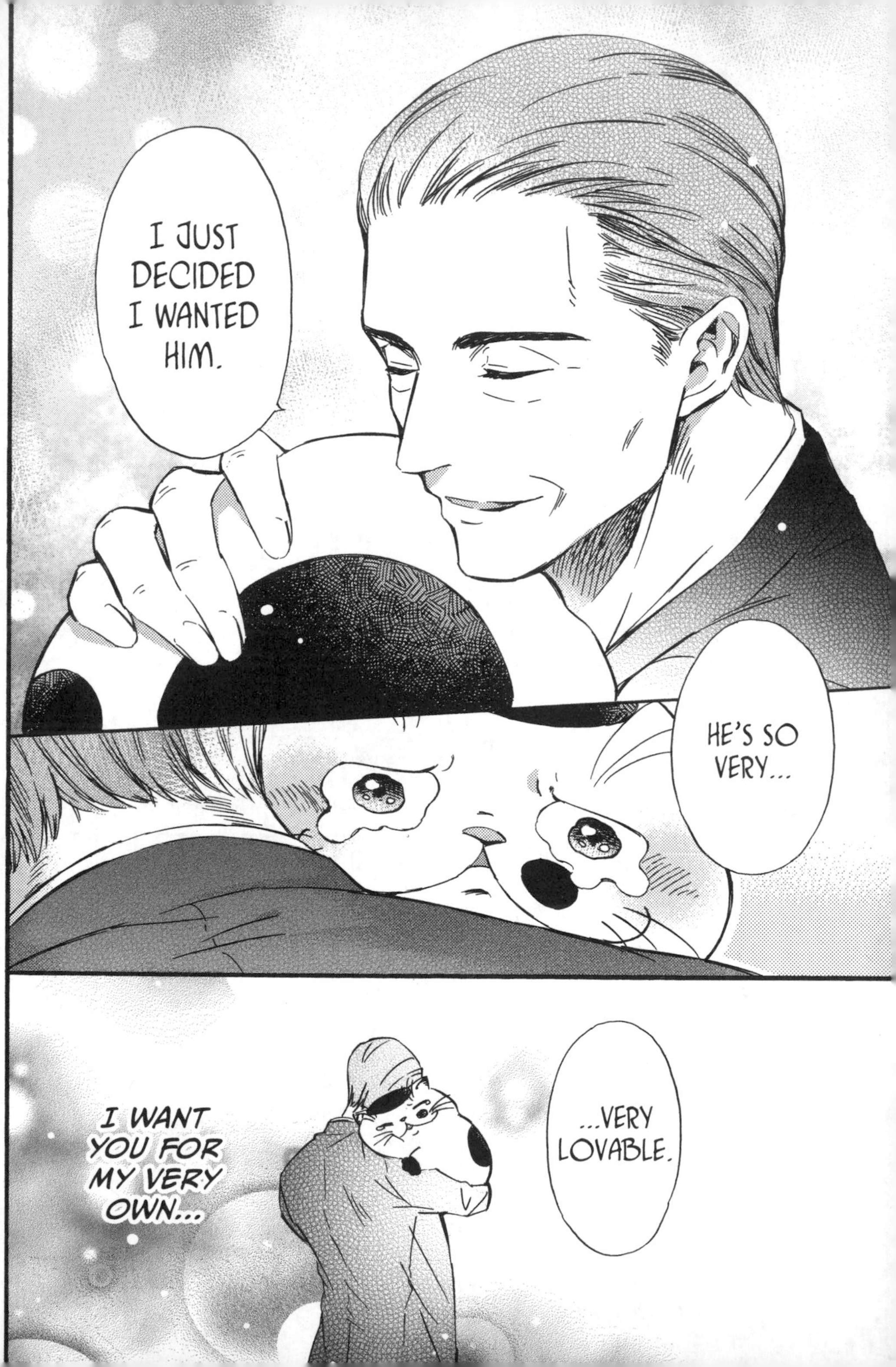
I JUST DECIDED I WANTED HIM.
HE'S SO VERY...
...VERY LOVABLE.
I WANT YOU FOR MY VERY OWN...

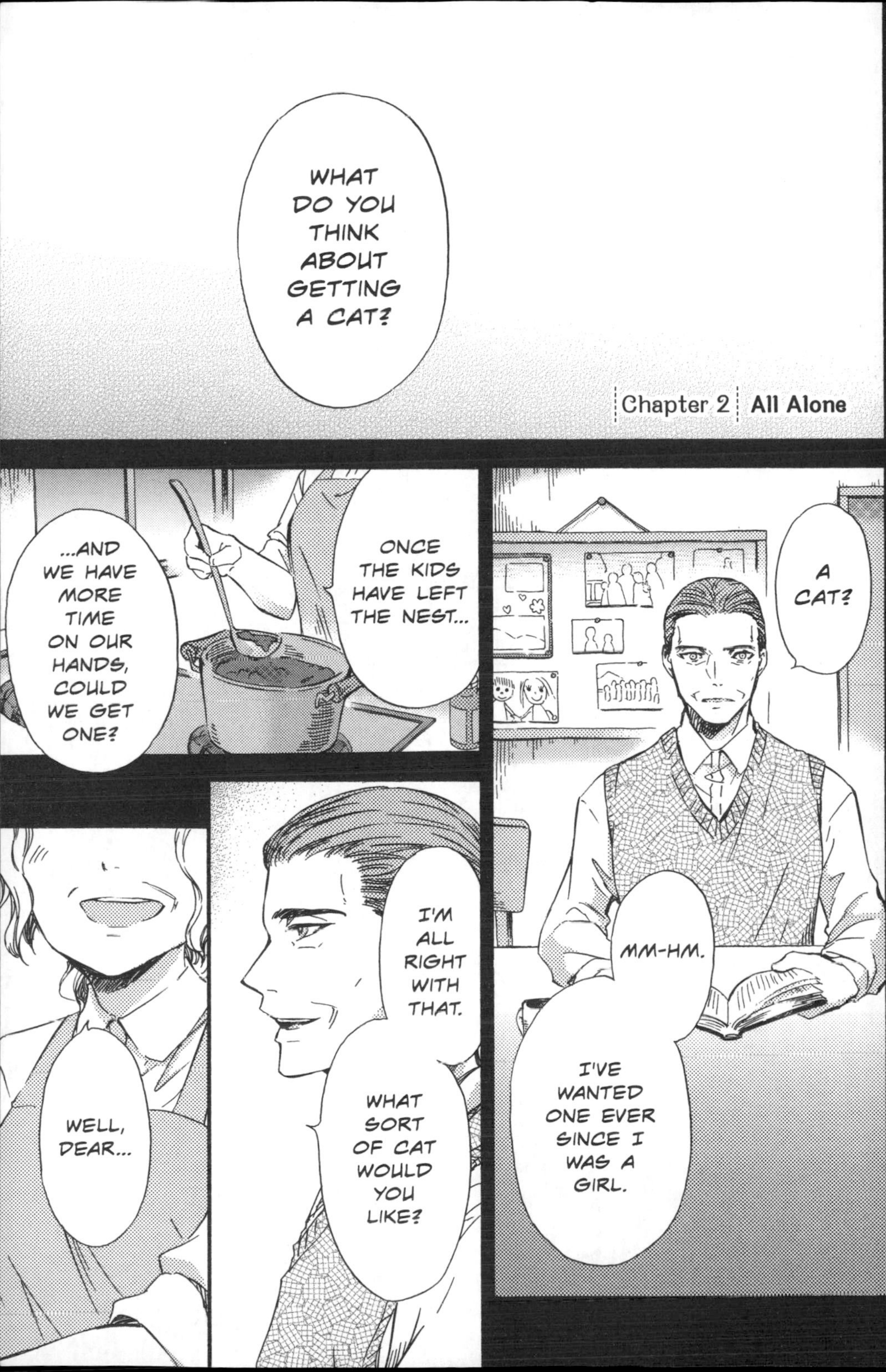
WHAT DO YOU THINK ABOUT GETTING A CAT?
Chapter 2 All Alone
A CAT?
MM-HM.
I'VE WANTED ONE EVER SINCE I WAS A GIRL.
ONCE THE KIDS HAVE LEFT THE NEST...
...AND WE HAVE MORE TIME ON OUR HANDS, COULD WE GET ONE?
I'M ALL RIGHT WITH THAT.
WHAT SORT OF CAT WOULD YOU LIKE?
WELL, DEAR...

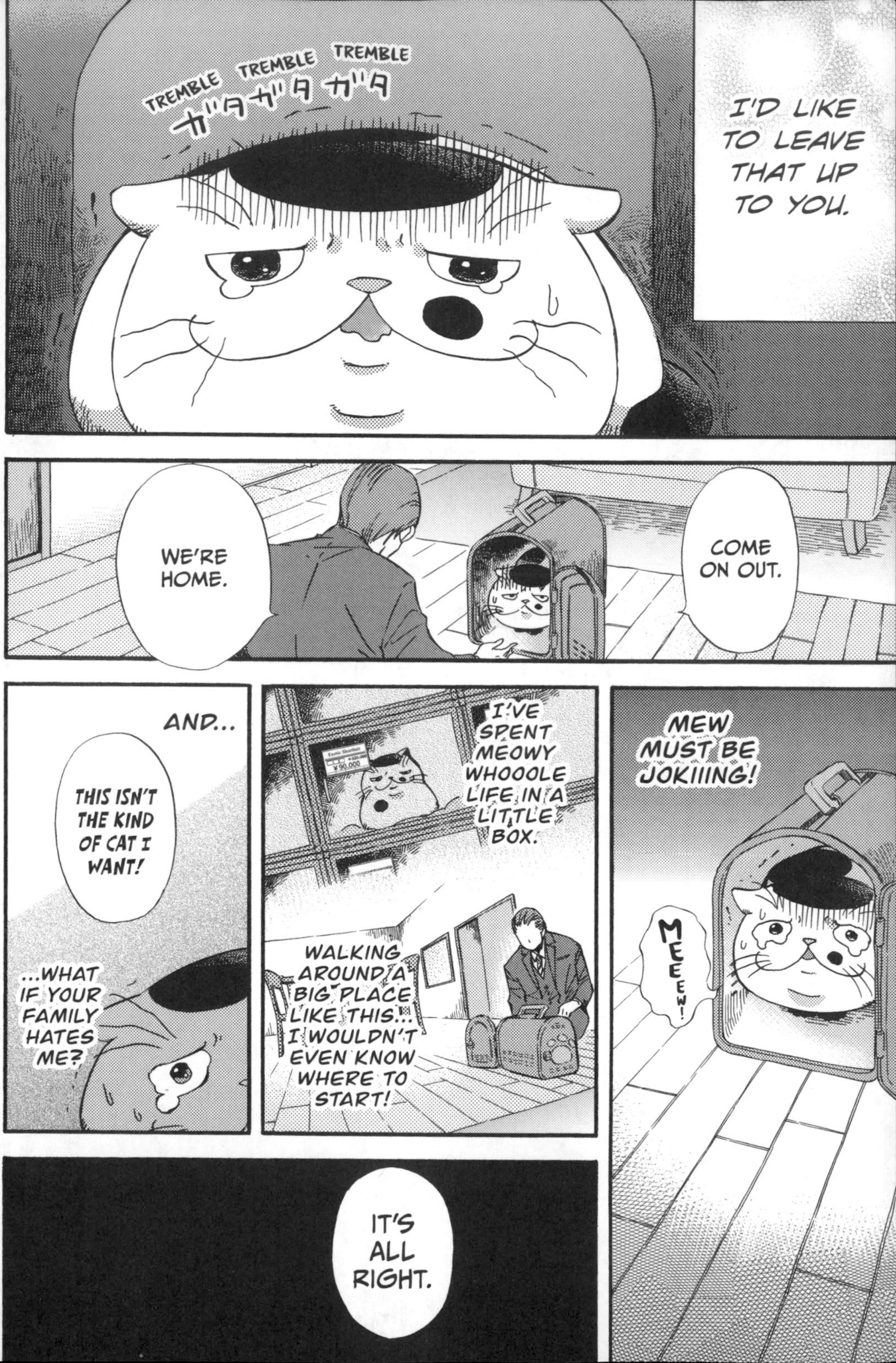
I'D LIKE TO LEAVE THAT UP TO YOU.
TREMBLE TREMBLE TREMBLE TREMBLE
ガタガタ ガタ
WE'RE HOME.
COME ON OUT.
MEW MUST BE JOKIIING!
MEEEEW!
I'VE SPENT MEOWY WHOOOLE LIFE IN A LITTLE BOX.
Exotic Shorthair
¥90,000
WALKING AROUND A BIG PLACE LIKE THIS... I WOULDN'T EVEN KNOW WHERE TO START!
AND...
THIS ISN'T THE KIND OF CAT I WANT!
...WHAT IF YOUR FAMILY HATES ME?
IT'S ALL RIGHT.

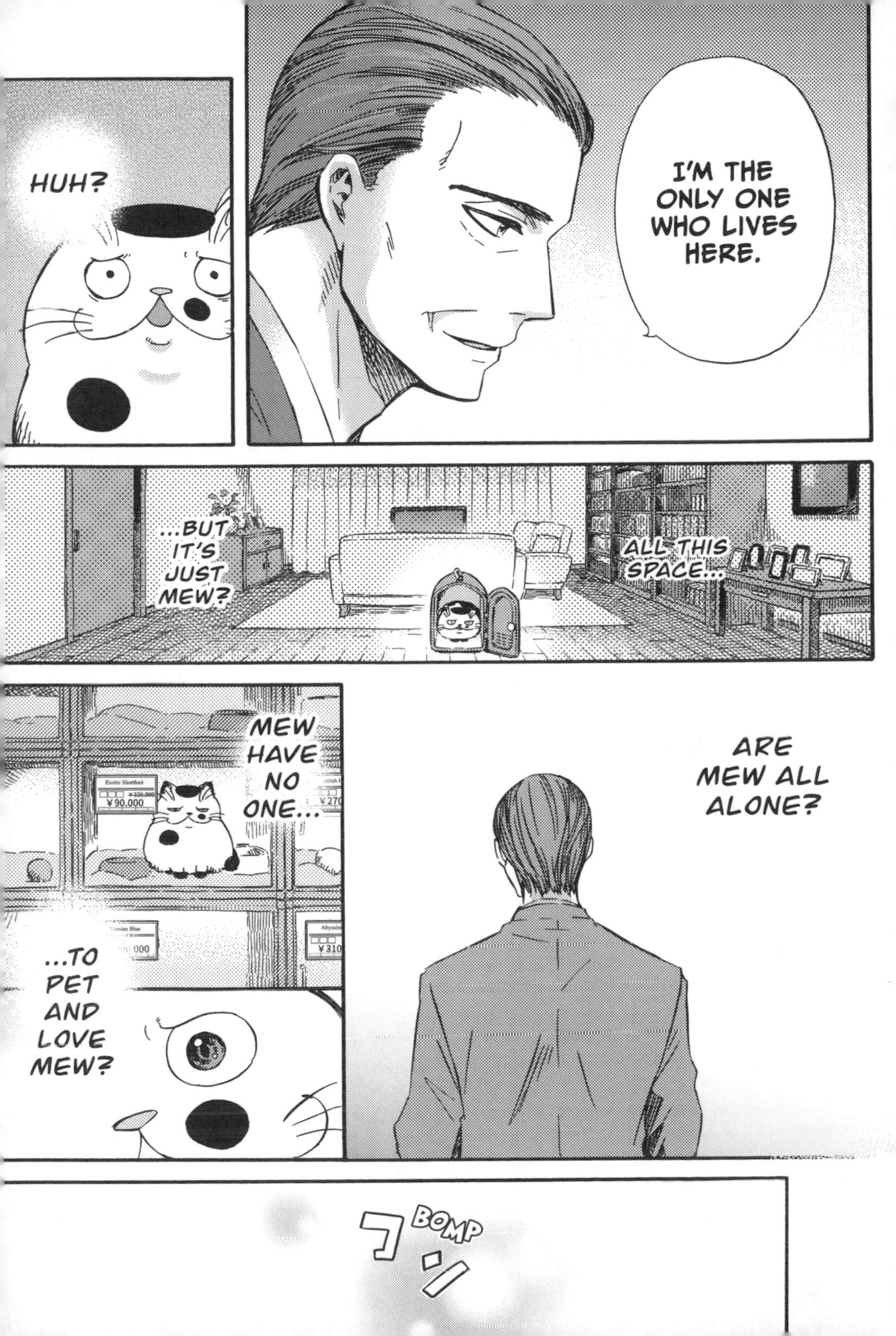
I'M THE ONLY ONE WHO LIVES HERE.
HUH?
ALL THIS SPACE...
...BUT IT'S JUST MEW?
ARE MEW ALL ALONE?
MEW HAVE NO ONE...
Exotic Shorthair
¥90.000
...TO PET AND LOVE MEW?
BOMP

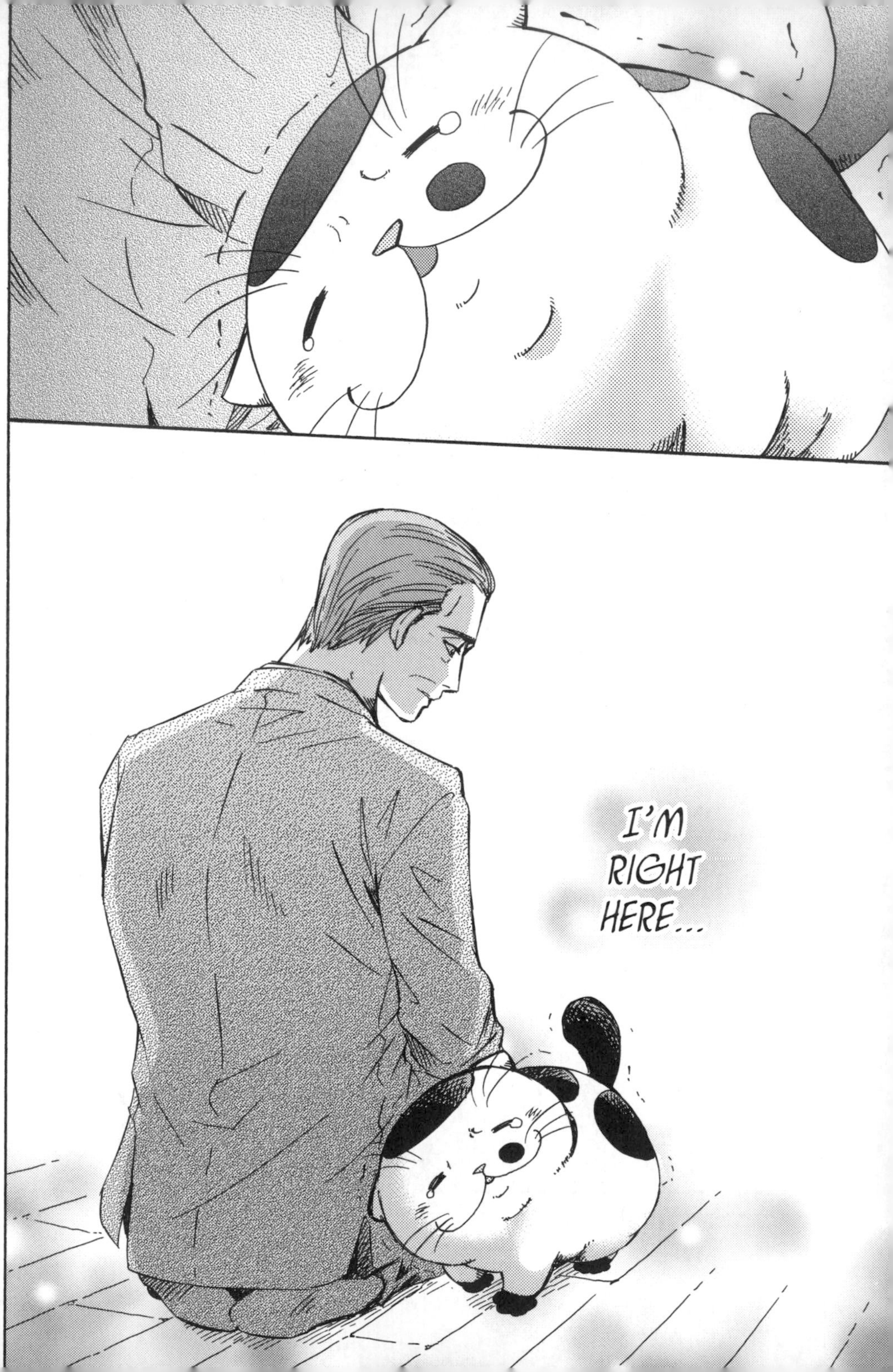
I'M RIGHT HERE...

# Chapter 3 The Cat's Name

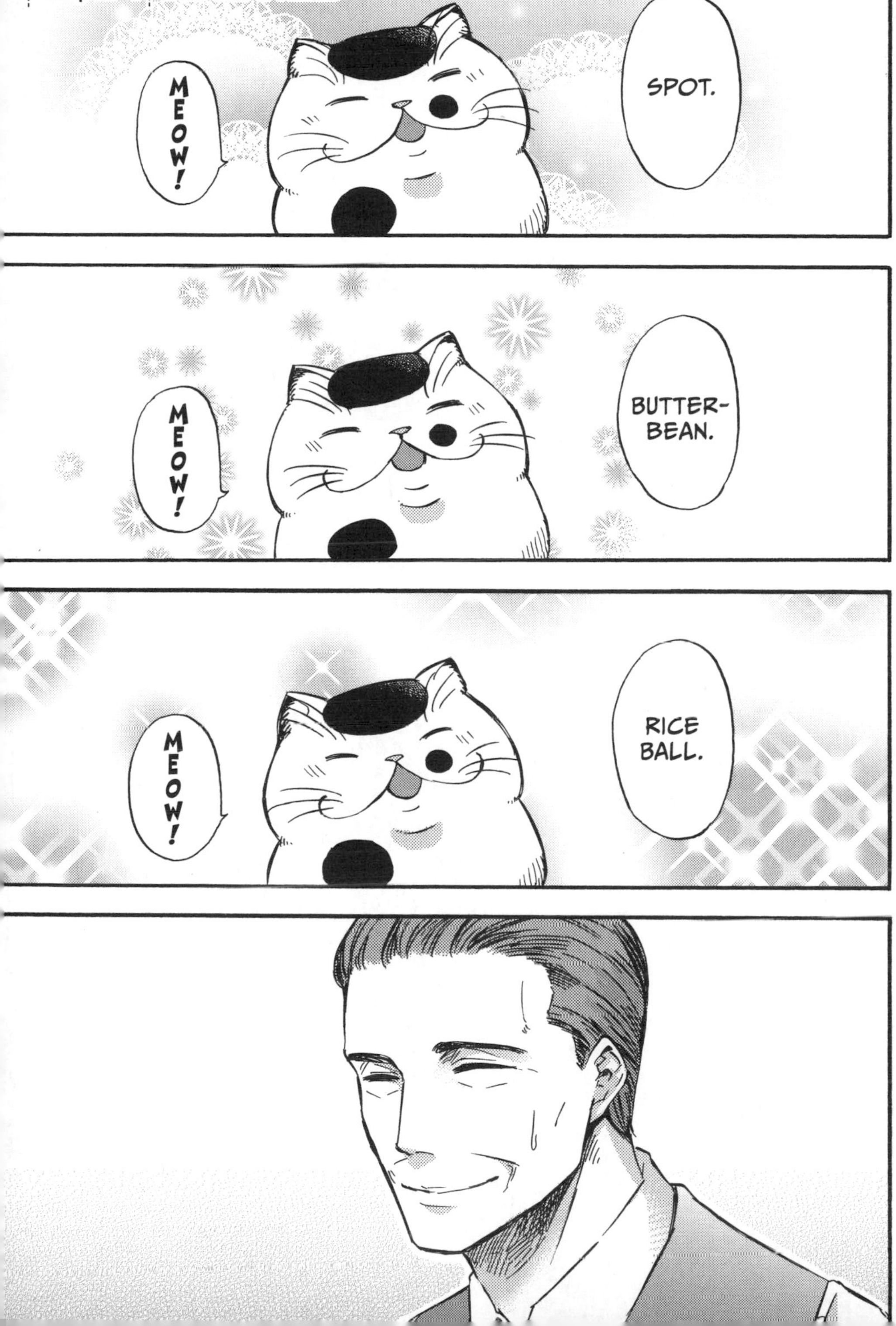
SPOT.
MEOW!
BUTTER-BEAN.
MEOW!
RICE BALL.
MEOW!

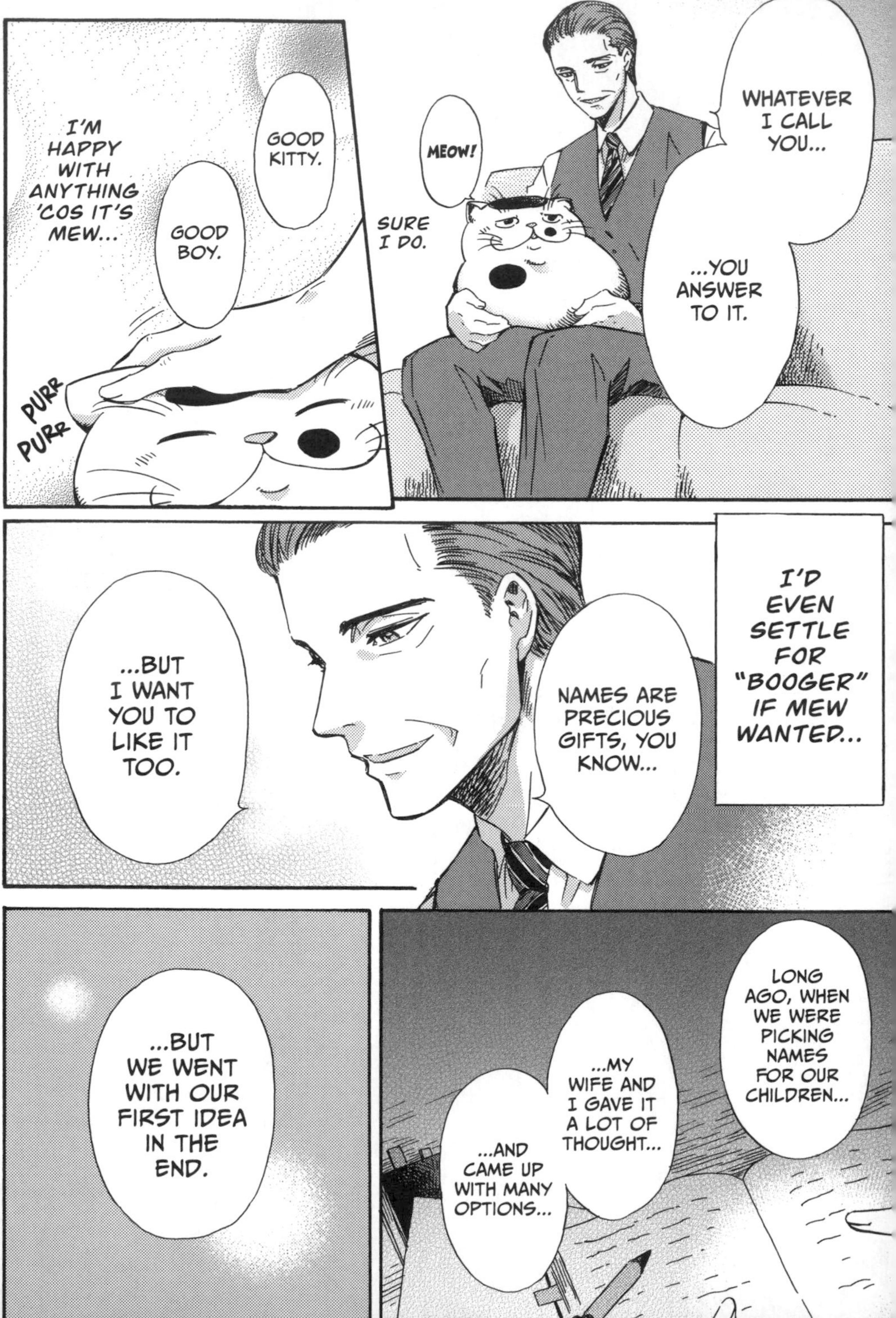
WHATEVER I CALL YOU...
...YOU ANSWER TO IT.
MEOW!
SURE I DO.
GOOD KITTY.
GOOD BOY.
I'M HAPPY WITH ANYTHING 'COS IT'S MEW...
PURR PURR
I'D EVEN SETTLE FOR "BOOGER" IF MEW WANTED...
NAMES ARE PRECIOUS GIFTS, YOU KNOW...
...BUT I WANT YOU TO LIKE IT TOO.
LONG AGO, WHEN WE WERE PICKING NAMES FOR OUR CHILDREN...
...MY WIFE AND I GAVE IT A LOT OF THOUGHT...
...AND CAME UP WITH MANY OPTIONS...
...BUT WE WENT WITH OUR FIRST IDEA IN THE END.

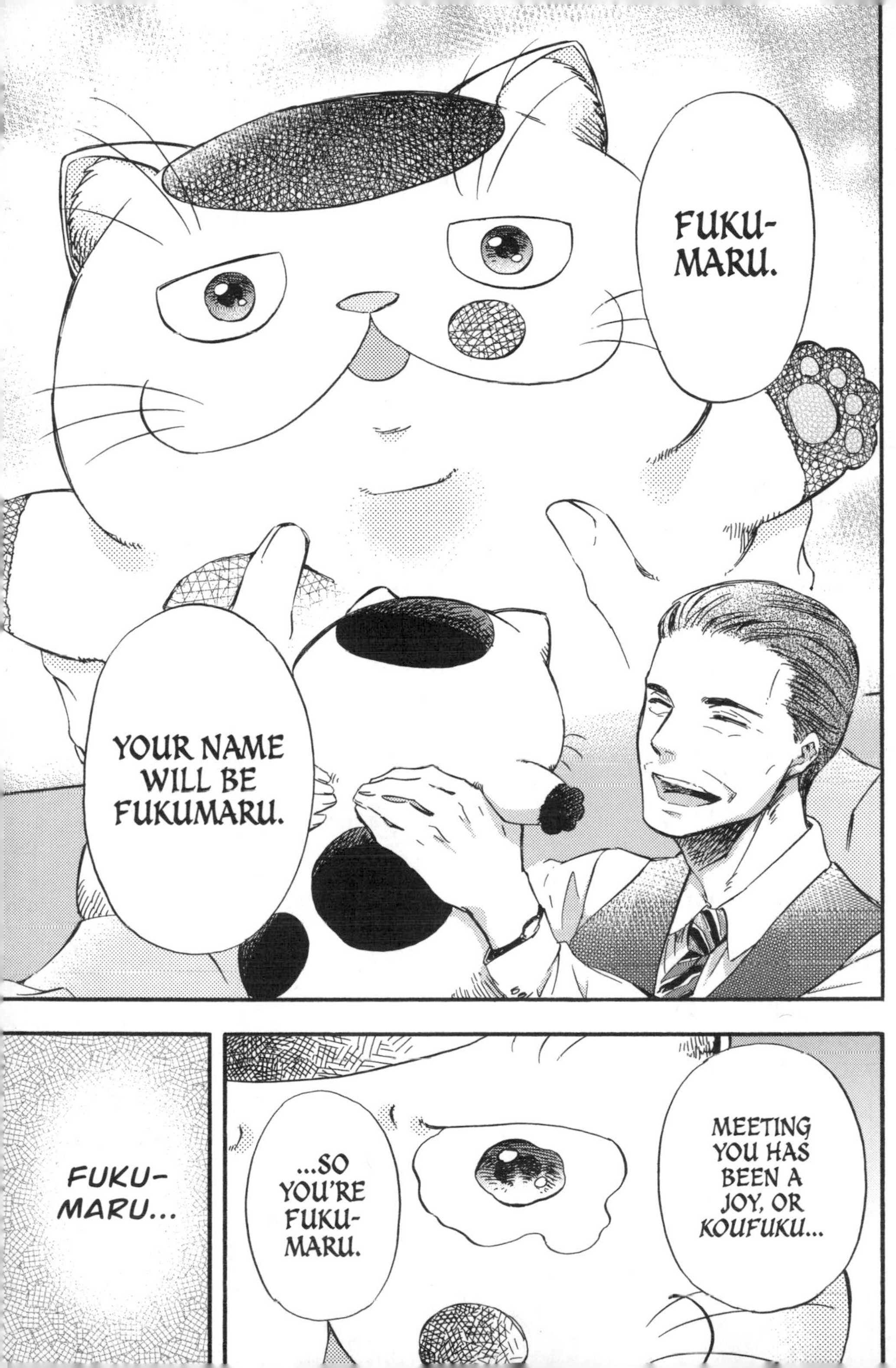
FUKU-MARU.
YOUR NAME WILL BE FUKUMARU.
MEETING YOU HAS BEEN A JOY, OR KOUFUKU...
...SO YOU'RE FUKU-MARU.
FUKU-MARU...

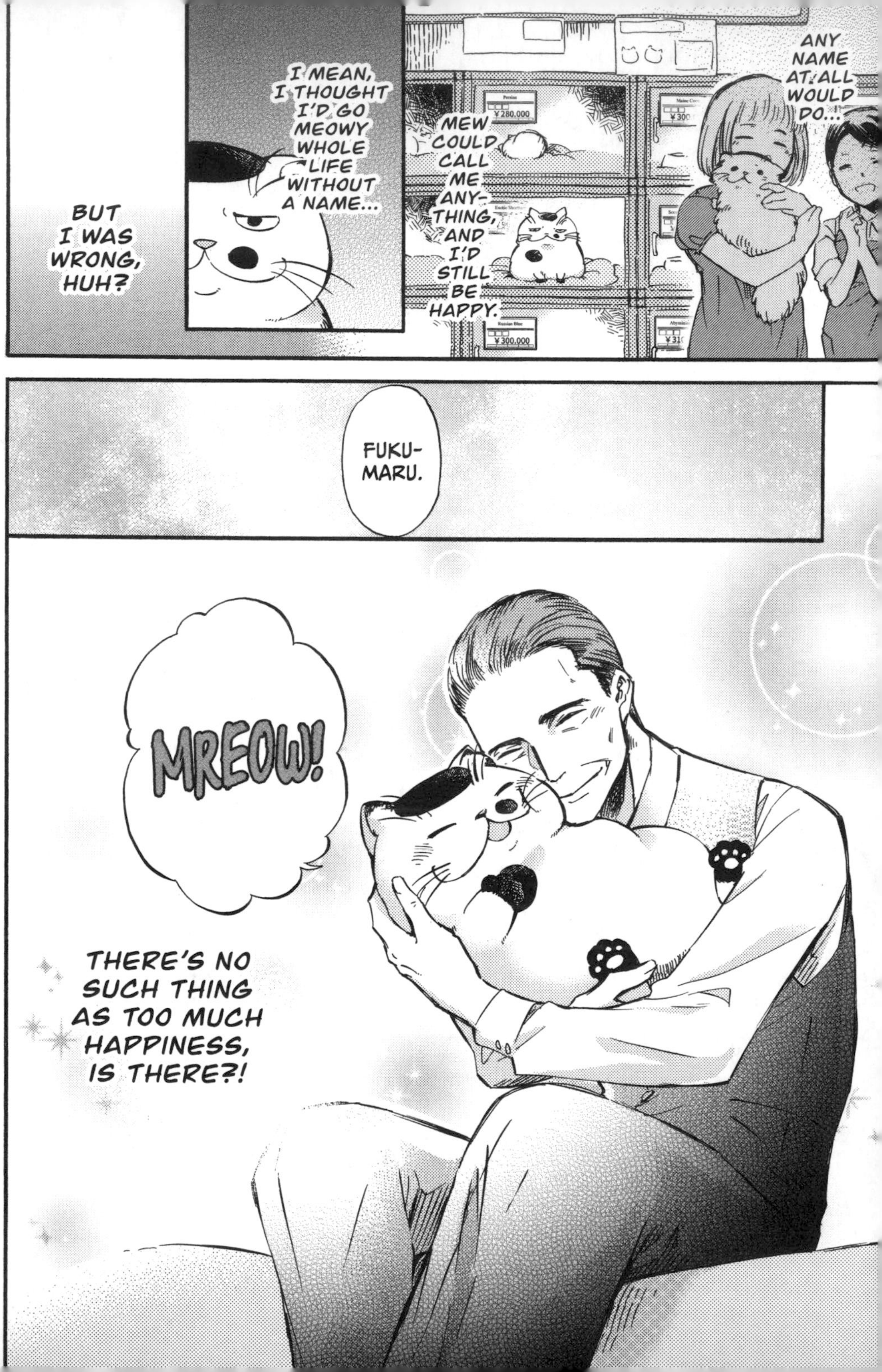
ANY NAME AT ALL WOULD DO...
MEW COULD CALL ME ANYTHING, AND I'D STILL BE HAPPY.
I MEAN, I THOUGHT I'D GO MEOWY WHOLE LIFE WITHOUT A NAME...
BUT I WAS WRONG, HUH?
FUKU-MARU.
MREOW!
THERE'S NO SUCH THING AS TOO MUCH HAPPINESS, IS THERE?!

Chapter 4 The Man Goes Shopping

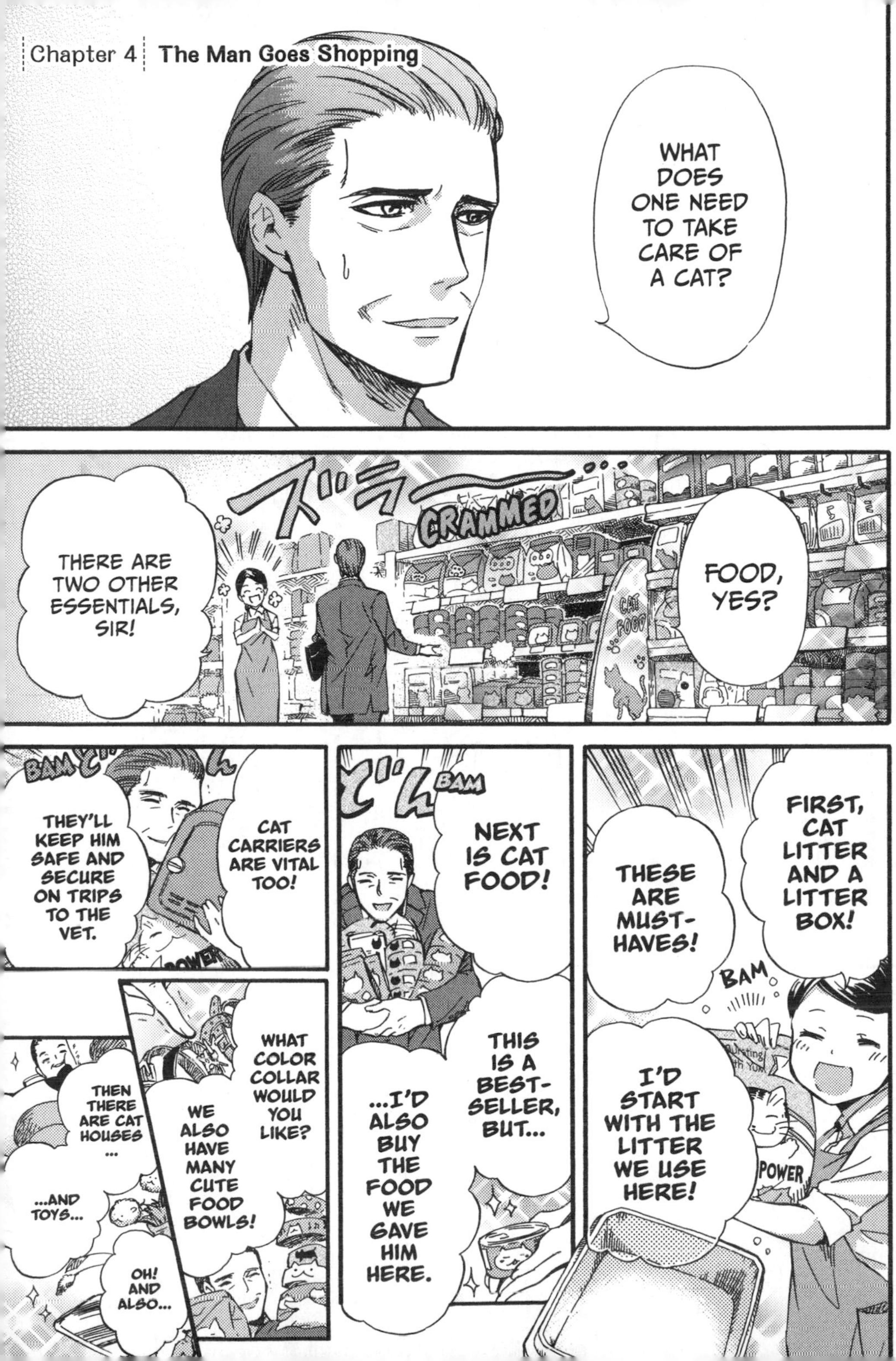
WHAT DOES ONE NEED TO TAKE CARE OF A CAT?
FOOD, YES?
CRAMMED
THERE ARE TWO OTHER ESSENTIALS, SIR!
FIRST, CAT LITTER AND A LITTER BOX!
THESE ARE MUST-HAVES!
BAM
I'D START WITH THE LITTER WE USE HERE!
POWER
BAM
NEXT IS CAT FOOD!
THIS IS A BEST-SELLER, BUT...
...I'D ALSO BUY THE FOOD WE GAVE HIM HERE.
BAM
CAT CARRIERS ARE VITAL TOO!
THEY'LL KEEP HIM SAFE AND SECURE ON TRIPS TO THE VET.
POWER
WHAT COLOR COLLAR WOULD YOU LIKE?
WE ALSO HAVE MANY CUTE FOOD BOWLS!
THEN THERE ARE CAT HOUSES ...
...AND TOYS...
OH! AND ALSO...

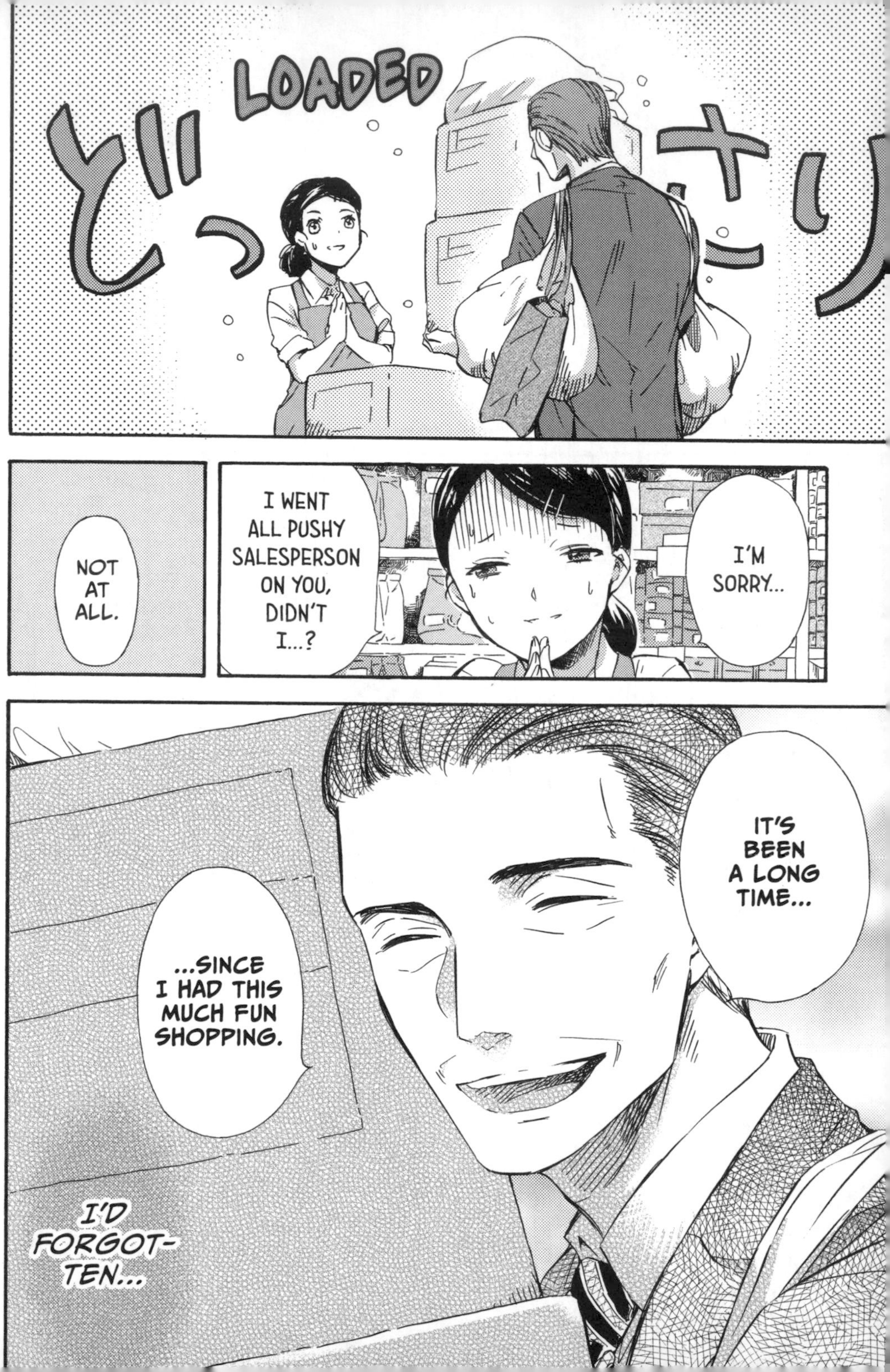
どっさり
LOADED
I'M SORRY...
I WENT ALL PUSHY SALESPERSON ON YOU, DIDN'T I...?
NOT AT ALL.
IT'S BEEN A LONG TIME...
...SINCE I HAD THIS MUCH FUN SHOPPING.
I'D FORGOT-TEN...

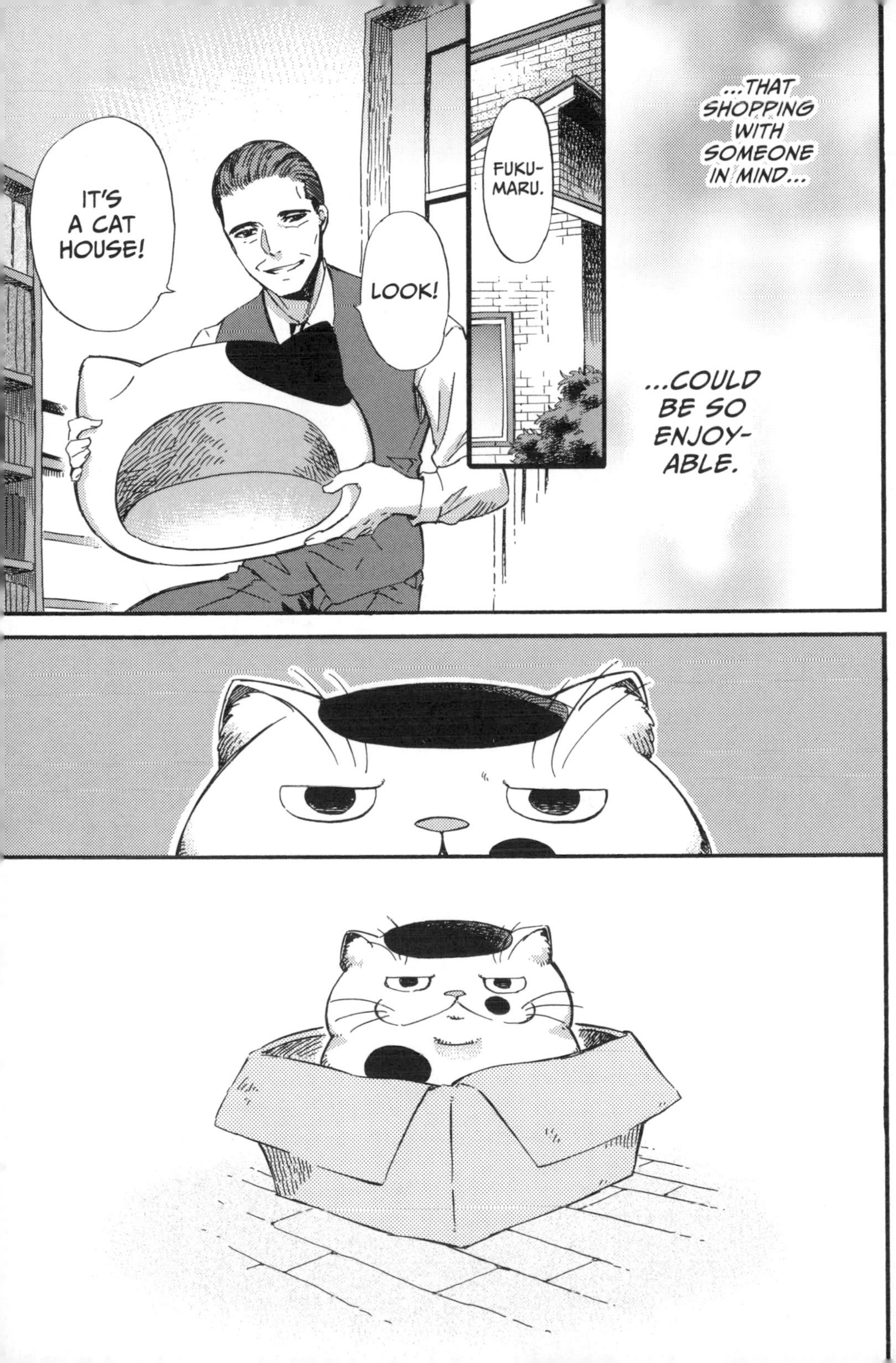

...THAT SHOPPING WITH SOMEONE IN MIND...
...COULD BE SO ENJOY-ABLE.
FUKU-MARU.
LOOK!
IT'S A CAT HOUSE!

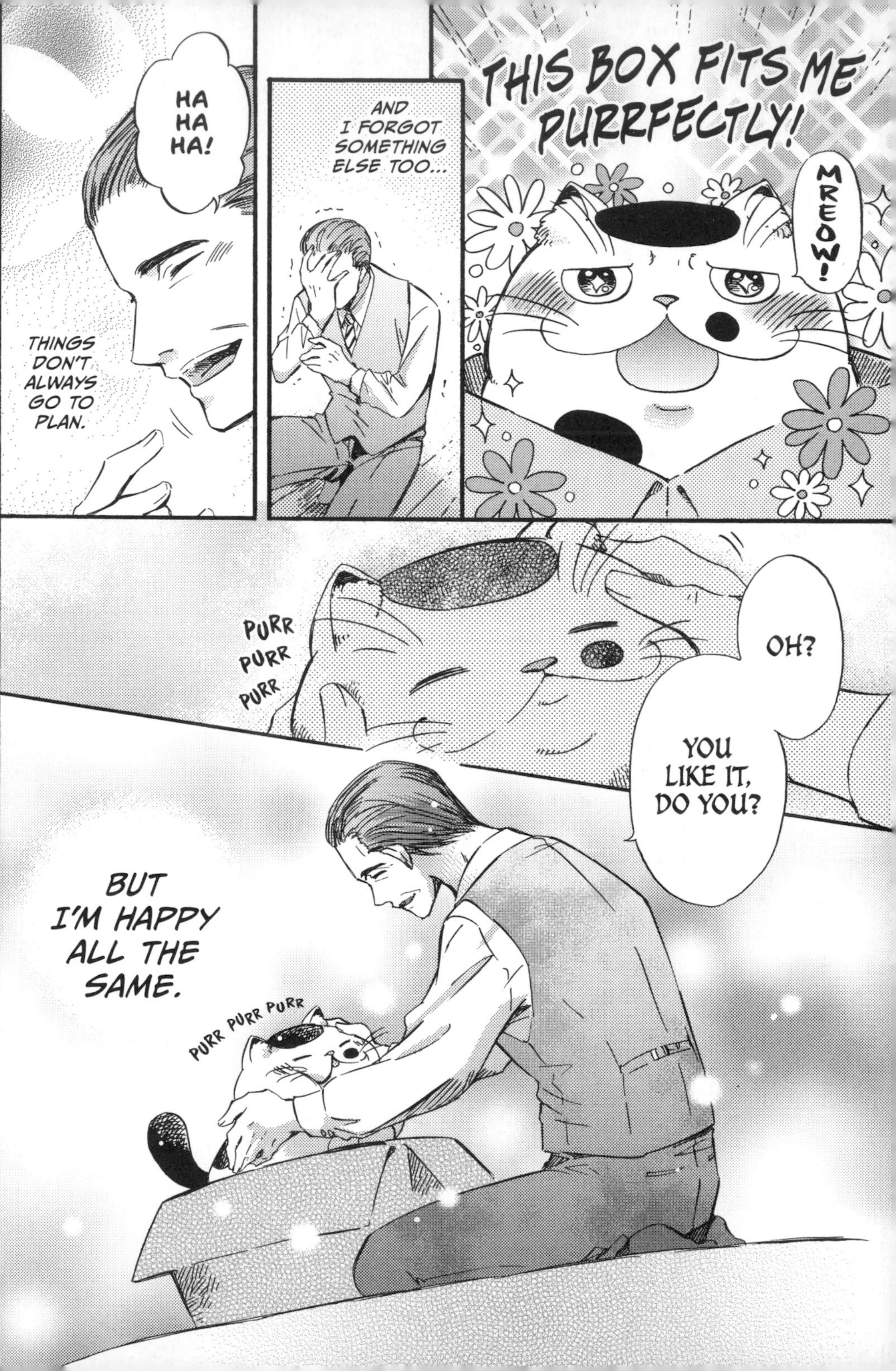
THIS BOX FITS ME PURRFECTLY!
MREOW!
AND I FORGOT SOMETHING ELSE TOO...
HA HA HA!
THINGS DON'T ALWAYS GO TO PLAN.
OH?
PURR PURR PURR
YOU LIKE IT, DO YOU?
BUT I'M HAPPY ALL THE SAME.
PURR PURR PURR

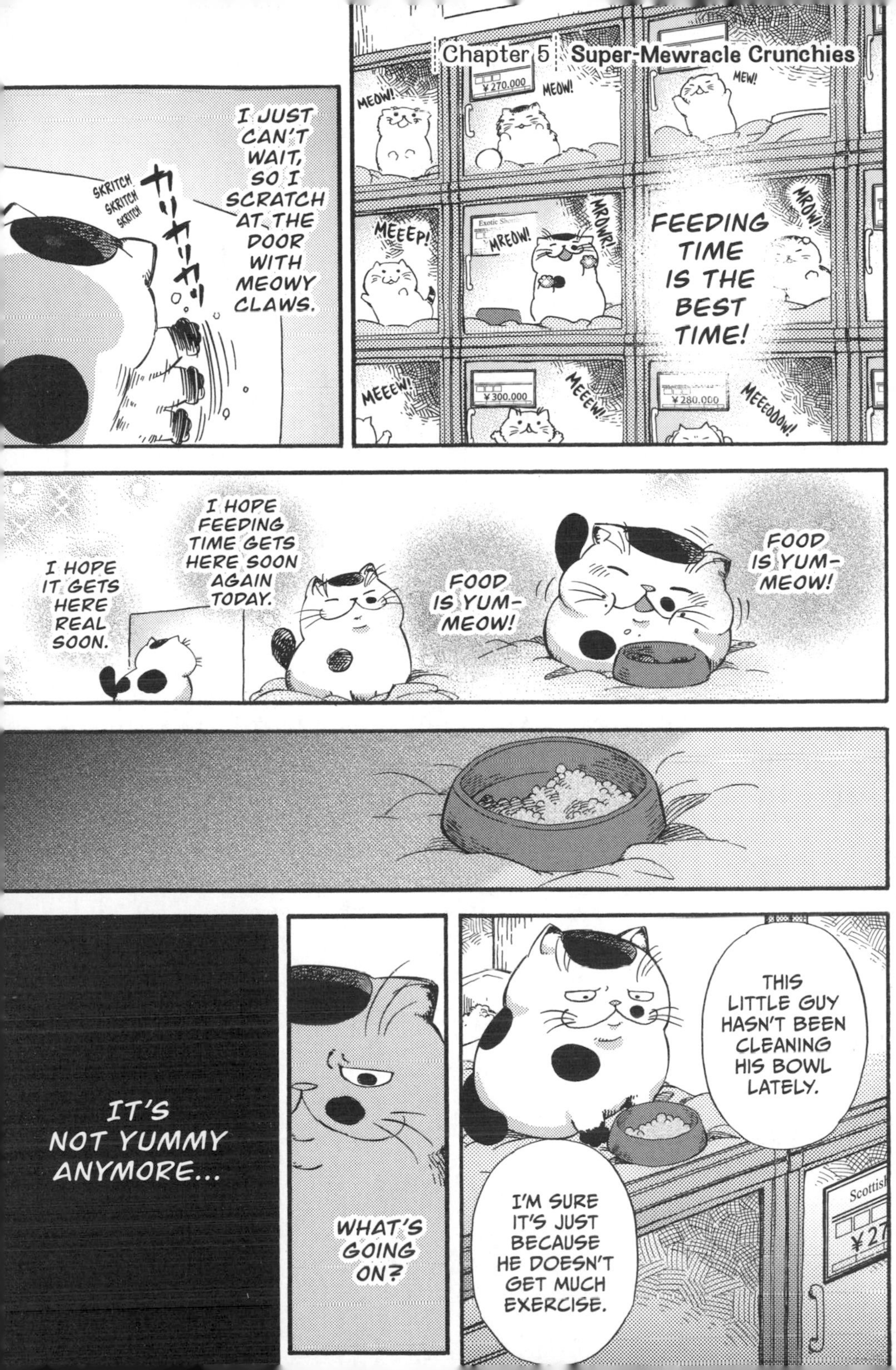
Chapter 5 Super-Mewracle Crunchies
MEW!
MEOW!
¥270,000
MEOW!
MROW!
FEEDING TIME IS THE BEST TIME!
MROWR!
MREOW!
MEEEP!
MEEEOOW!
¥280,000
MEEEW!
¥300,000
MEEEW!
I JUST CAN'T WAIT, SO I SCRATCH AT THE DOOR WITH MEOWY CLAWS.
SKRITCH SKRITCH SKRITCH
FOOD IS YUM-MEOW!
FOOD IS YUM-MEOW!
I HOPE FEEDING TIME GETS HERE SOON AGAIN TODAY.
I HOPE IT GETS HERE REAL SOON.
THIS LITTLE GUY HASN'T BEEN CLEANING HIS BOWL LATELY.
I'M SURE IT'S JUST BECAUSE HE DOESN'T GET MUCH EXERCISE.
WHAT'S GOING ON?
IT'S NOT YUMMY ANYMORE...

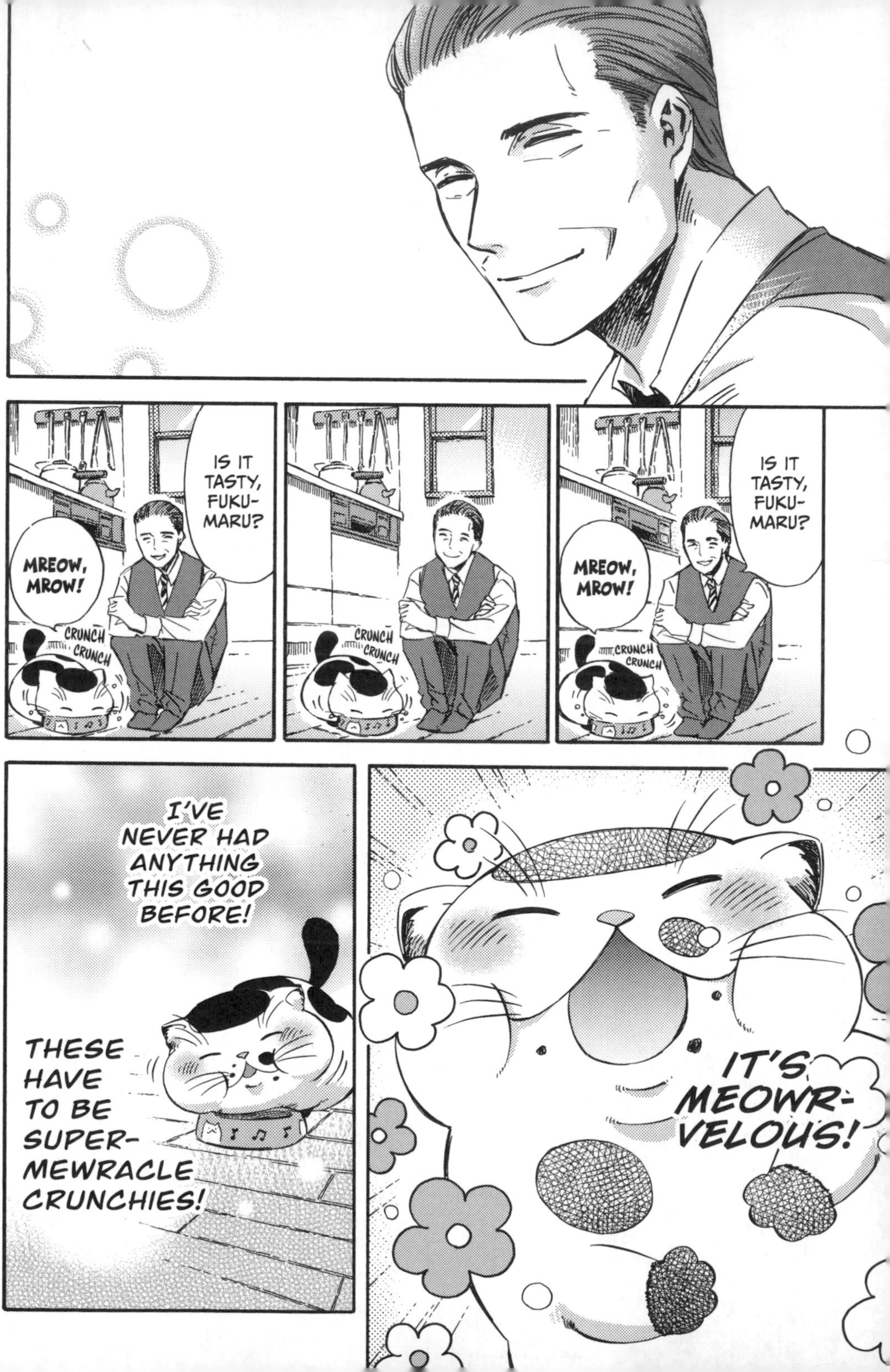
IS IT TASTY, FUKU-MARU?
MREOW, MROW!
CRUNCH CRUNCH
CRUNCH CRUNCH
IS IT TASTY, FUKU-MARU?
MREOW, MROW!
CRUNCH CRUNCH
IT'S MEOWR-VELOUS!
I'VE NEVER HAD ANYTHING THIS GOOD BEFORE!
THESE HAVE TO BE SUPER-MEWRACLE CRUNCHIES!

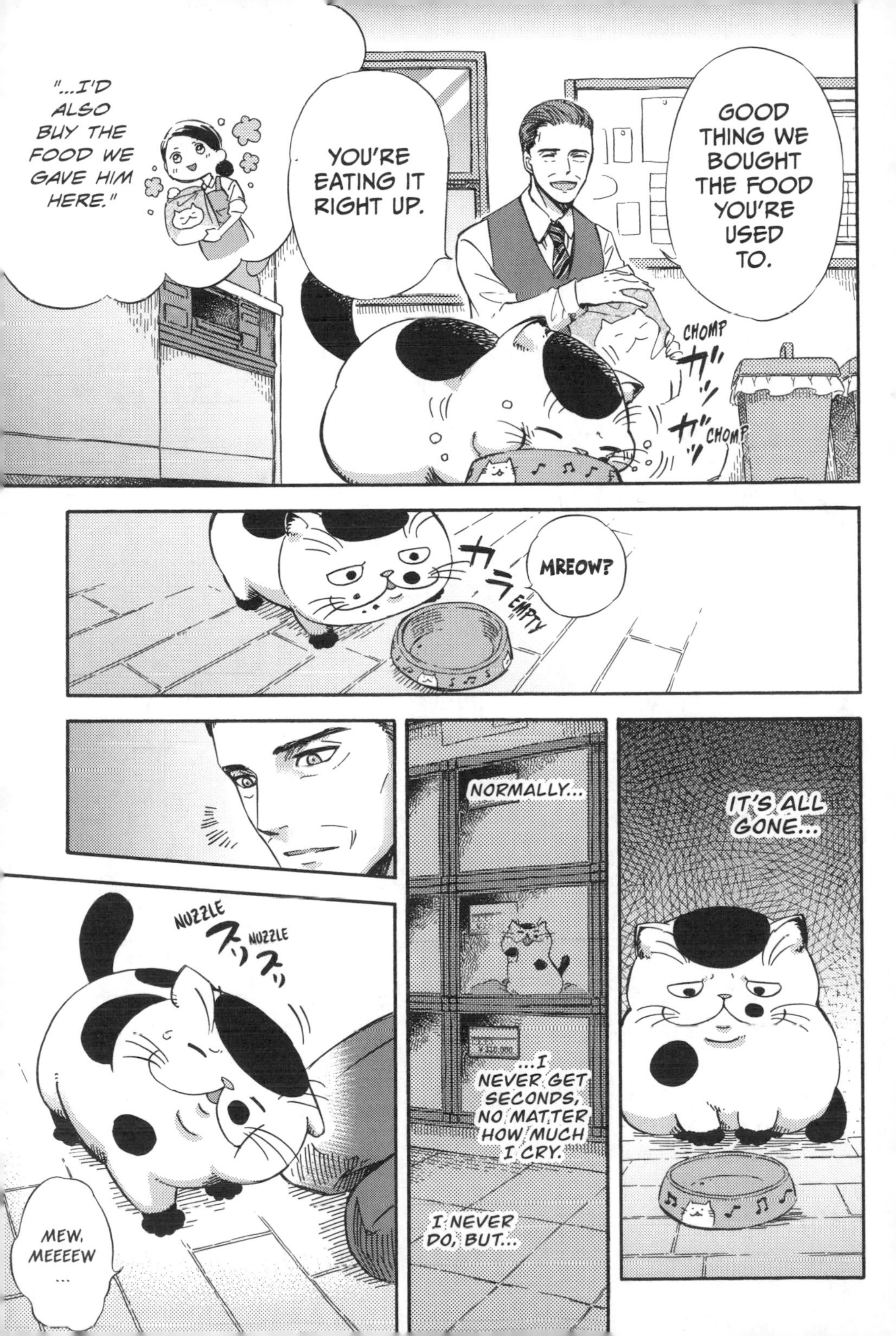
GOOD THING WE BOUGHT THE FOOD YOU'RE USED TO.
YOU'RE EATING IT RIGHT UP.
"...I'D ALSO BUY THE FOOD WE GAVE HIM HERE."
CHOMP
CHOMP
EMPTY
MREOW?
IT'S ALL GONE...
NORMALLY...
...I NEVER GET SECONDS, NO MATTER HOW MUCH I CRY.
I NEVER DO, BUT...
NUZZLE
NUZZLE
MEW, MEEEEW...

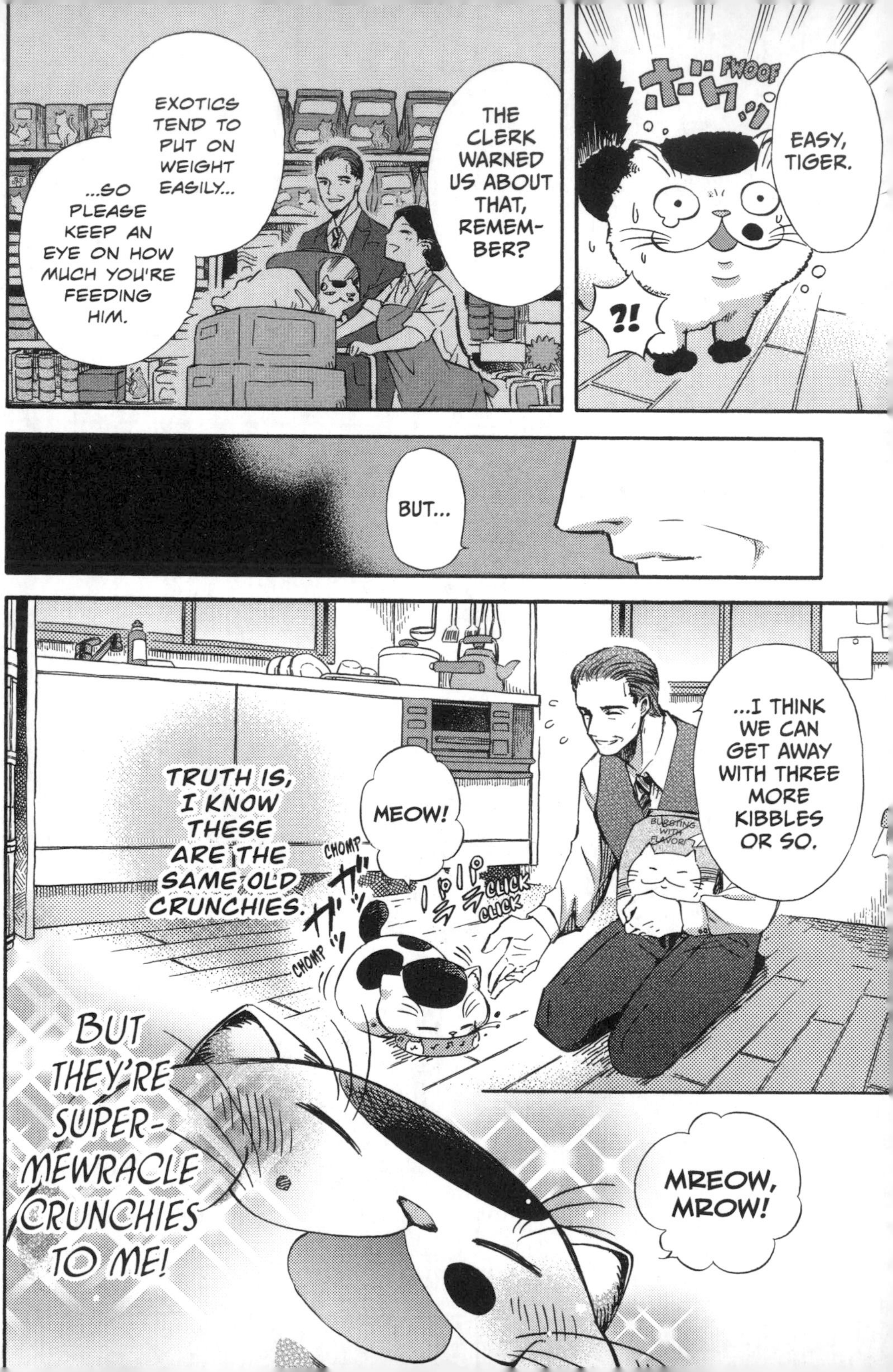
FWOOF
EASY, TIGER.
?!
THE CLERK WARNED US ABOUT THAT, REMEMBER?
EXOTICS TEND TO PUT ON WEIGHT EASILY...
...SO PLEASE KEEP AN EYE ON HOW MUCH YOU'RE FEEDING HIM.
BUT...
...I THINK WE CAN GET AWAY WITH THREE MORE KIBBLES OR SO.
BURSTING WITH FLAVOR!
MEOW!
CLICK CLICK
CHOMP
TRUTH IS, I KNOW THESE ARE THE SAME OLD CRUNCHIES.
CHOMP
MREOW, MROW!
BUT THEY'RE SUPER-MEWRACLE CRUNCHIES TO ME!

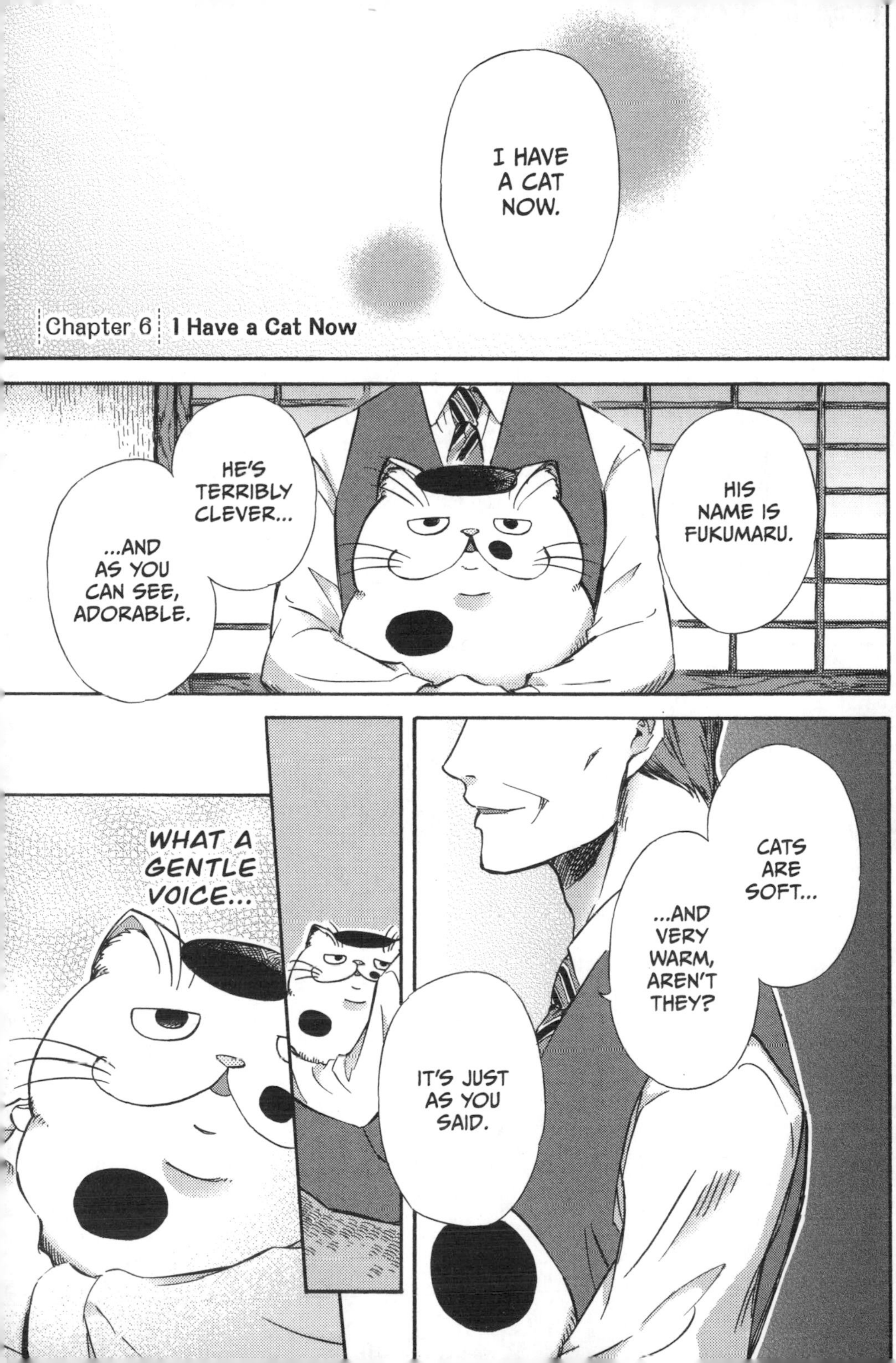
I HAVE A CAT NOW.
Chapter 6 I Have a Cat Now
HIS NAME IS FUKUMARU.
HE'S TERRIBLY CLEVER...
...AND AS YOU CAN SEE, ADORABLE.
CATS ARE SOFT...
...AND VERY WARM, AREN'T THEY?
IT'S JUST AS YOU SAID.
WHAT A GENTLE VOICE...

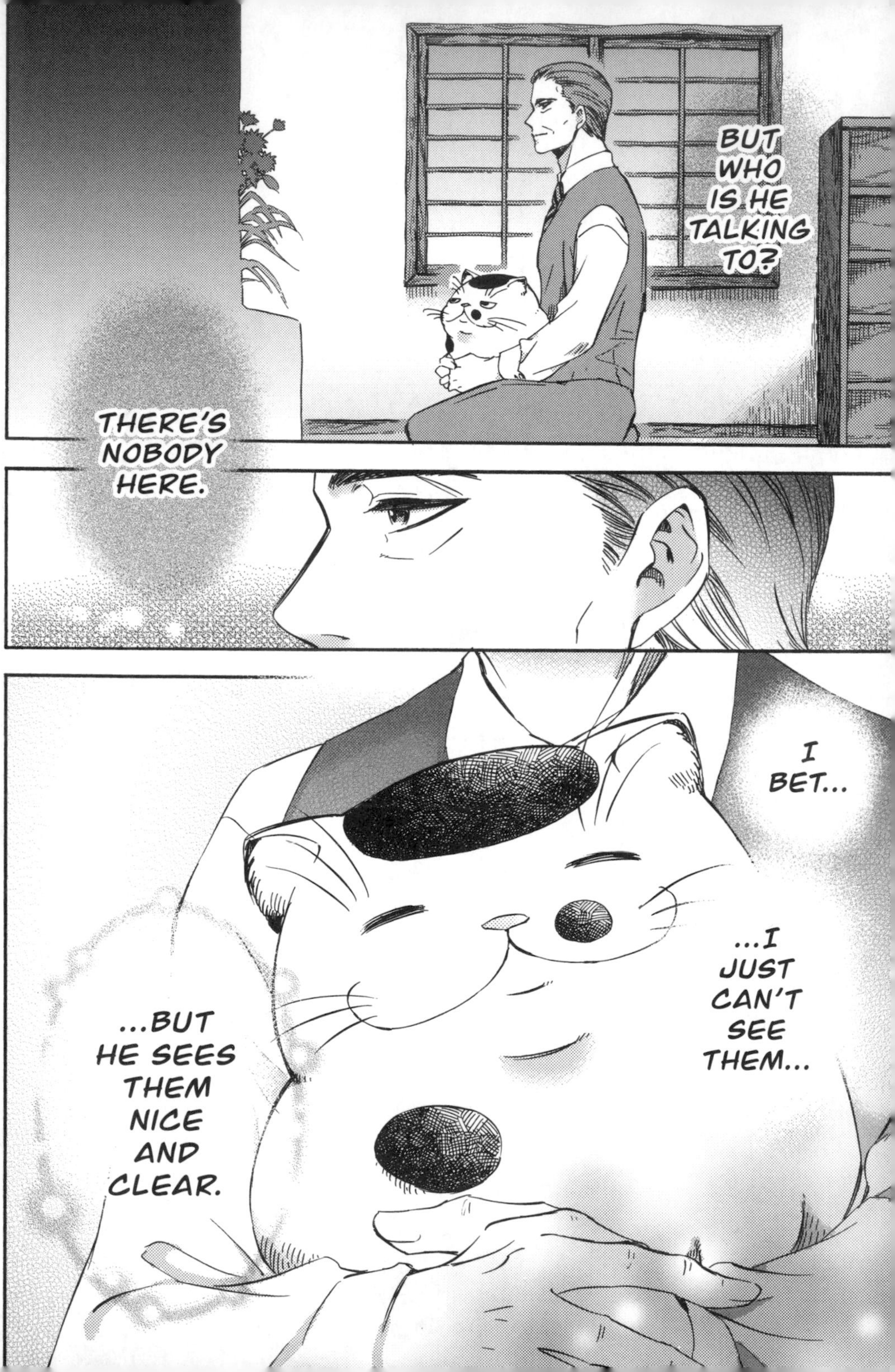
BUT WHO IS HE TALKING TO?
THERE'S NOBODY HERE.
I BET...
...I JUST CAN'T SEE THEM...
...BUT HE SEES THEM NICE AND CLEAR.

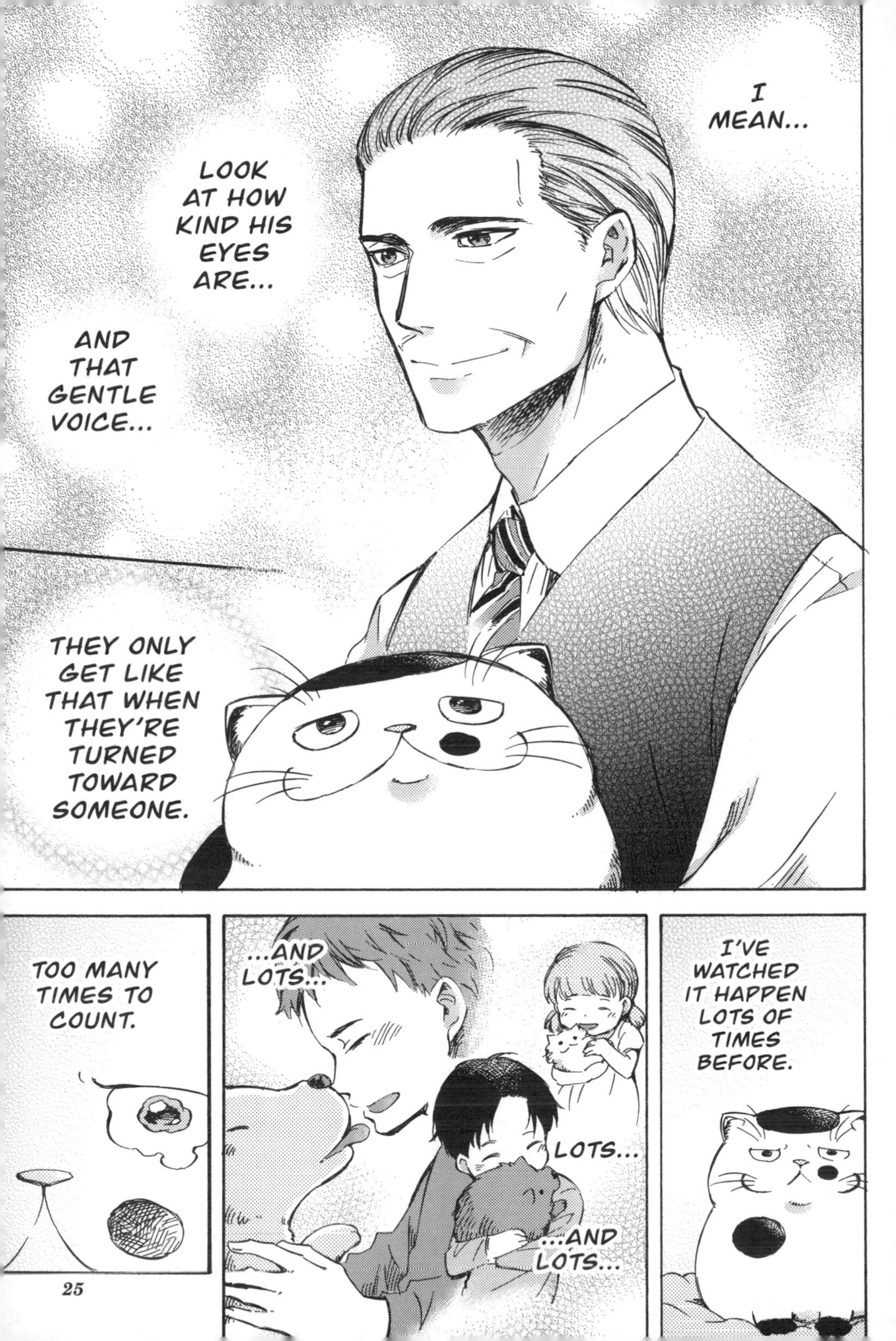
I MEAN...
LOOK AT HOW KIND HIS EYES ARE...
AND THAT GENTLE VOICE...
THEY ONLY GET LIKE THAT WHEN THEY'RE TURNED TOWARD SOMEONE.
I'VE WATCHED IT HAPPEN LOTS OF TIMES BEFORE.
LOTS...
...AND LOTS...
...AND LOTS...
TOO MANY TIMES TO COUNT.

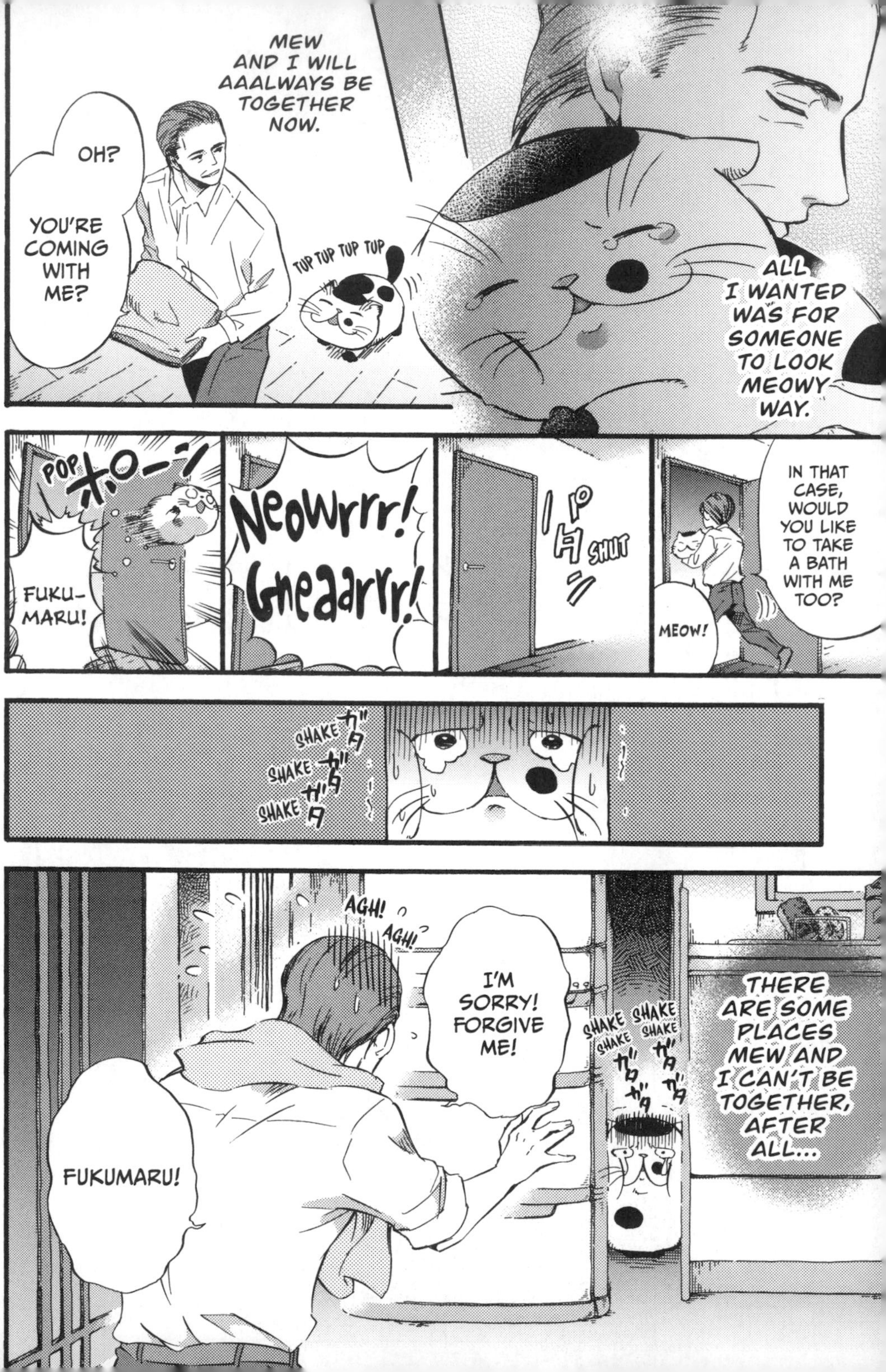
ALL I WANTED WAS FOR SOMEONE TO LOOK MEOWY WAY.
MEW AND I WILL AAALWAYS BE TOGETHER NOW.
OH?
YOU'RE COMING WITH ME?
TUP TUP TUP TUP
IN THAT CASE, WOULD YOU LIKE TO TAKE A BATH WITH ME TOO?
MEOW!
SHUT
Neowrrr! Gneaarrr!
POP
FUKU-MARU!
SHAKE
SHAKE
SHAKE
THERE ARE SOME PLACES MEW AND I CAN'T BE TOGETHER, AFTER ALL...
SHAKE SHAKE
SHAKE SHAKE
AGH! AGH!
I'M SORRY! FORGIVE ME!
FUKUMARU!

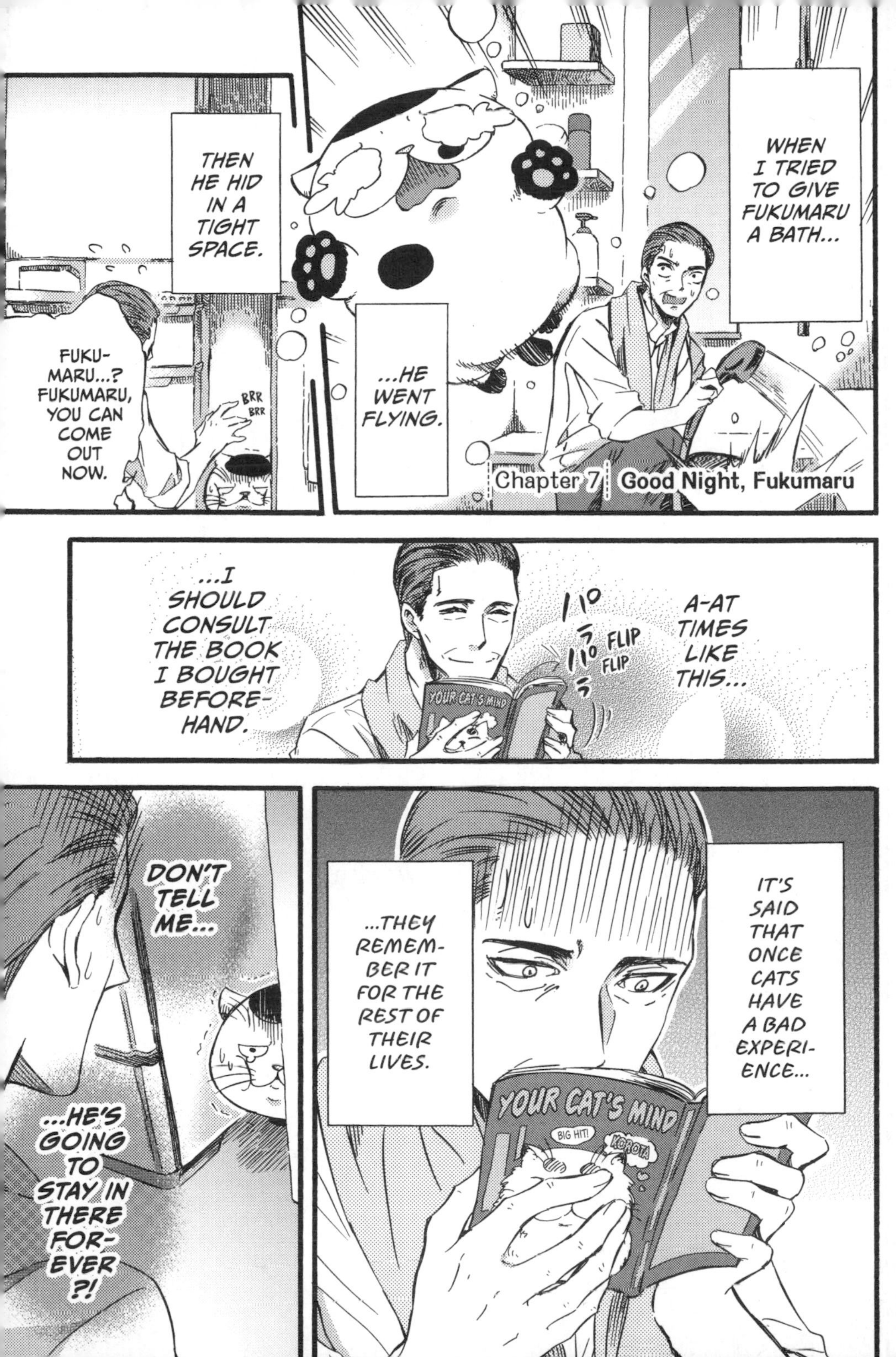
WHEN I TRIED TO GIVE FUKUMARU A BATH...
Chapter 7 Good Night, Fukumaru
...HE WENT FLYING.
THEN HE HID IN A TIGHT SPACE.
FUKUMARU...? FUKUMARU, YOU CAN COME OUT NOW.
BRR BRR
A-AT TIMES LIKE THIS...
FLIP FLIP
...I SHOULD CONSULT THE BOOK I BOUGHT BEFOREHAND.
YOUR CAT'S MIND
IT'S SAID THAT ONCE CATS HAVE A BAD EXPERIENCE...
...THEY REMEMBER IT FOR THE REST OF THEIR LIVES.
YOUR CAT'S MIND
BIG HIT!
KOROTA
DON'T TELL ME...
...HE'S GOING TO STAY IN THERE FOREVER?!

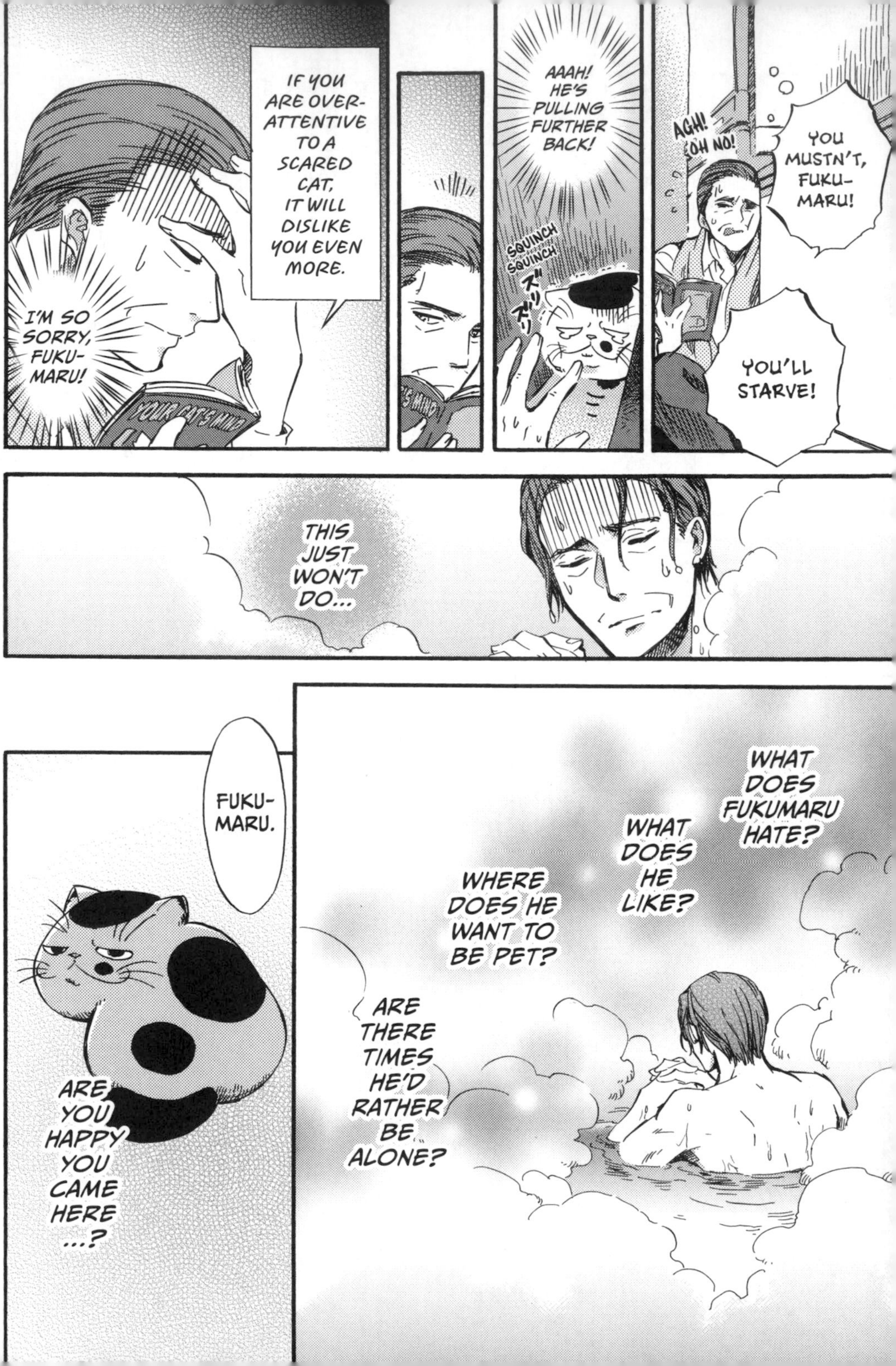
AGH! OH NO!
YOU MUSTN'T, FUKUMARU!
YOU'LL STARVE!
AAAH! HE'S PULLING FURTHER BACK!
SQUINCH SQUINCH
ズリ ズリ
YOUR CAT'S MIND
IF YOU ARE OVER-ATTENTIVE TO A SCARED CAT, IT WILL DISLIKE YOU EVEN MORE.
I'M SO SORRY, FUKUMARU!
THIS JUST WON'T DO...
WHAT DOES FUKUMARU HATE?
WHAT DOES HE LIKE?
WHERE DOES HE WANT TO BE PET?
ARE THERE TIMES HE'D RATHER BE ALONE?
FUKUMARU.
ARE YOU HAPPY YOU CAME HERE ...?

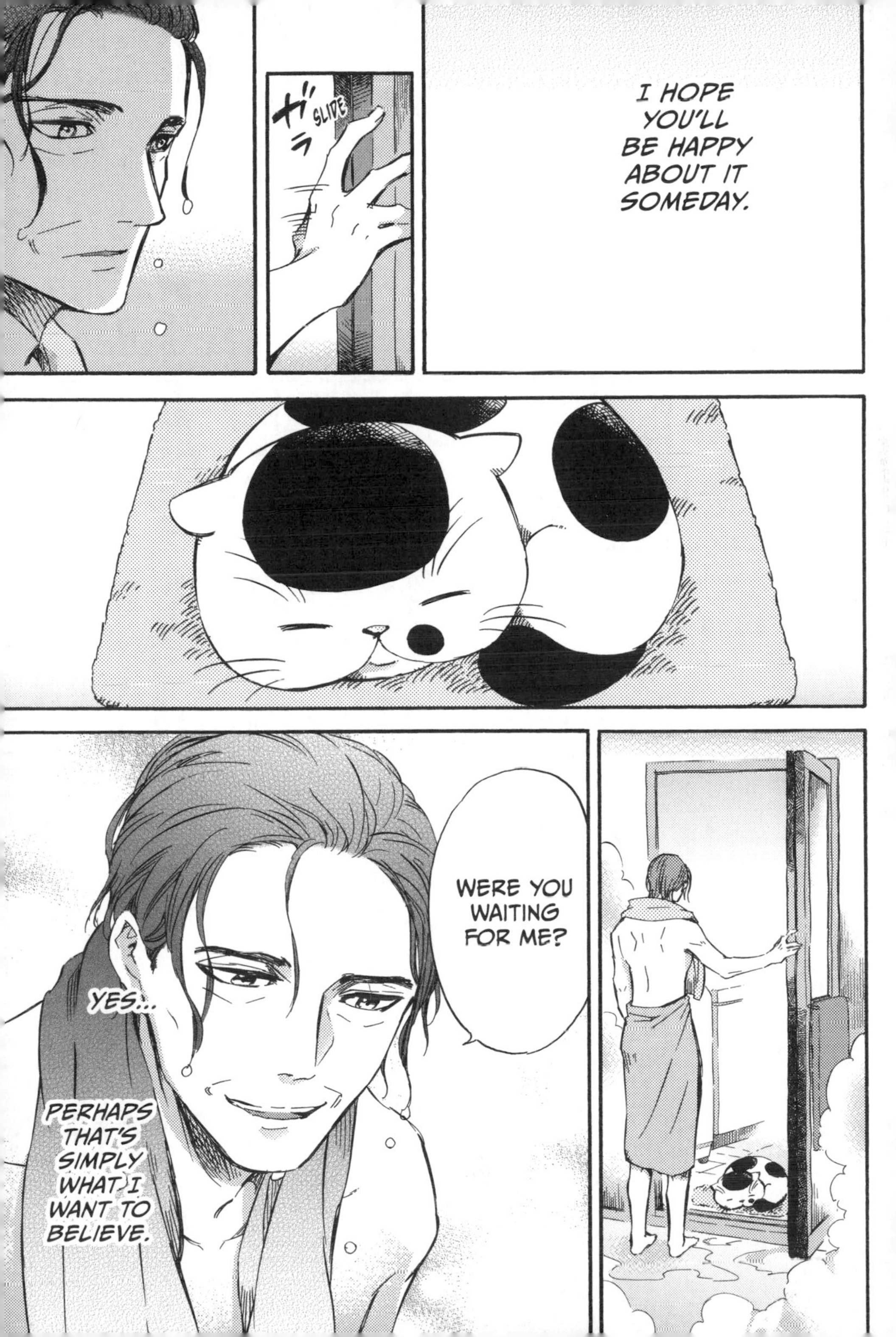
I HOPE YOU'LL BE HAPPY ABOUT IT SOMEDAY.
ガラ
SLIDE
WERE YOU WAITING FOR ME?
YES...
PERHAPS THAT'S SIMPLY WHAT I WANT TO BELIEVE.

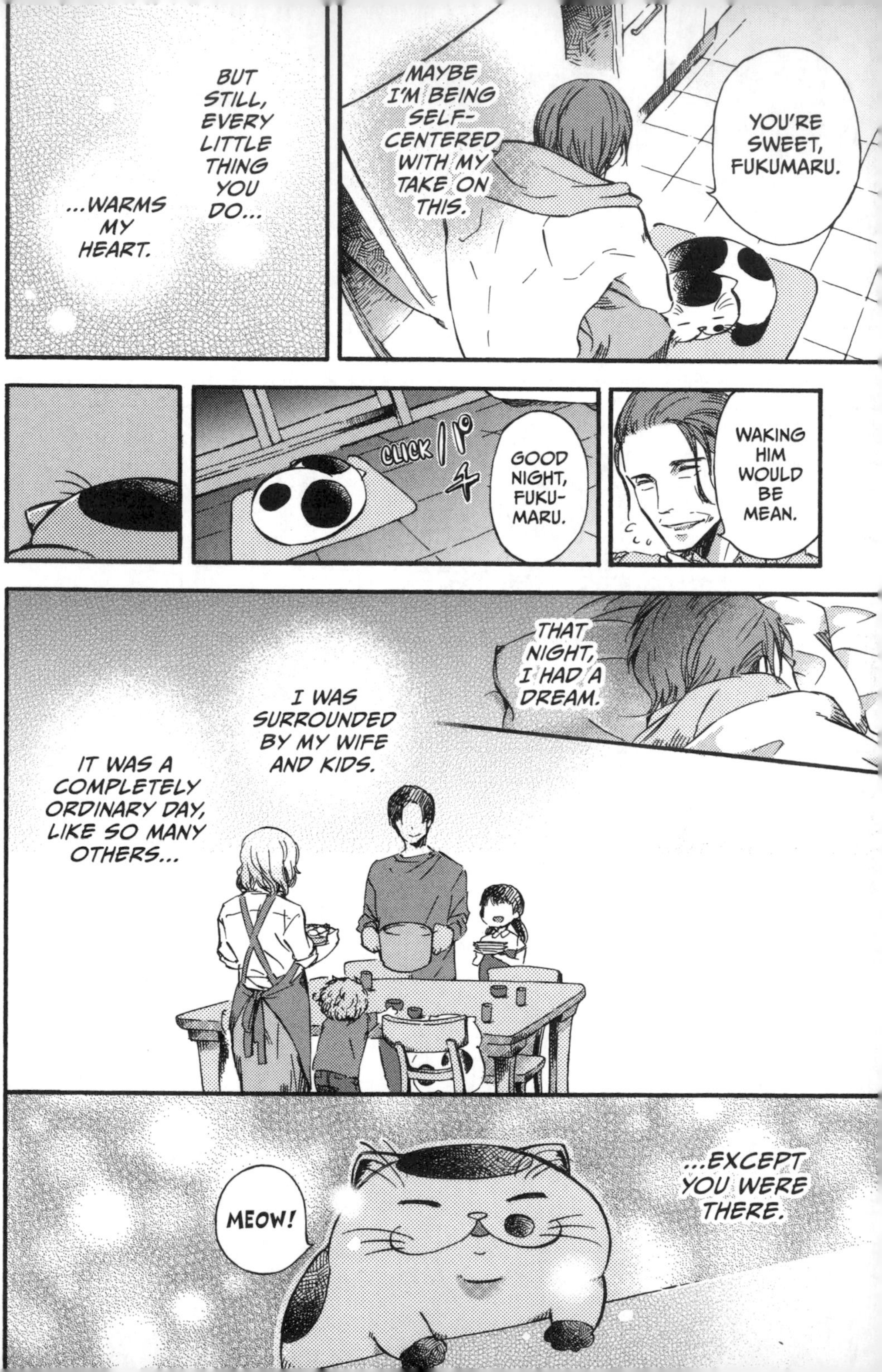

YOU'RE SWEET, FUKUMARU.
MAYBE I'M BEING SELF-CENTERED WITH MY TAKE ON THIS.
BUT STILL, EVERY LITTLE THING YOU DO...
...WARMS MY HEART.
WAKING HIM WOULD BE MEAN.
GOOD NIGHT, FUKU-MARU.
CLICK
THAT NIGHT, I HAD A DREAM.
I WAS SURROUNDED BY MY WIFE AND KIDS.
IT WAS A COMPLETELY ORDINARY DAY, LIKE SO MANY OTHERS...
...EXCEPT YOU WERE THERE.
MEOW!

# Chapter 8 Good Night, Mister

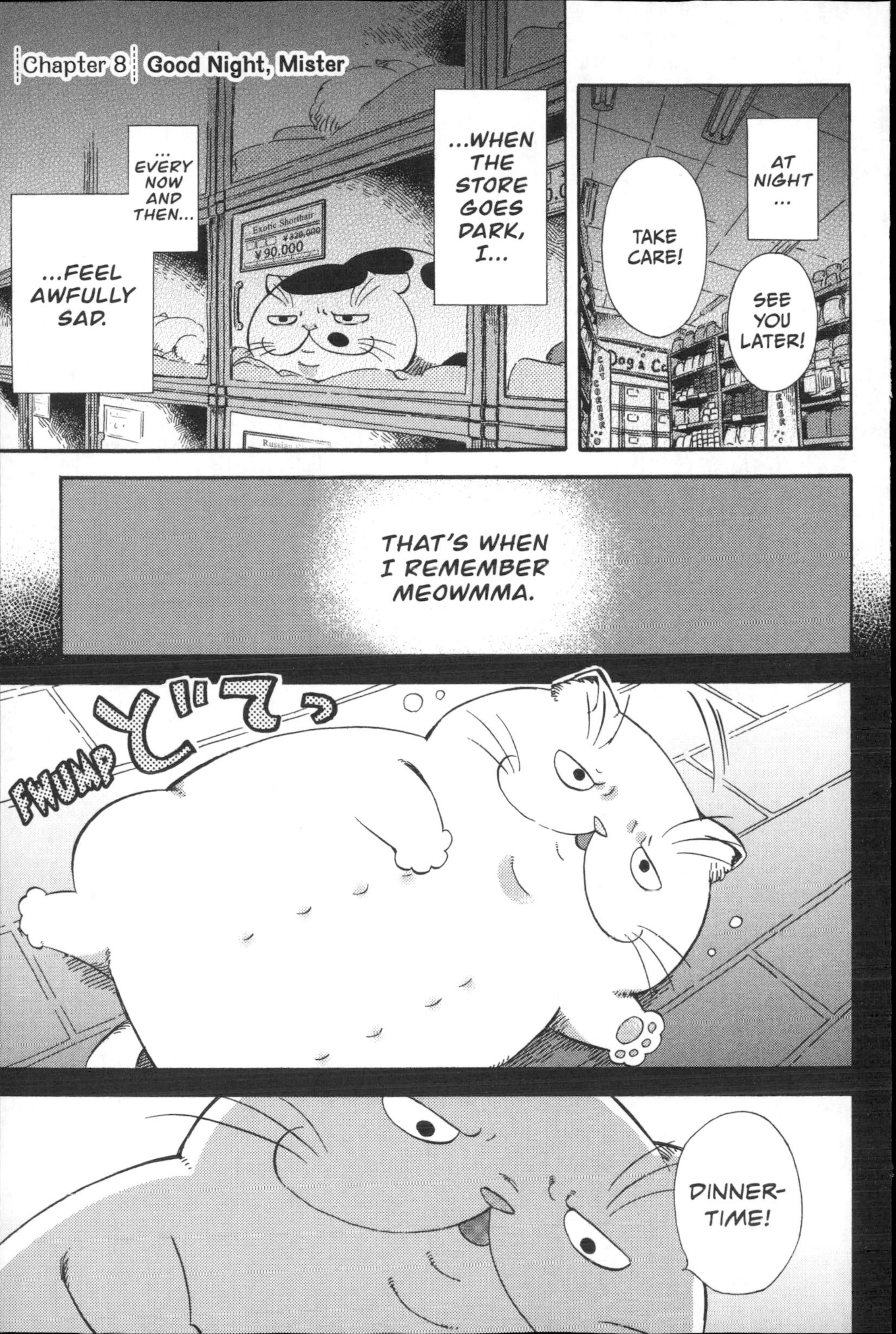
AT NIGHT...
TAKE CARE!
SEE YOU LATER!
...WHEN THE STORE GOES DARK, I...
...EVERY NOW AND THEN...
Exotic Shorthair
¥90.000
...FEEL AWFULLY SAD.
THAT'S WHEN I REMEMBER MEOWMMA.
FWUMP どでっ
DINNER-TIME!

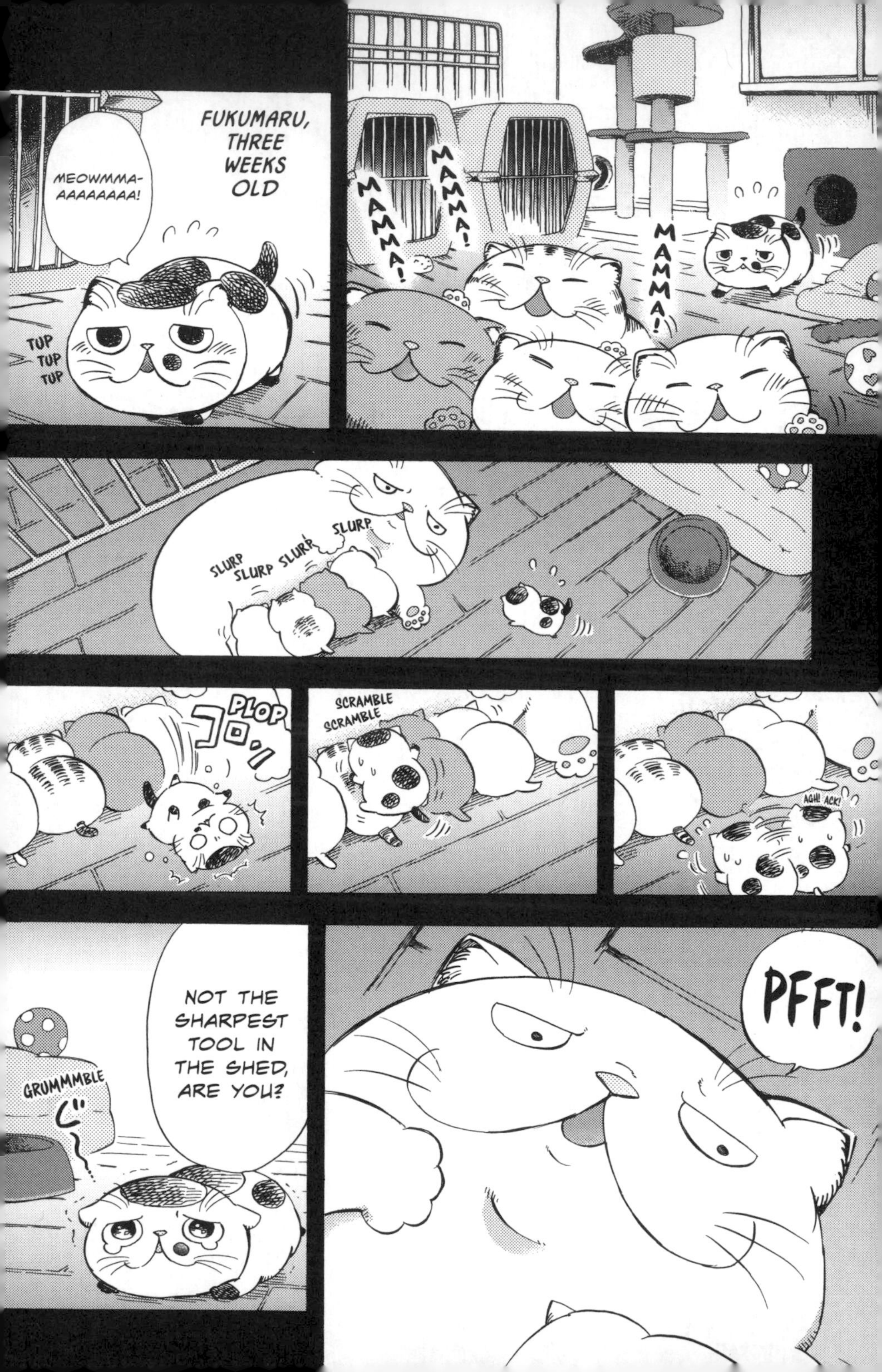
MAMMA!
MAMMA!
MAMMA!
FUKUMARU, THREE WEEKS OLD
MEOWMMA-AAAAAAAAA!
TUP TUP TUP
SLURP
SLURP
SLURP
SLURP
AGH! ACK!
SCRAMBLE SCRAMBLE
PLOP
PFFT!
NOT THE SHARPEST TOOL IN THE SHED, ARE YOU?
GRUMMMBLE

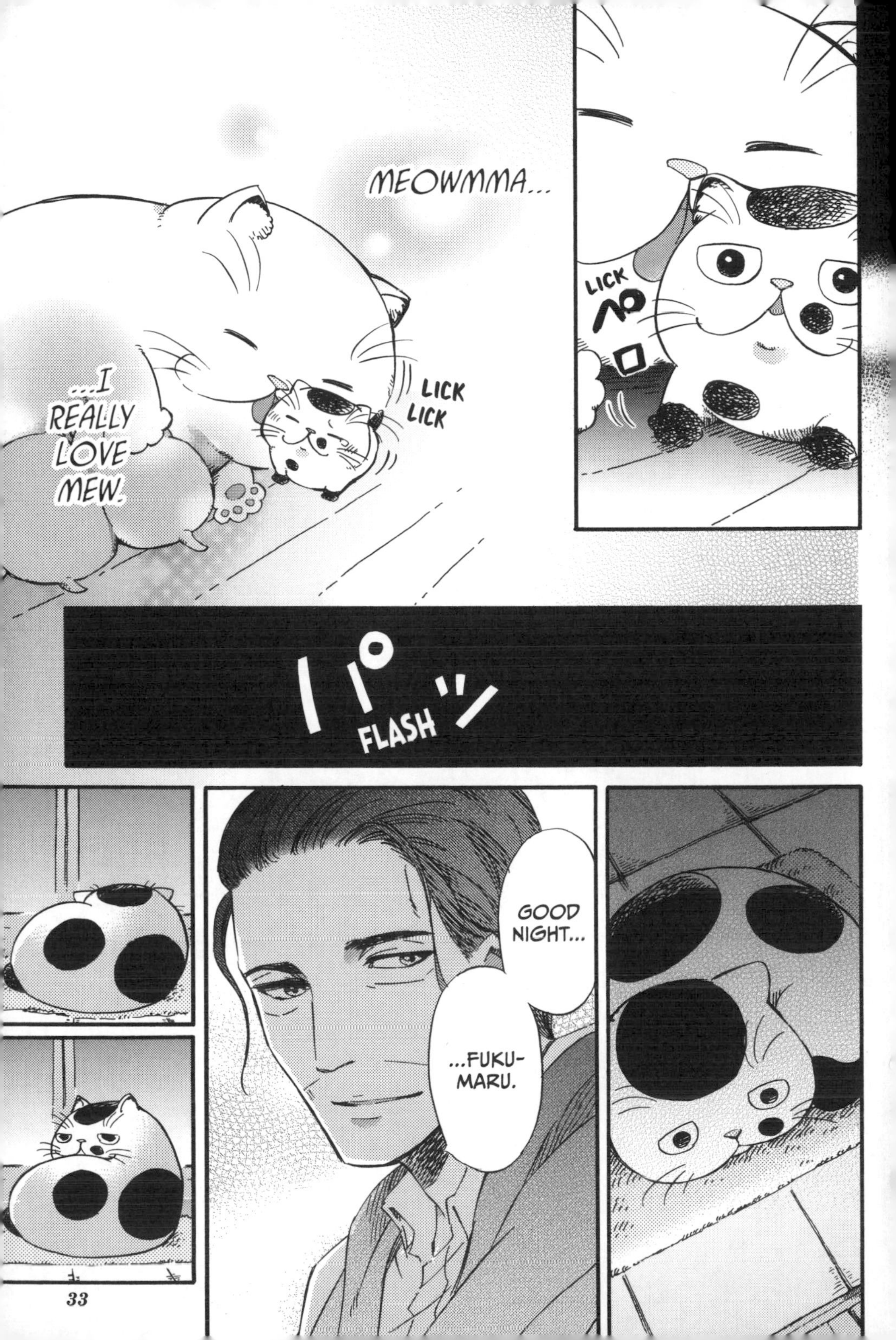
LICK
ペロ
MEOWMMA...
LICK LICK
...I REALLY LOVE MEW.
パッ
FLASH
GOOD NIGHT...
...FUKU-MARU.

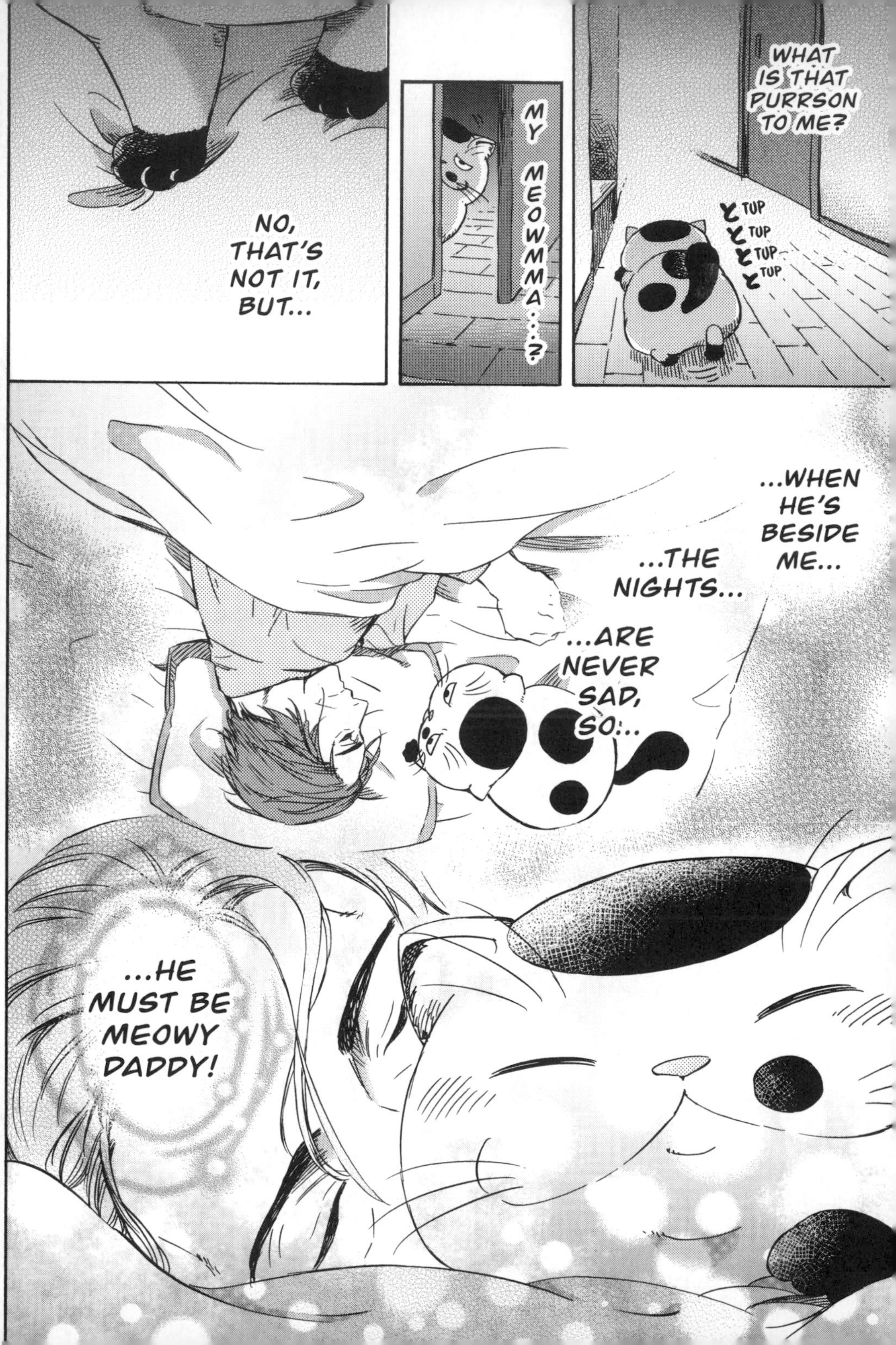
WHAT IS THAT PURRSON TO ME?
と TUP と TUP と TUP と TUP
MY MEOWMMA...?
NO, THAT'S NOT IT, BUT...
...WHEN HE'S BESIDE ME...
...THE NIGHTS...
...ARE NEVER SAD, SO...
...HE MUST BE MEOWY DADDY!

THE NOBLE FELINE IN THE BATHROOM (PART 1)

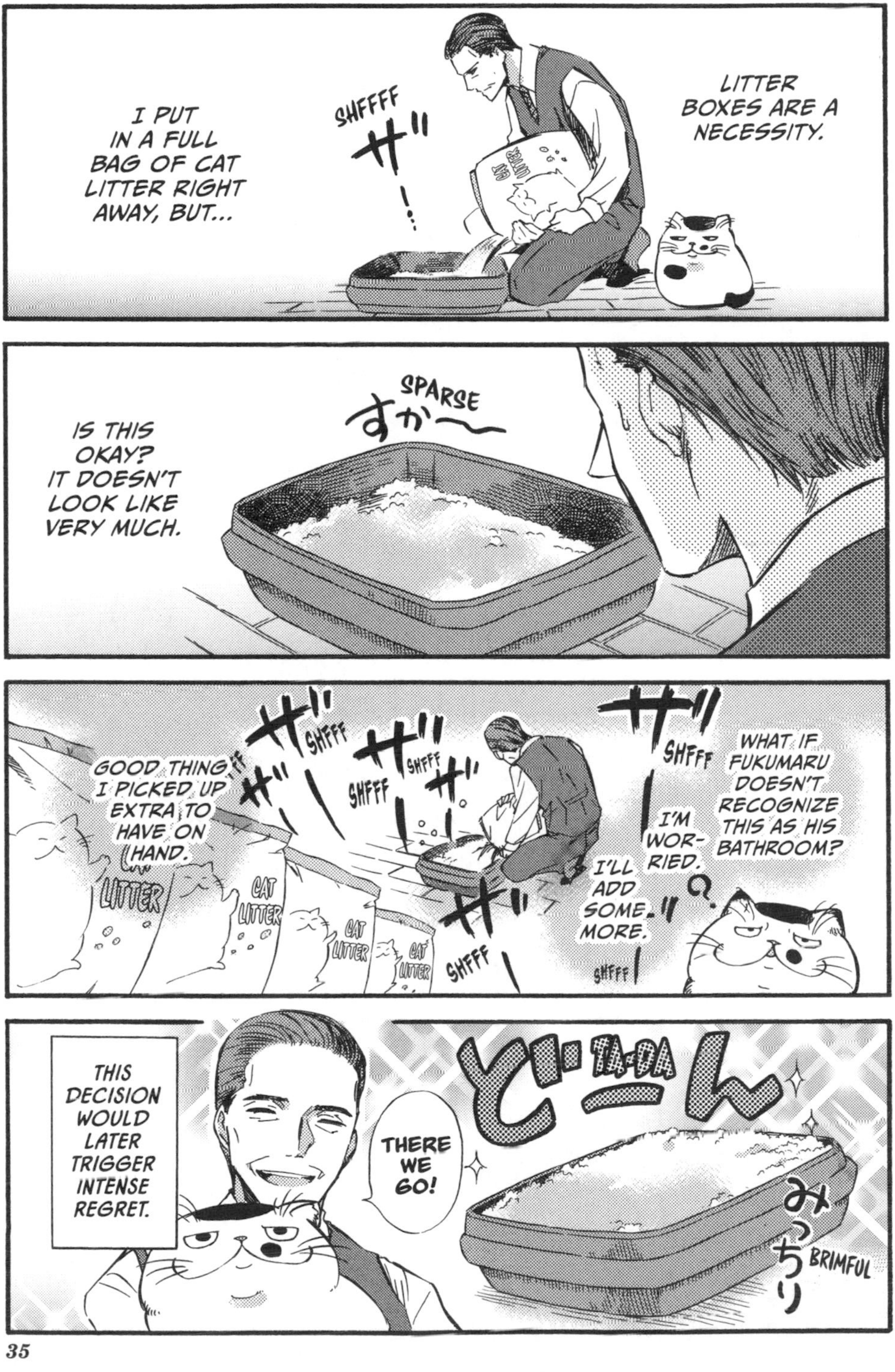
LITTER BOXES ARE A NECESSITY.
SHFFFF
ザ
I PUT IN A FULL BAG OF CAT LITTER RIGHT AWAY, BUT...
SPARSE
すか〜
IS THIS OKAY? IT DOESN'T LOOK LIKE VERY MUCH.
ザ
SHFFF
WHAT IF FUKUMARU DOESN'T RECOGNIZE THIS AS HIS BATHROOM?
I'M WOR-RIED.
I'LL ADD SOME MORE.
SHFFF
ザ
SHFFF
ザ
SHFFF
ザ
SHFFF
ザ
SHFFF
GOOD THING I PICKED UP EXTRA TO HAVE ON HAND.
CAT LITTER
CAT LITTER
CAT LITTER
どーん
TA-DA
みっちり
BRIMFUL
THERE WE GO!
THIS DECISION WOULD LATER TRIGGER INTENSE REGRET.

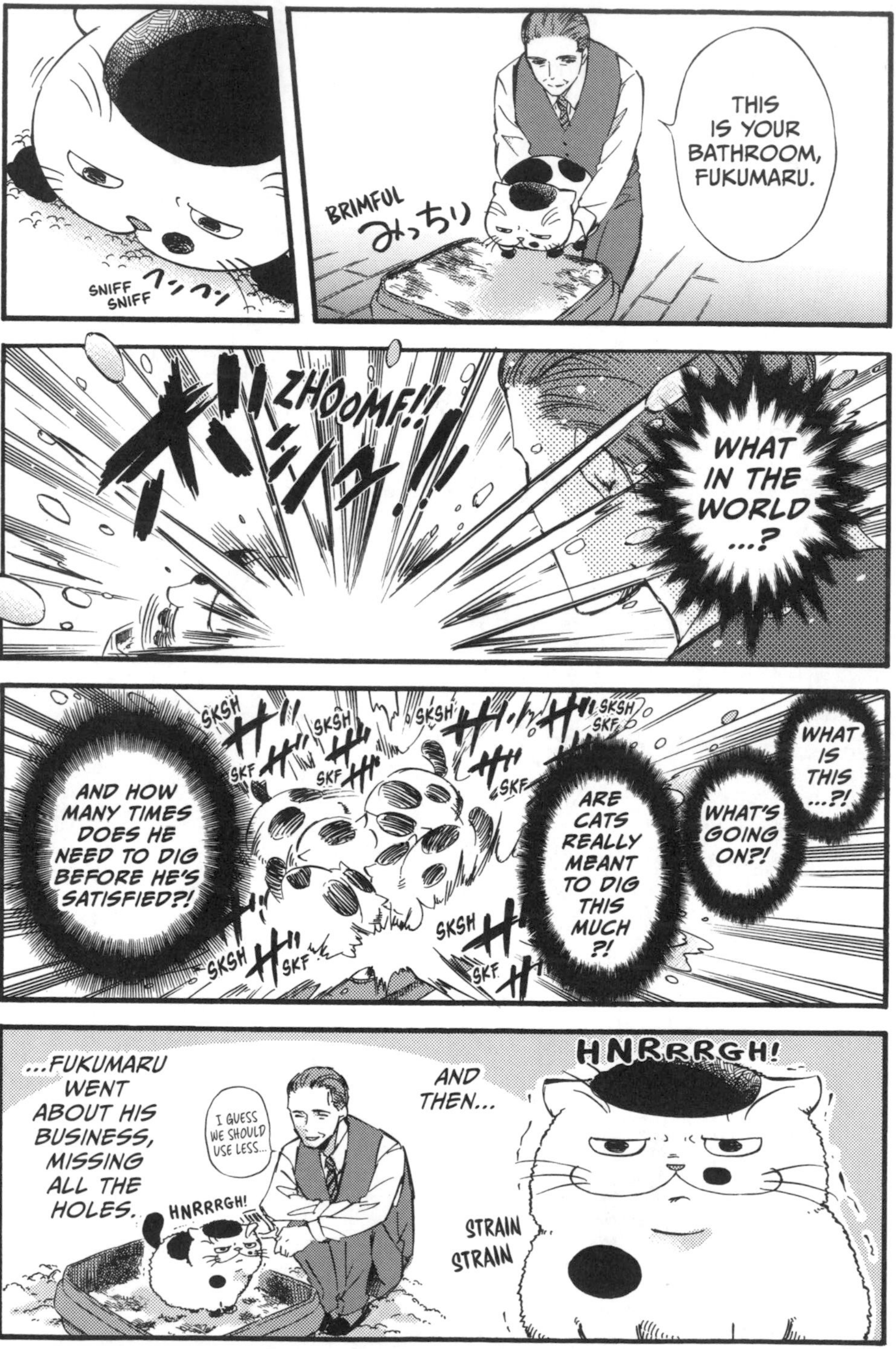
THIS IS YOUR BATHROOM, FUKUMARU.
BRIMFUL
みっちり
SNIFF SNIFF
フンフン
WHAT IN THE WORLD ...?
ZHOOMF!!
WHAT IS THIS ...?!
WHAT'S GOING ON?!
ARE CATS REALLY MEANT TO DIG THIS MUCH ?!
SKSH SKF
SKSH
SKF
SKSH
SKF
SKSH
SKF
SKSH
SKF
SKSH
SKF
AND HOW MANY TIMES DOES HE NEED TO DIG BEFORE HE'S SATISFIED?!
HNRRRGH!
STRAIN STRAIN
AND THEN...
I GUESS WE SHOULD USE LESS...
HNRRRGH!
...FUKUMARU WENT ABOUT HIS BUSINESS, MISSING ALL THE HOLES.

# THE NOBLE FELINE IN THE BATHROOM (PART 2)

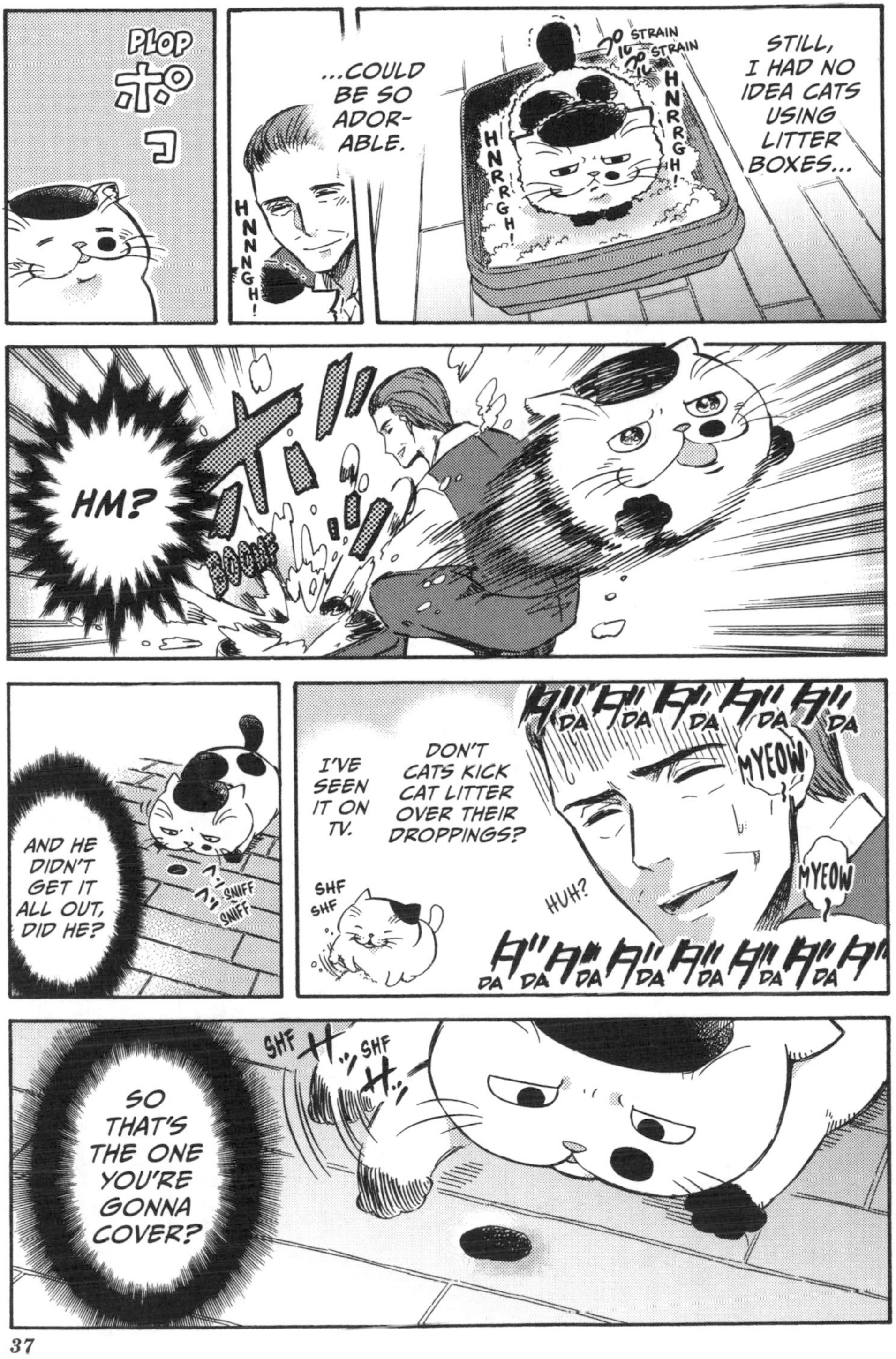
STILL, I HAD NO IDEA CATS USING LITTER BOXES...
STRAIN
STRAIN
HNRRGH!
HNRRGH!
...COULD BE SO ADORABLE.
HNNNGH!
PLOP
HM?
DA DA DA DA DA
DON'T CATS KICK CAT LITTER OVER THEIR DROPPINGS?
I'VE SEEN IT ON TV.
MYEOW
MYEOW
HUH?
SHF SHF
DA DA DA DA DA DA DA
SNIFF SNIFF
AND HE DIDN'T GET IT ALL OUT, DID HE?
SHF
SHF
SO THAT'S THE ONE YOU'RE GONNA COVER?

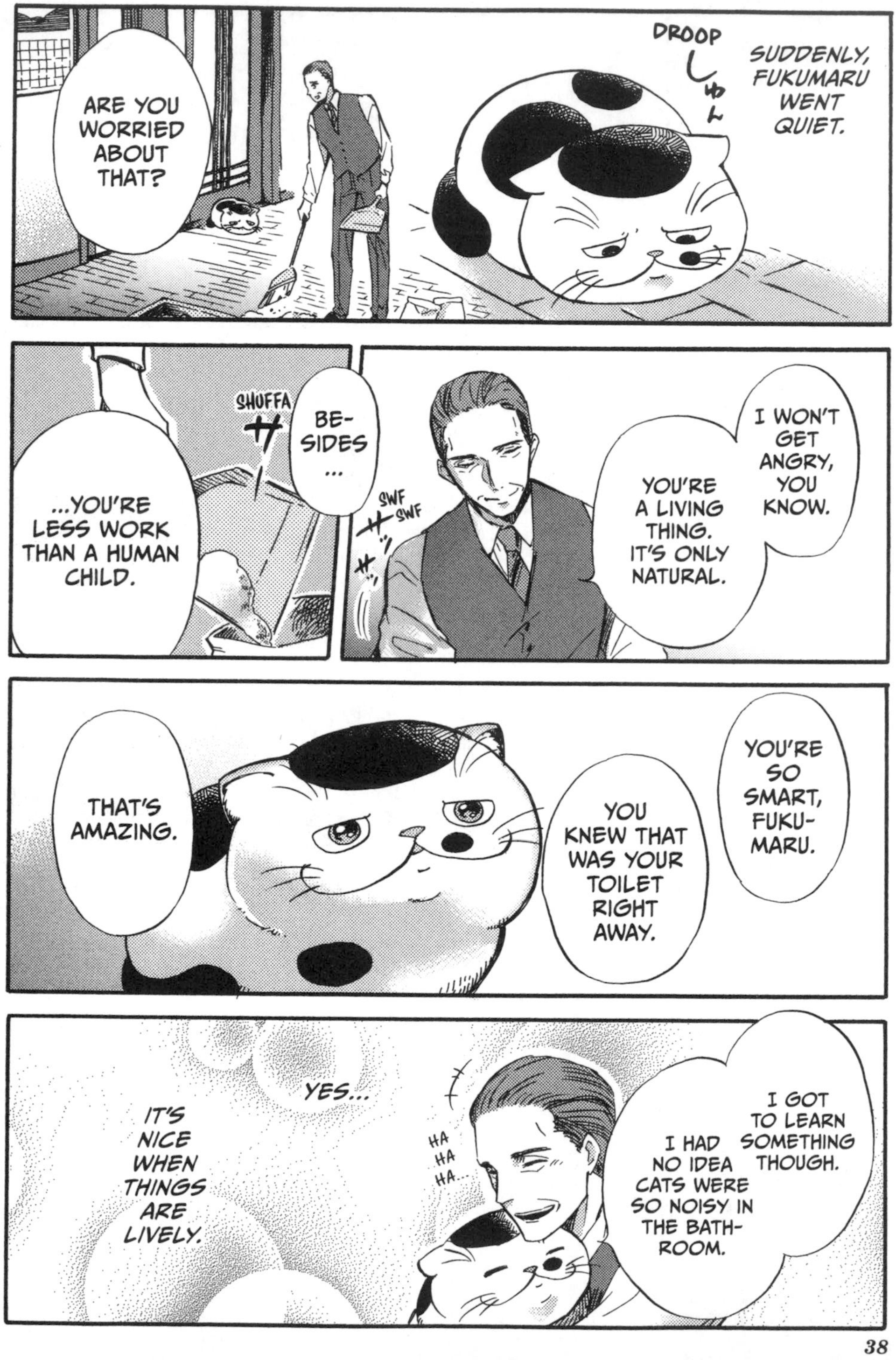
SUDDENLY, FUKUMARU WENT QUIET.
DROOP しゅん
ARE YOU WORRIED ABOUT THAT?
I WON'T GET ANGRY, YOU KNOW.
YOU'RE A LIVING THING. IT'S ONLY NATURAL.
SWF SWF
BE-SIDES...
SHUFFA
...YOU'RE LESS WORK THAN A HUMAN CHILD.
YOU'RE SO SMART, FUKU-MARU.
YOU KNEW THAT WAS YOUR TOILET RIGHT AWAY.
THAT'S AMAZING.
I GOT TO LEARN SOMETHING THOUGH.
I HAD NO IDEA CATS WERE SO NOISY IN THE BATH-ROOM.
HA HA HA...
YES...
IT'S NICE WHEN THINGS ARE LIVELY.

## THE NOBLE FELINE IN THE BATHROOM, AFTERWARD

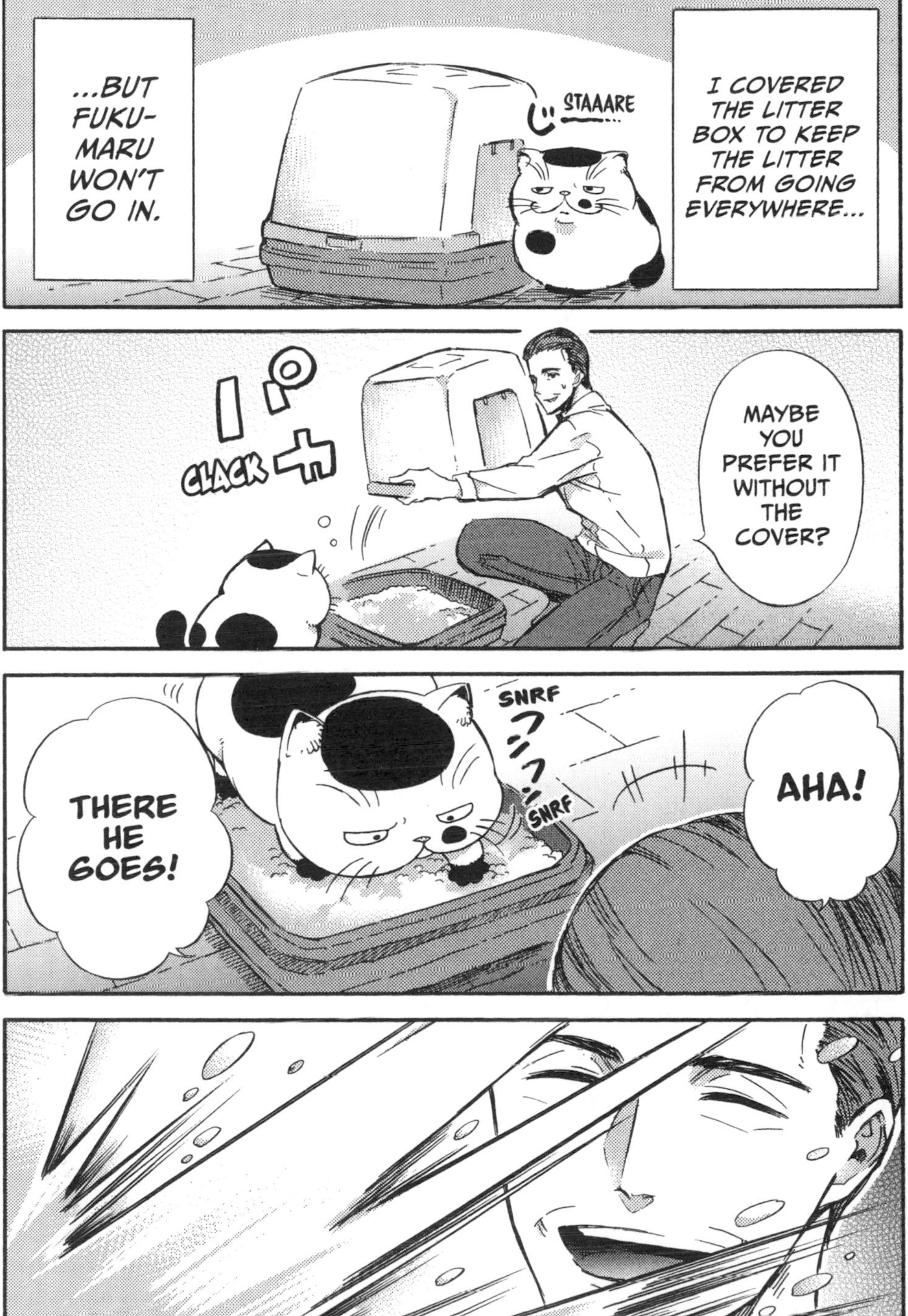
I COVERED THE LITTER BOX TO KEEP THE LITTER FROM GOING EVERYWHERE...
STAAARE
...BUT FUKU-MARU WON'T GO IN.
MAYBE YOU PREFER IT WITHOUT THE COVER?
CLACK
AHA!
SNRF
SNRF
THERE HE GOES!

AND SO THE PAIR'S
LONG DAY CAME
TO AN END.

## Chapter 9 Kneady-Kneady Fukumaru

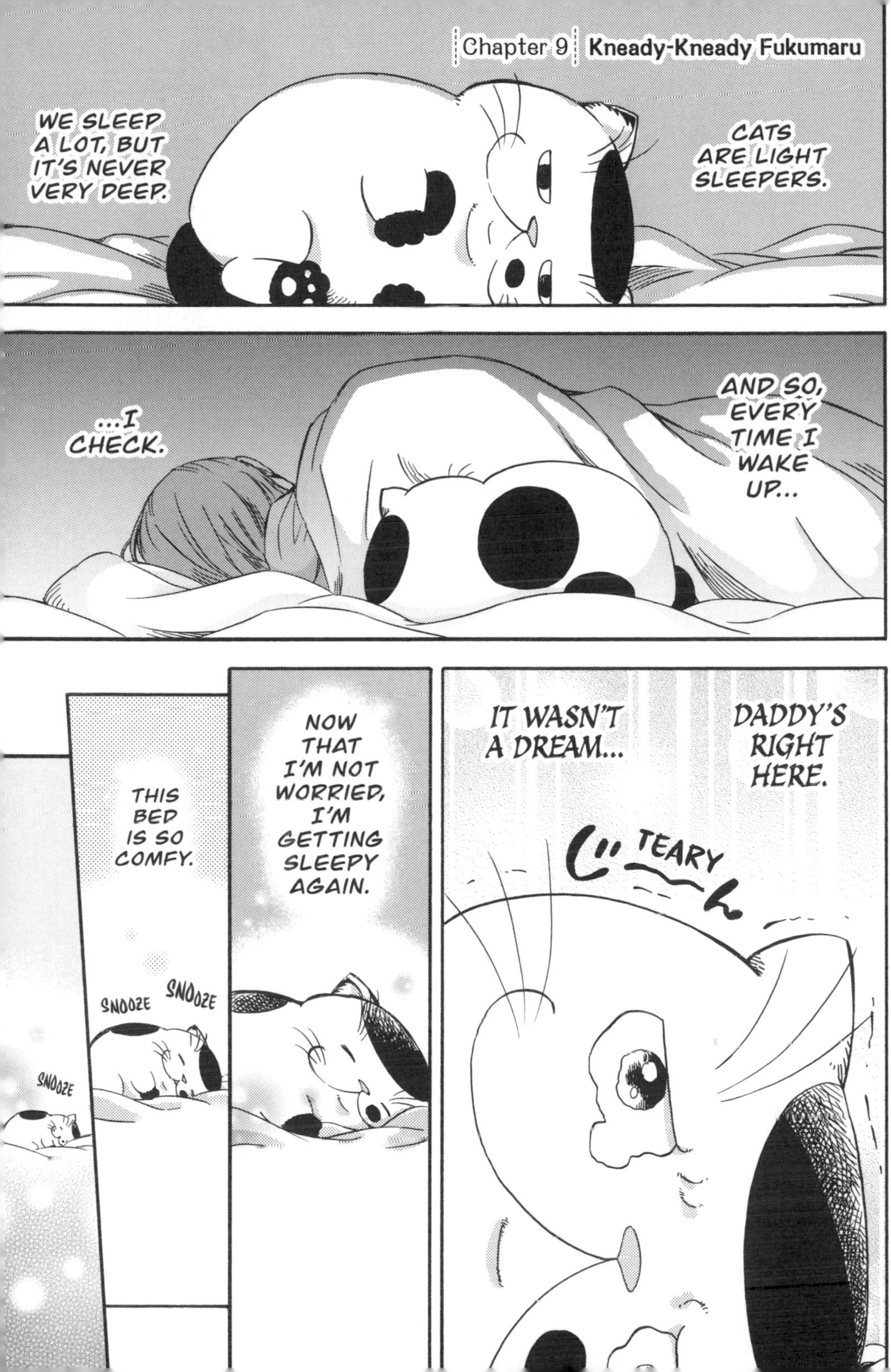
CATS ARE LIGHT SLEEPERS.
WE SLEEP A LOT, BUT IT'S NEVER VERY DEEP.
AND SO, EVERY TIME I WAKE UP...
...I CHECK.
DADDY'S RIGHT HERE.
IT WASN'T A DREAM...
TEARY
NOW THAT I'M NOT WORRIED, I'M GETTING SLEEPY AGAIN.
THIS BED IS SO COMFY.
SNOOZE
SNOOZE
SNOOZE

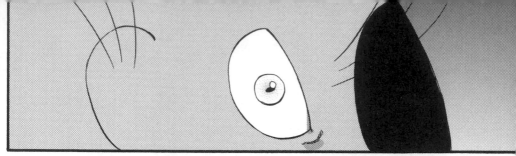

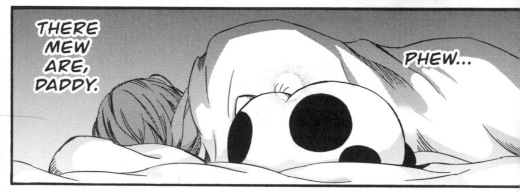

PHEW...
THERE MEW ARE, DADDY.
...BUT ARE MEW REALLY HERE?
I'M NOT DREAMING, AM I?
LET ME JUST MAKE SURE.
うにょ～ん STREEETCH
PAT
もみもみ KNEADY KNEADY
KNEADY KNEADY もみもみ
WRIGGLE SQUIRM

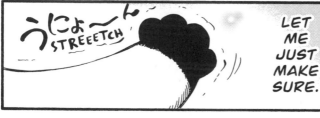

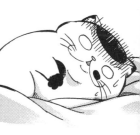

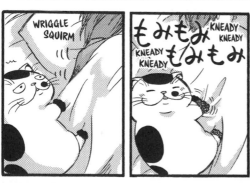

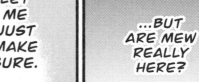

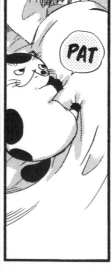

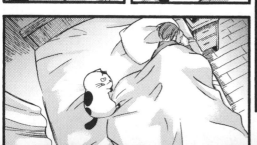

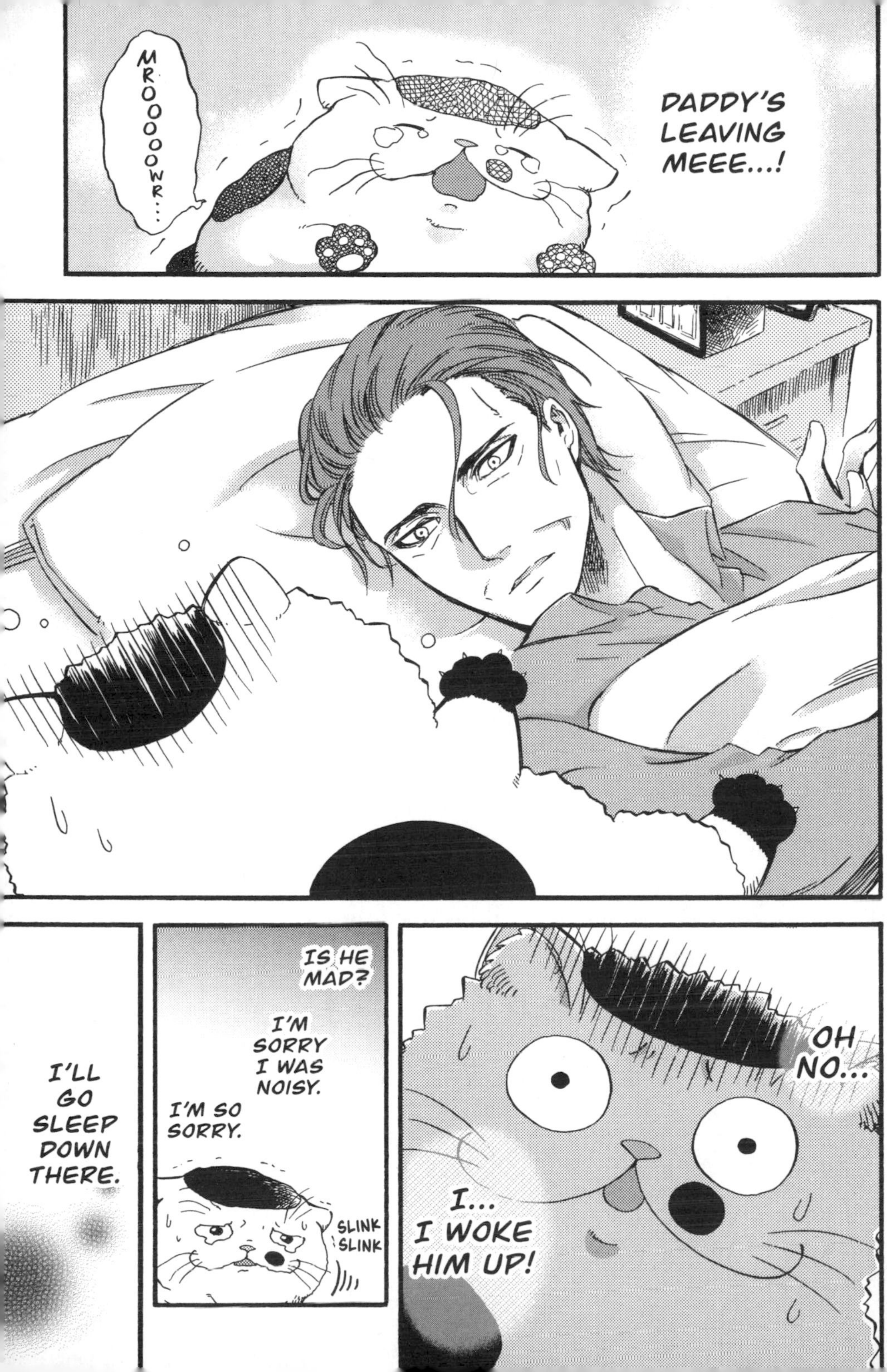
DADDY'S LEAVING MEEE...!
MROOOOOWR...
OH NO...
I... I WOKE HIM UP!
IS HE MAD?
I'M SORRY I WAS NOISY.
I'M SO SORRY.
SLINK SLINK
I'LL GO SLEEP DOWN THERE.

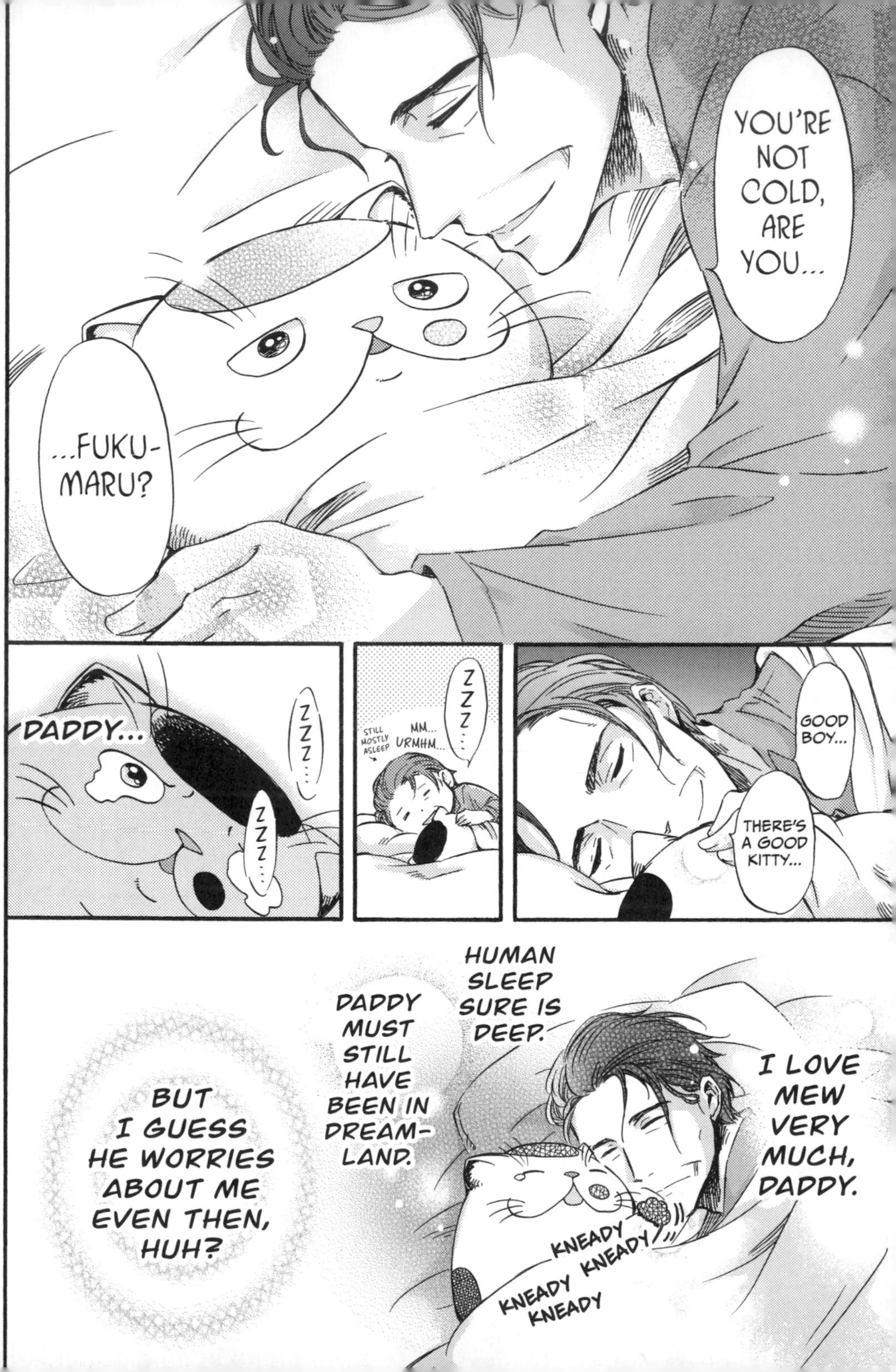
YOU'RE NOT COLD, ARE YOU...
...FUKU-MARU?
GOOD BOY...
THERE'S A GOOD KITTY...
Z Z Z...
MM... URMHM...
STILL MOSTLY ASLEEP
DADDY...
Z Z Z...
Z Z Z...
I LOVE MEW VERY MUCH, DADDY.
HUMAN SLEEP SURE IS DEEP.
DADDY MUST STILL HAVE BEEN IN DREAM-LAND.
BUT I GUESS HE WORRIES ABOUT ME EVEN THEN, HUH?
KNEADY KNEADY KNEADY KNEADY

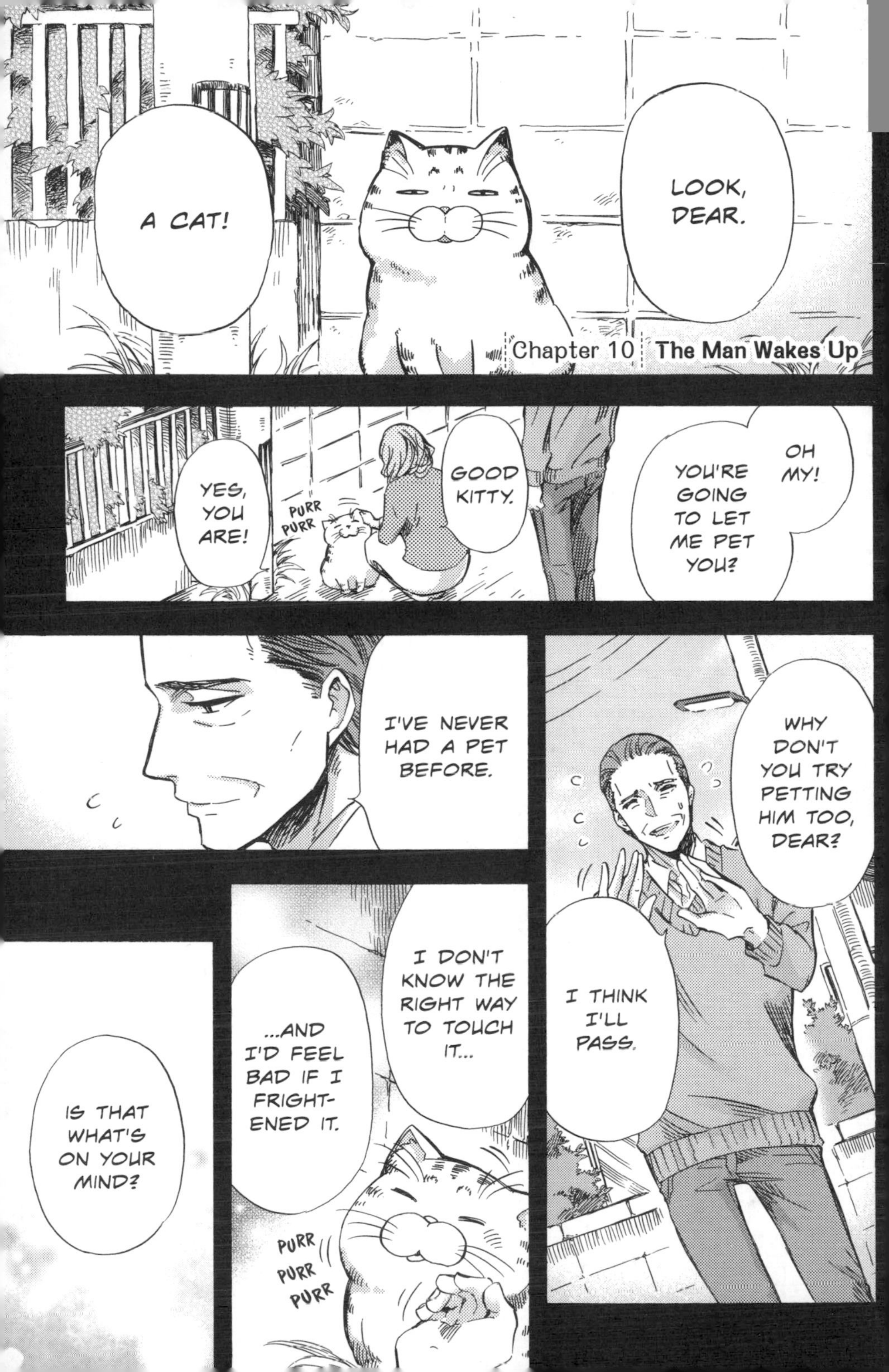
LOOK, DEAR.
A CAT!
Chapter 10 The Man Wakes Up
OH MY!
YOU'RE GOING TO LET ME PET YOU?
GOOD KITTY.
PURR PURR
YES, YOU ARE!
WHY DON'T YOU TRY PETTING HIM TOO, DEAR?
I THINK I'LL PASS.
I'VE NEVER HAD A PET BEFORE.
I DON'T KNOW THE RIGHT WAY TO TOUCH IT...
...AND I'D FEEL BAD IF I FRIGHT-ENED IT.
PURR PURR PURR
IS THAT WHAT'S ON YOUR MIND?

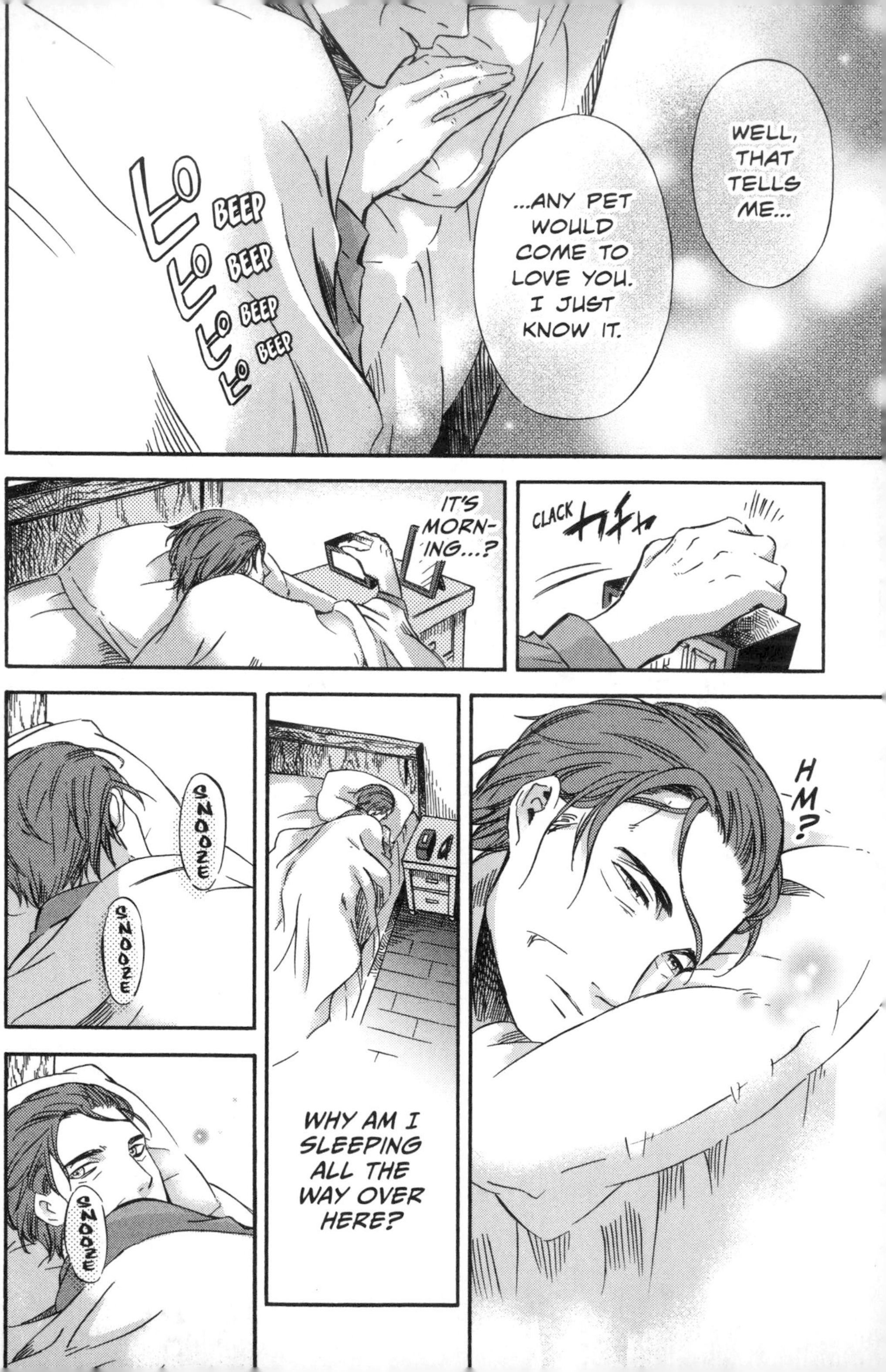
WELL, THAT TELLS ME...
...ANY PET WOULD COME TO LOVE YOU. I JUST KNOW IT.
BEEP
BEEP
BEEP
BEEP
CLACK カチャ
IT'S MORN-ING...?
HM?
WHY AM I SLEEPING ALL THE WAY OVER HERE?
SNOOZE
SNOOZE
SNOOZE

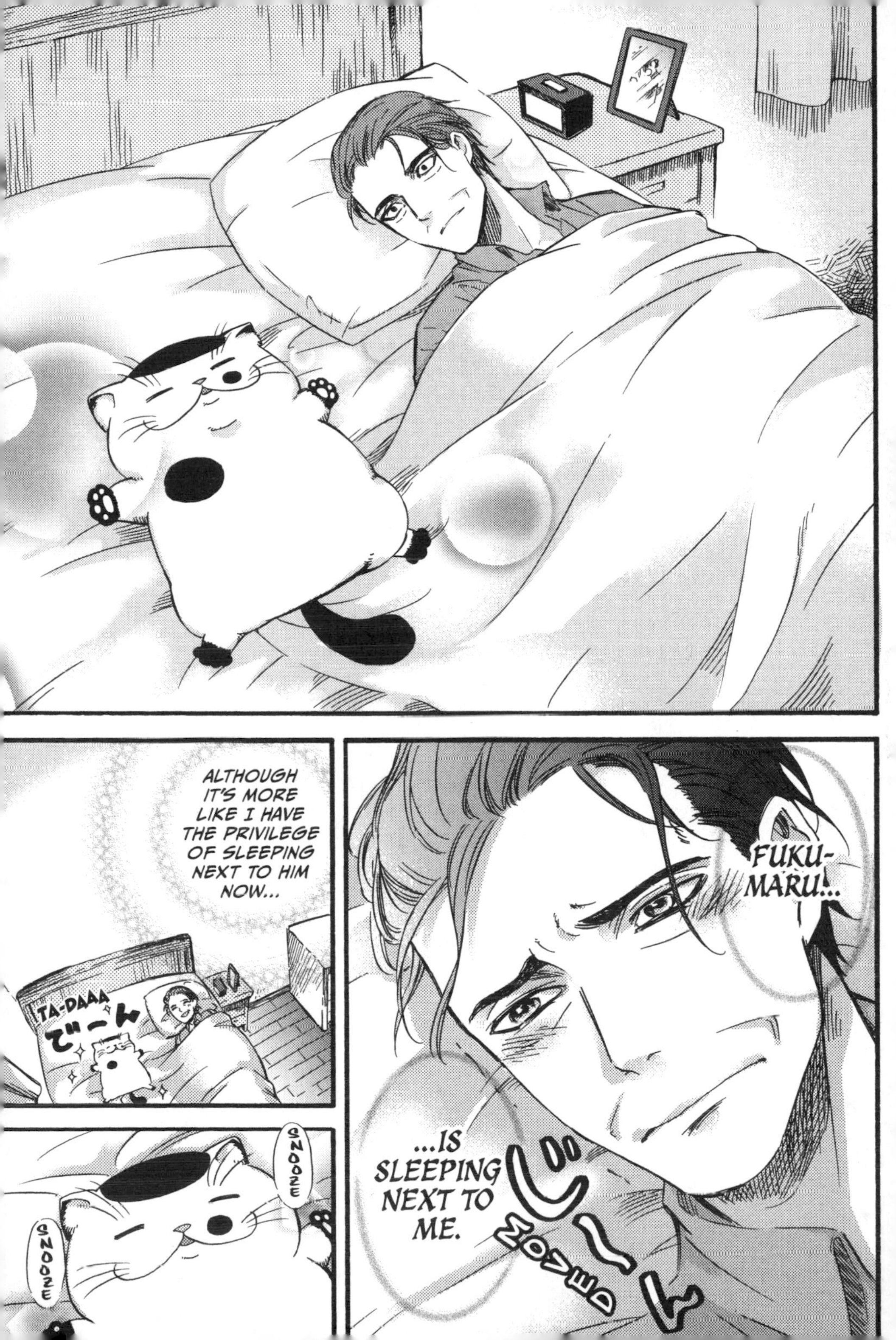
FUKU-MARU...
...IS SLEEPING NEXT TO ME.
じーん
MOVED
ALTHOUGH IT'S MORE LIKE I HAVE THE PRIVILEGE OF SLEEPING NEXT TO HIM NOW...
TA-DAAA
でーん
SNOOZE
SNOOZE

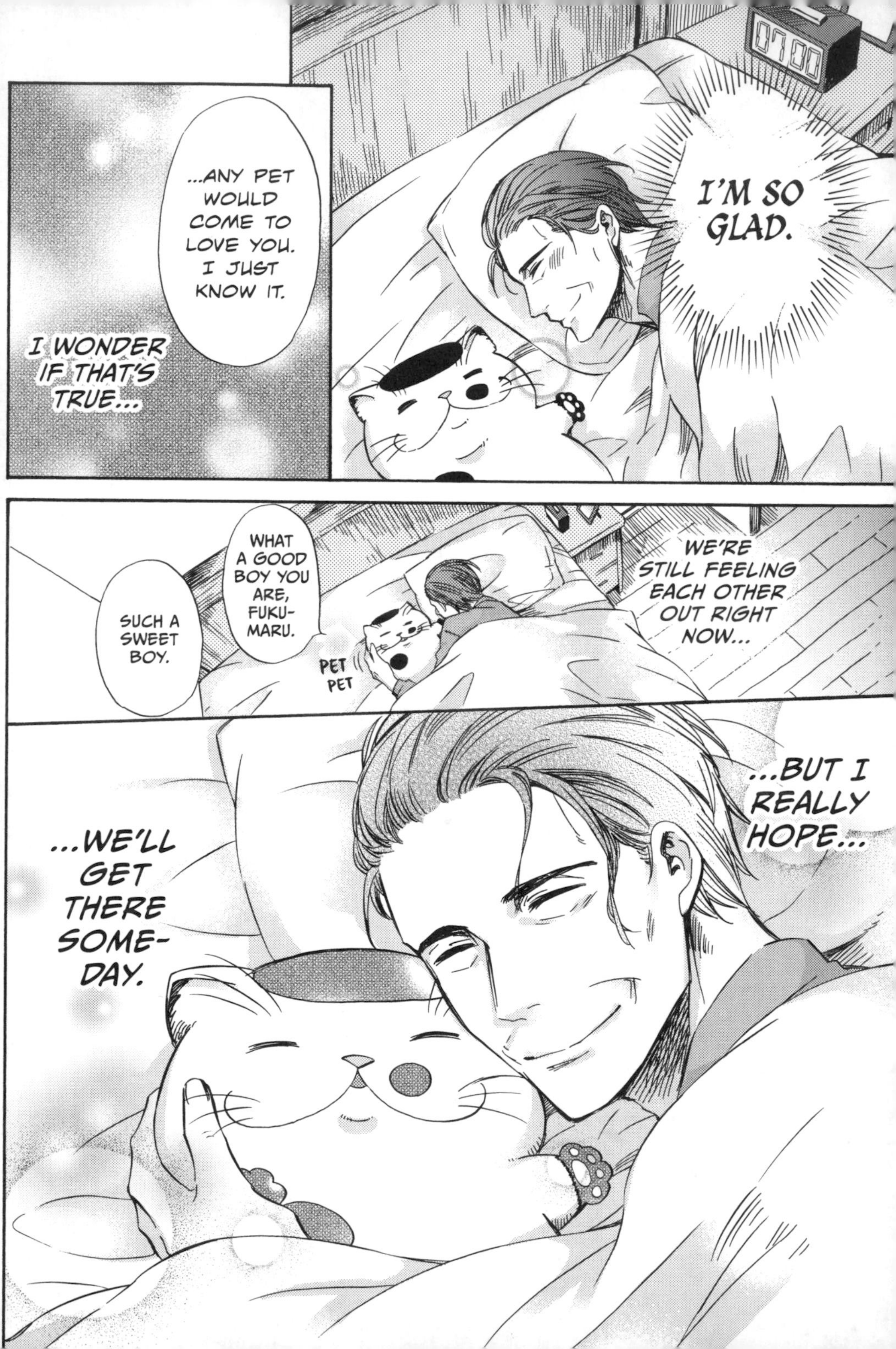
I'M SO GLAD.
...ANY PET WOULD COME TO LOVE YOU. I JUST KNOW IT.
I WONDER IF THAT'S TRUE...
WE'RE STILL FEELING EACH OTHER OUT RIGHT NOW...
WHAT A GOOD BOY YOU ARE, FUKU-MARU.
PET PET
SUCH A SWEET BOY.
...BUT I REALLY HOPE...
...WE'LL GET THERE SOME-DAY.

## WANTED: FUKUMARU PHOTOS

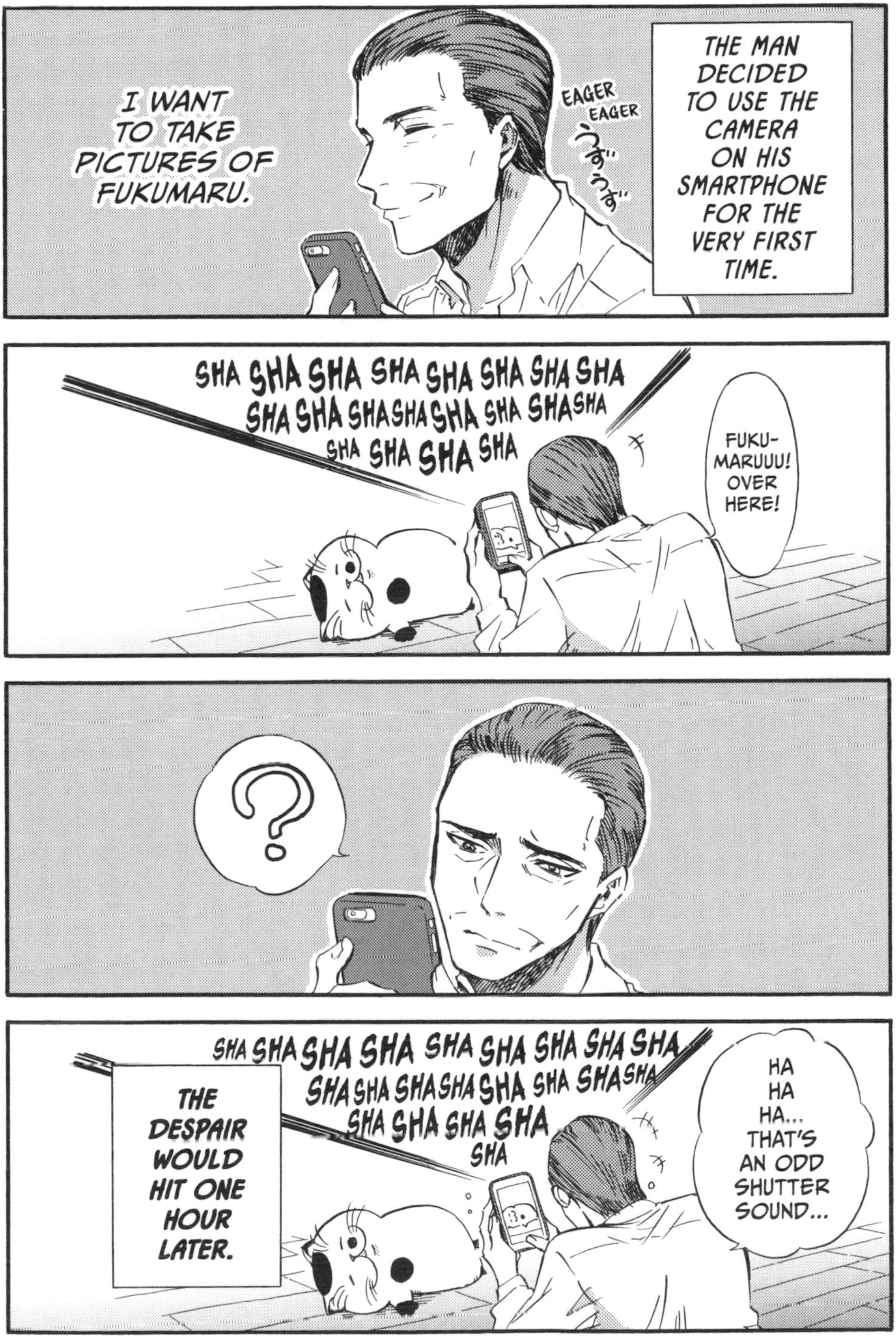
THE MAN DECIDED TO USE THE CAMERA ON HIS SMARTPHONE FOR THE VERY FIRST TIME.
EAGER EAGER
うずうず
I WANT TO TAKE PICTURES OF FUKUMARU.
FUKU-MARUUU! OVER HERE!
SHA SHA SHA SHA SHA SHA SHA SHA
SHA SHA SHASHA SHA SHA SHASHA
SHA SHA SHA SHA
?
HA HA HA... THAT'S AN ODD SHUTTER SOUND...
SHA SHA SHA SHA SHA SHA SHA SHA SHA
SHA SHA SHASHA SHA SHA SHASHA
SHA SHA SHA SHA
SHA
THE DESPAIR WOULD HIT ONE HOUR LATER.

## FUKUMARU STOOD UP!

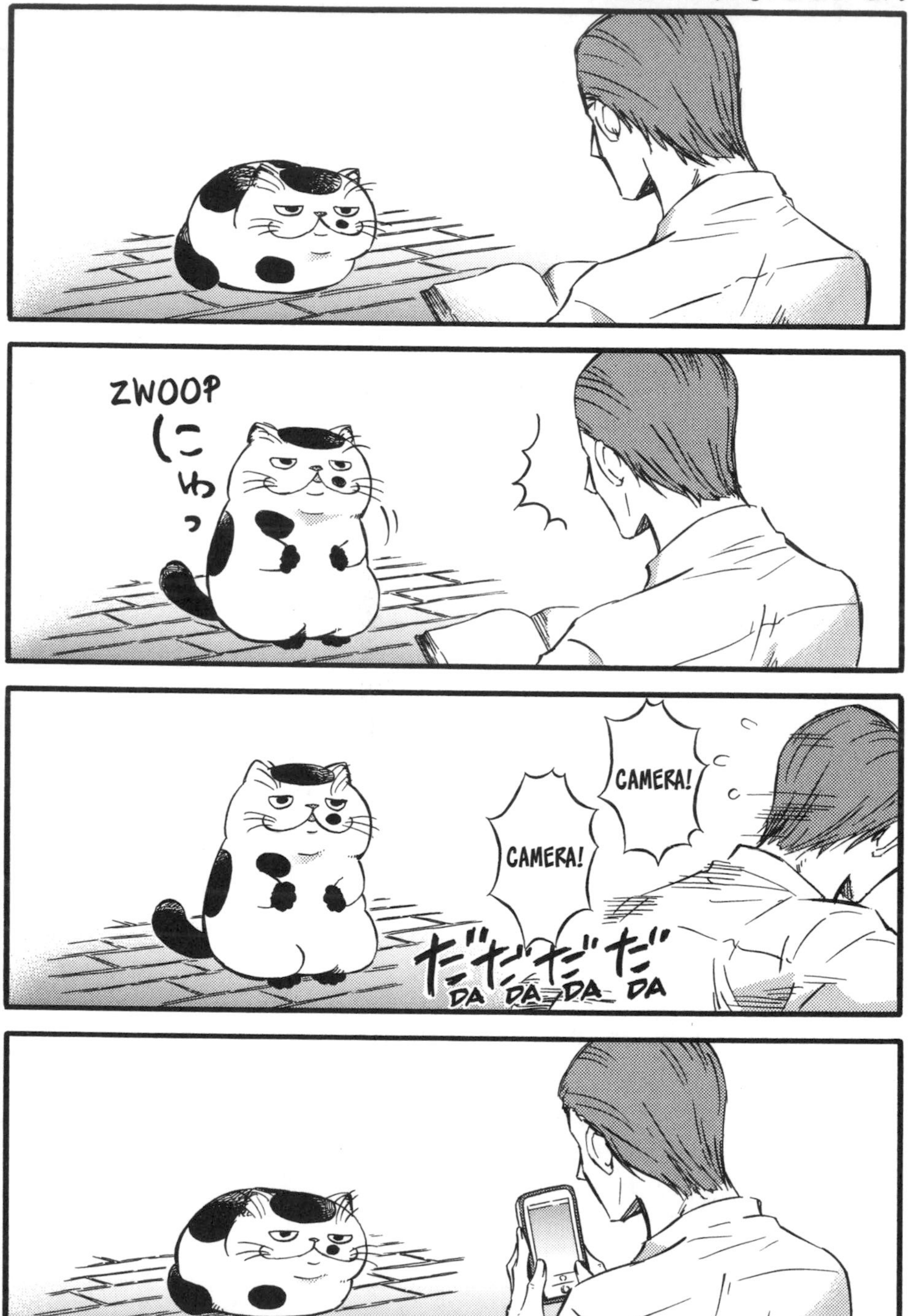
ZWOOP
にゅっ
CAMERA!
CAMERA!
だだだだ
DA DA DA DA

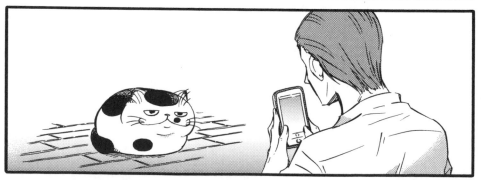

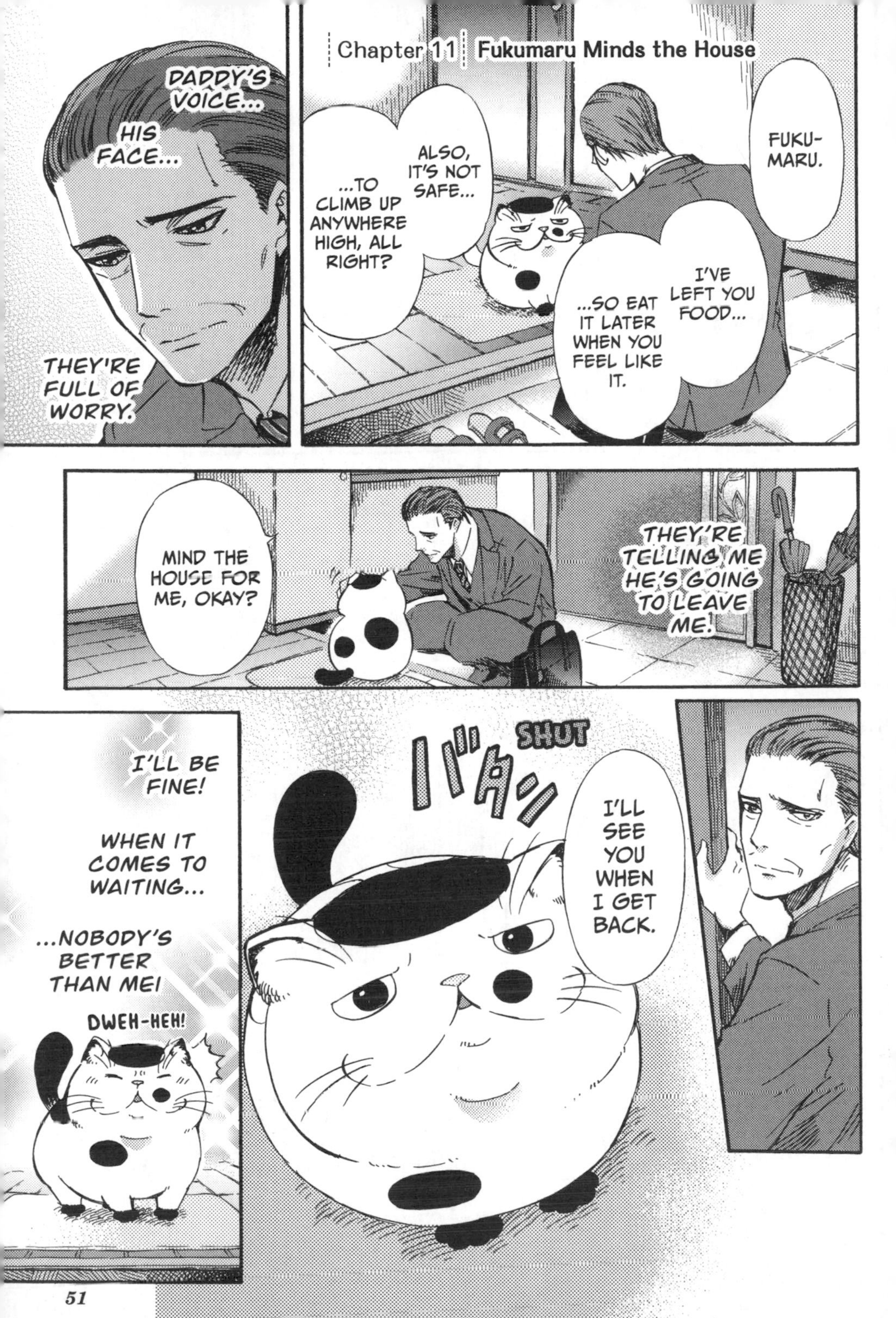
Chapter 11 Fukumaru Minds the House
FUKU-MARU.
I'VE LEFT YOU FOOD...
...SO EAT IT LATER WHEN YOU FEEL LIKE IT.
ALSO, IT'S NOT SAFE...
...TO CLIMB UP ANYWHERE HIGH, ALL RIGHT?
DADDY'S VOICE...
HIS FACE...
THEY'RE FULL OF WORRY.
THEY'RE TELLING ME HE'S GOING TO LEAVE ME!
MIND THE HOUSE FOR ME, OKAY?
I'LL SEE YOU WHEN I GET BACK.
SHUT
I'LL BE FINE!
WHEN IT COMES TO WAITING...
...NOBODY'S BETTER THAN ME!
DWEH-HEH!

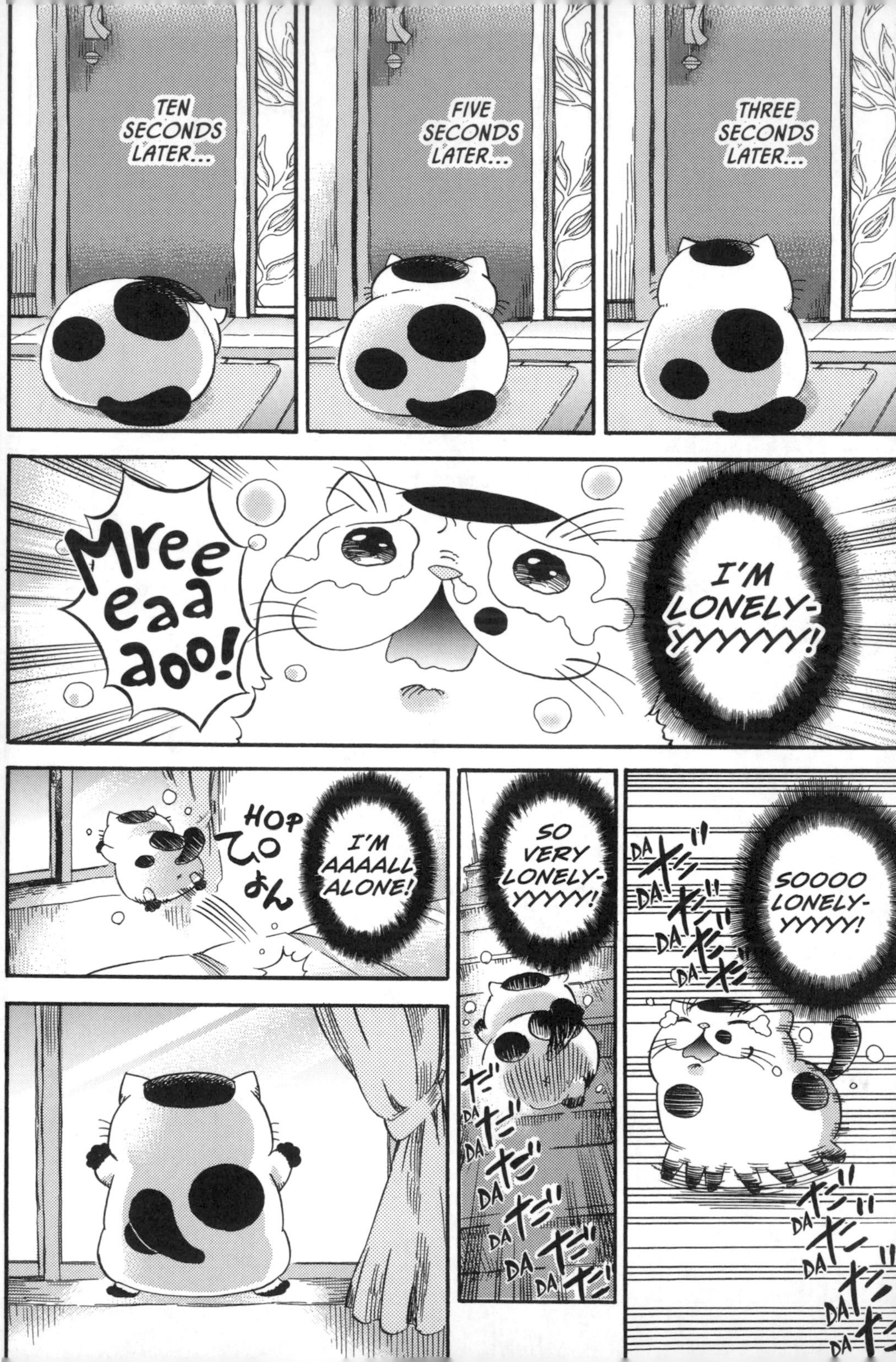
THREE SECONDS LATER...
FIVE SECONDS LATER...
TEN SECONDS LATER...
I'M LONELY-YYYYYY!
Mreeeaaaoo!
SOOOO LONELY-YYYYY!
DA DA DA DA
DA DA DA DA
SO VERY LONELY-YYYYY!
DA DA DA DA DA DA
I'M AAAALL ALONE!
HOP
ぴょん

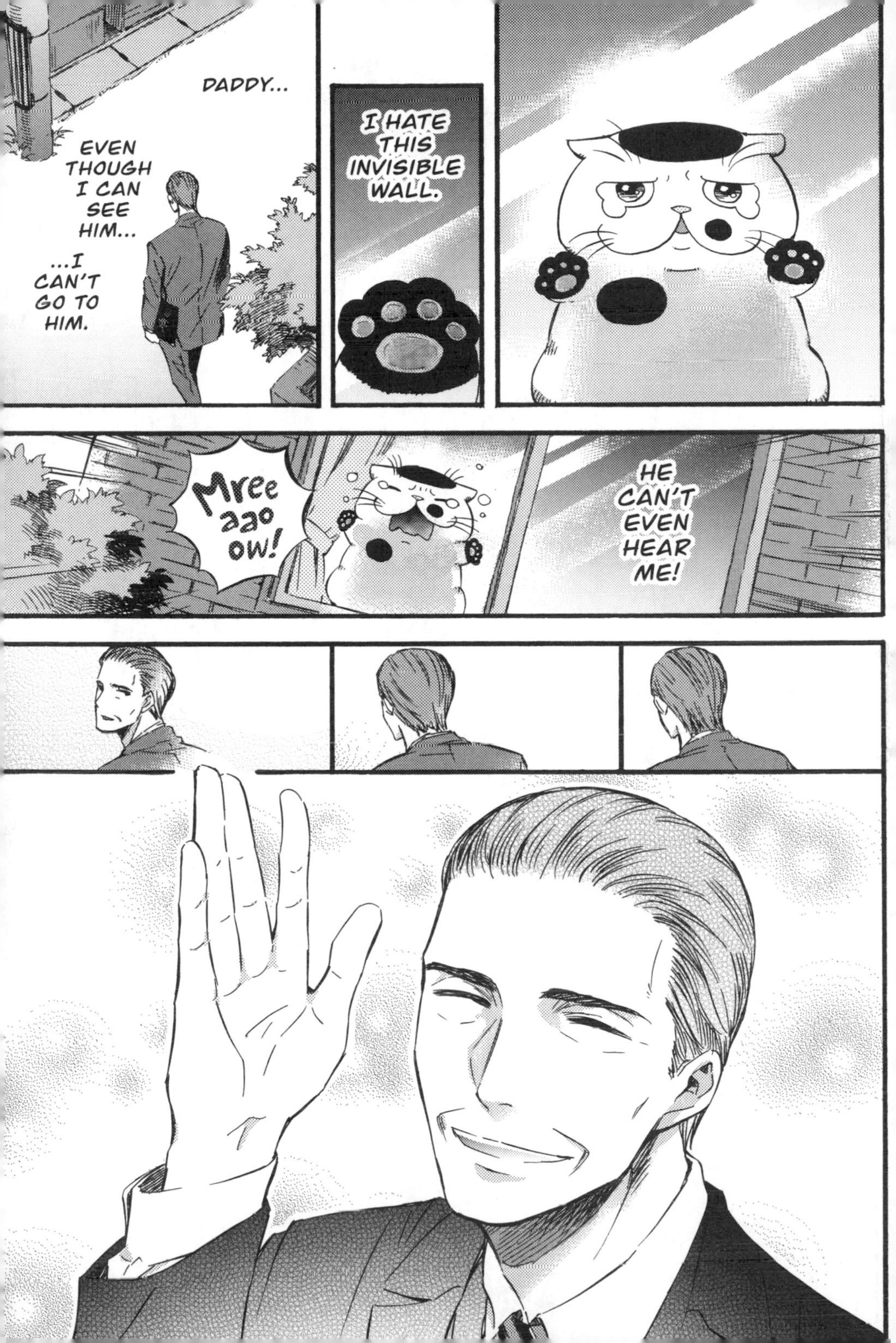
I HATE THIS INVISIBLE WALL.
DADDY...
EVEN THOUGH I CAN SEE HIM...
...I CAN'T GO TO HIM.
HE CAN'T EVEN HEAR ME!
Mreeaaoow!

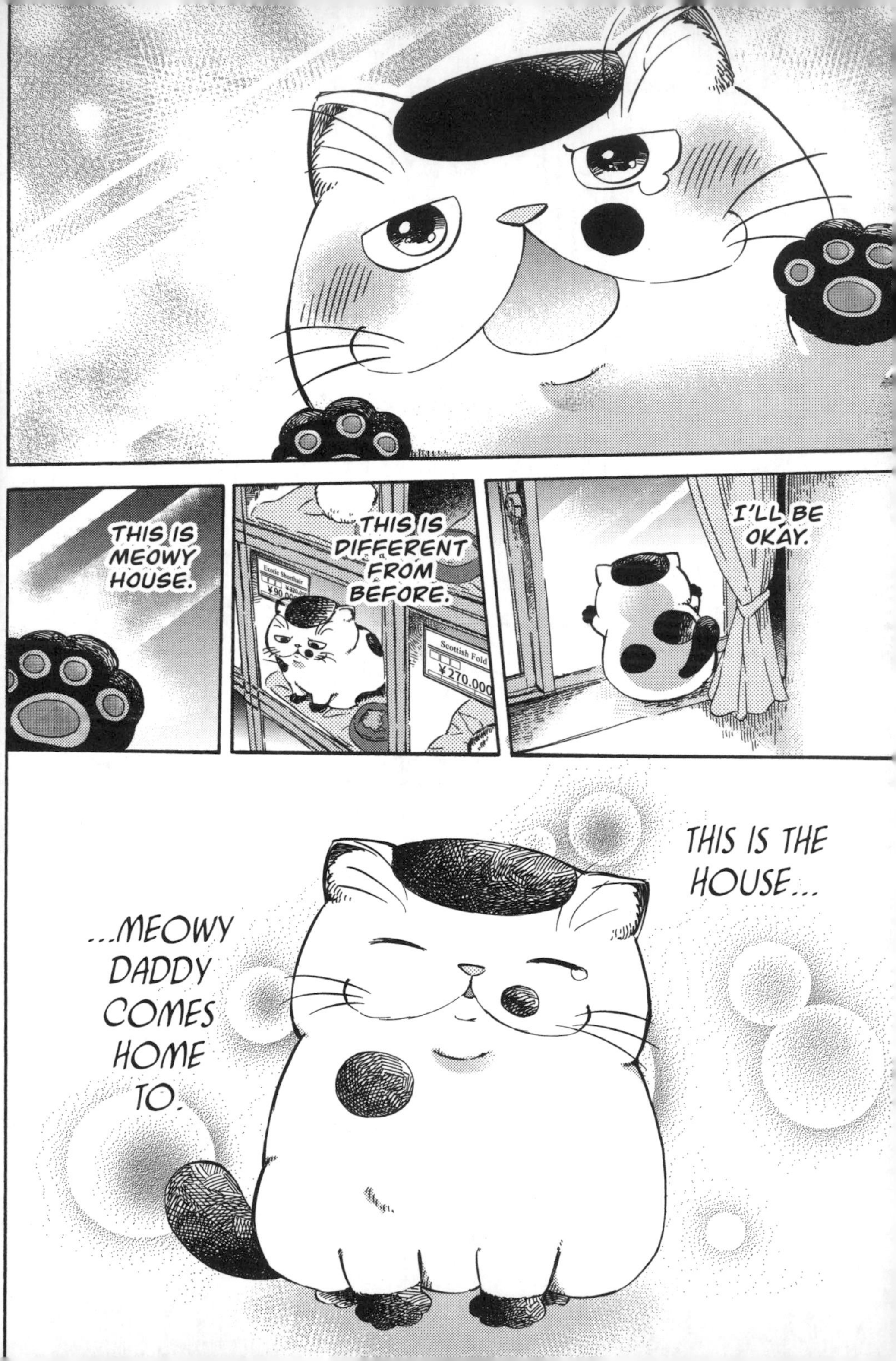
I'LL BE OKAY.
THIS IS DIFFERENT FROM BEFORE.
Exotic Shorthair
Scottish Fold
¥270,000
THIS IS MEOWY HOUSE.
THIS IS THE HOUSE...
...MEOWY DADDY COMES HOME TO.

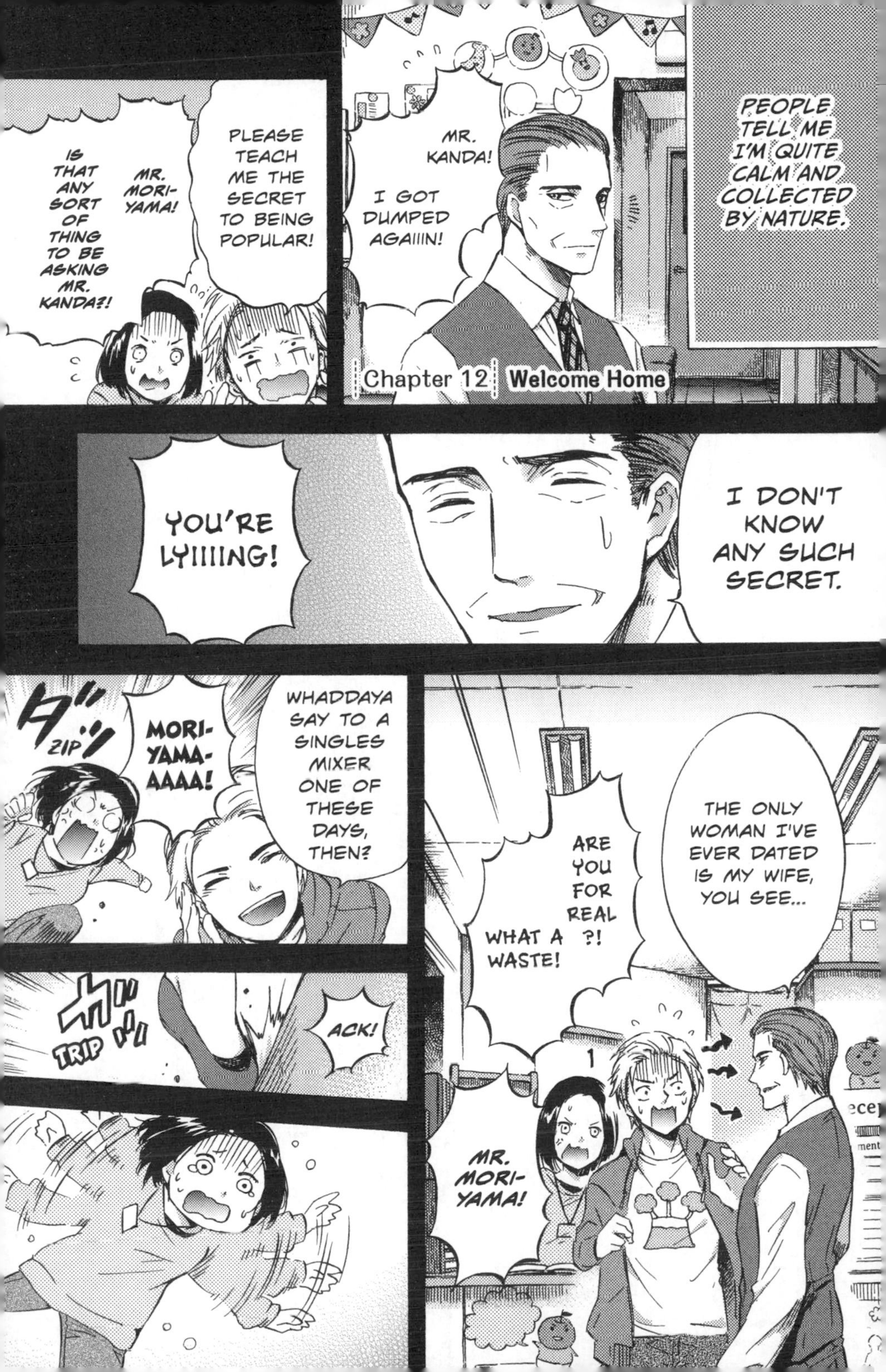
PEOPLE TELL ME I'M QUITE CALM AND COLLECTED BY NATURE.
MR. KANDA!
I GOT DUMPED AGAIIIN!
Chapter 12 Welcome Home
PLEASE TEACH ME THE SECRET TO BEING POPULAR!
MR. MORI-YAMA!
IS THAT ANY SORT OF THING TO BE ASKING MR. KANDA?!
I DON'T KNOW ANY SUCH SECRET.
YOU'RE LYIIIING!
THE ONLY WOMAN I'VE EVER DATED IS MY WIFE, YOU SEE...
ARE YOU FOR REAL?!
WHAT A WASTE!
MR. MORI-YAMA!
WHADDAYA SAY TO A SINGLES MIXER ONE OF THESE DAYS, THEN?
MORI-YAMA-AAAA!
ZIP
ACK!
TRIP

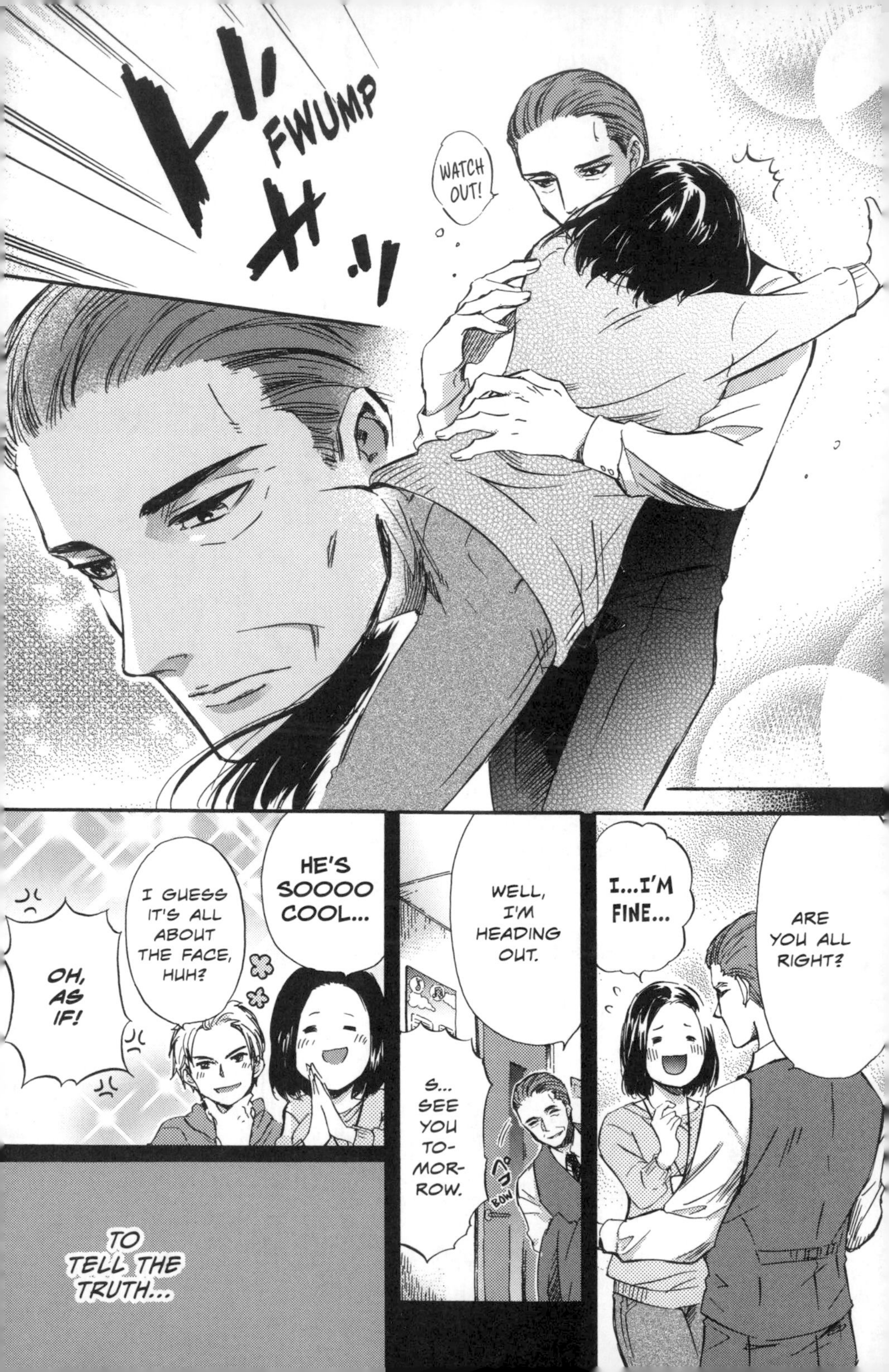
WATCH OUT!
ドサッ
FWUMP
ARE YOU ALL RIGHT?
I...I'M FINE...
WELL, I'M HEADING OUT.
S... SEE YOU TO-MOR-ROW.
BOW
HE'S SOOOO COOL...
I GUESS IT'S ALL ABOUT THE FACE, HUH?
OH, AS IF!
TO TELL THE TRUTH...

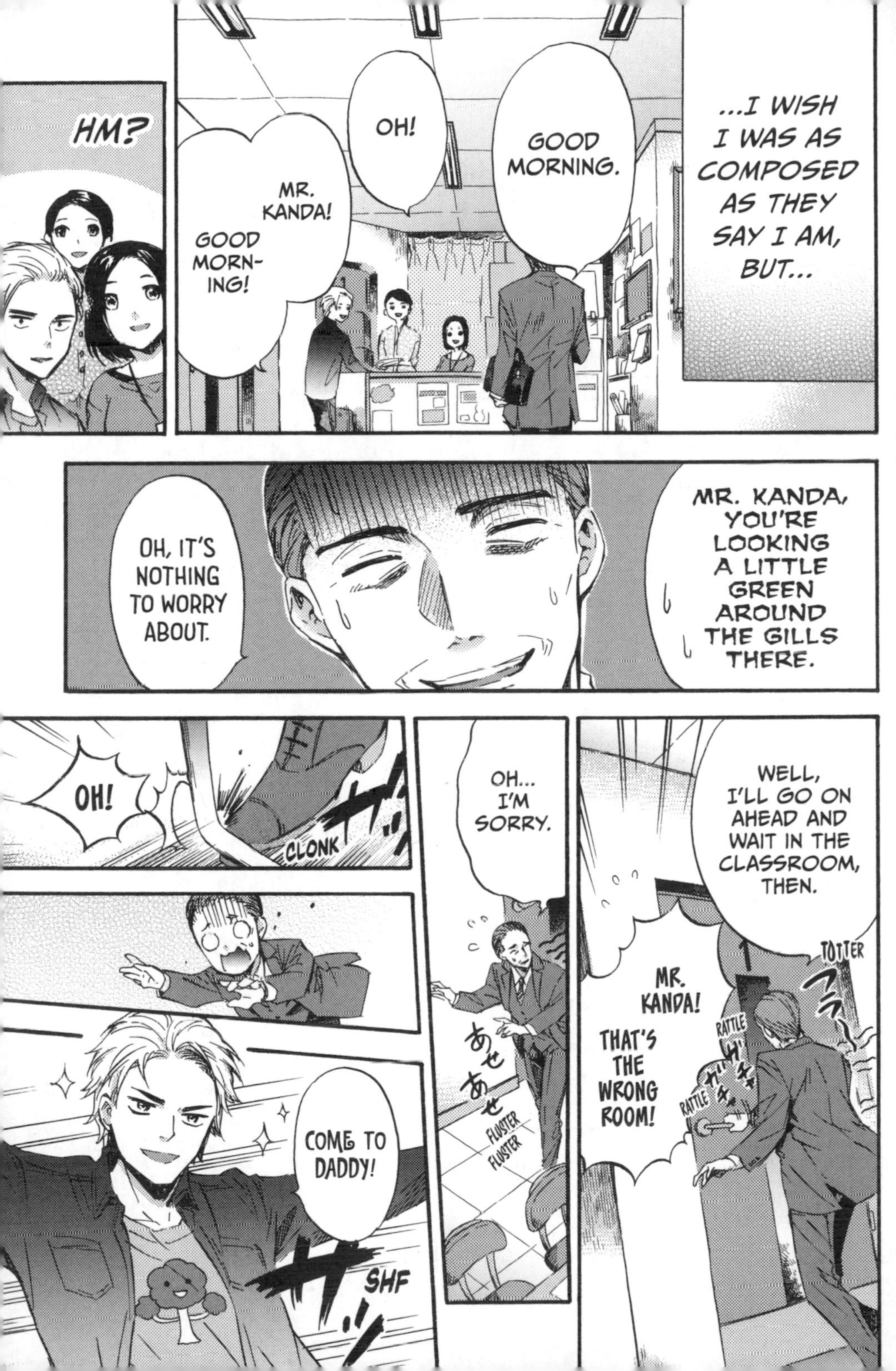
...I WISH I WAS AS COMPOSED AS THEY SAY I AM, BUT...
GOOD MORNING.
OH!
MR. KANDA!
GOOD MORN-ING!
HM?
MR. KANDA, YOU'RE LOOKING A LITTLE GREEN AROUND THE GILLS THERE.
OH, IT'S NOTHING TO WORRY ABOUT.
WELL, I'LL GO ON AHEAD AND WAIT IN THE CLASSROOM, THEN.
TOTTER
RATTLE
RATTLE
MR. KANDA!
THAT'S THE WRONG ROOM!
OH... I'M SORRY.
あせ あせ
FLUSTER FLUSTER
OH!
CLONK
COME TO DADDY!
SHF

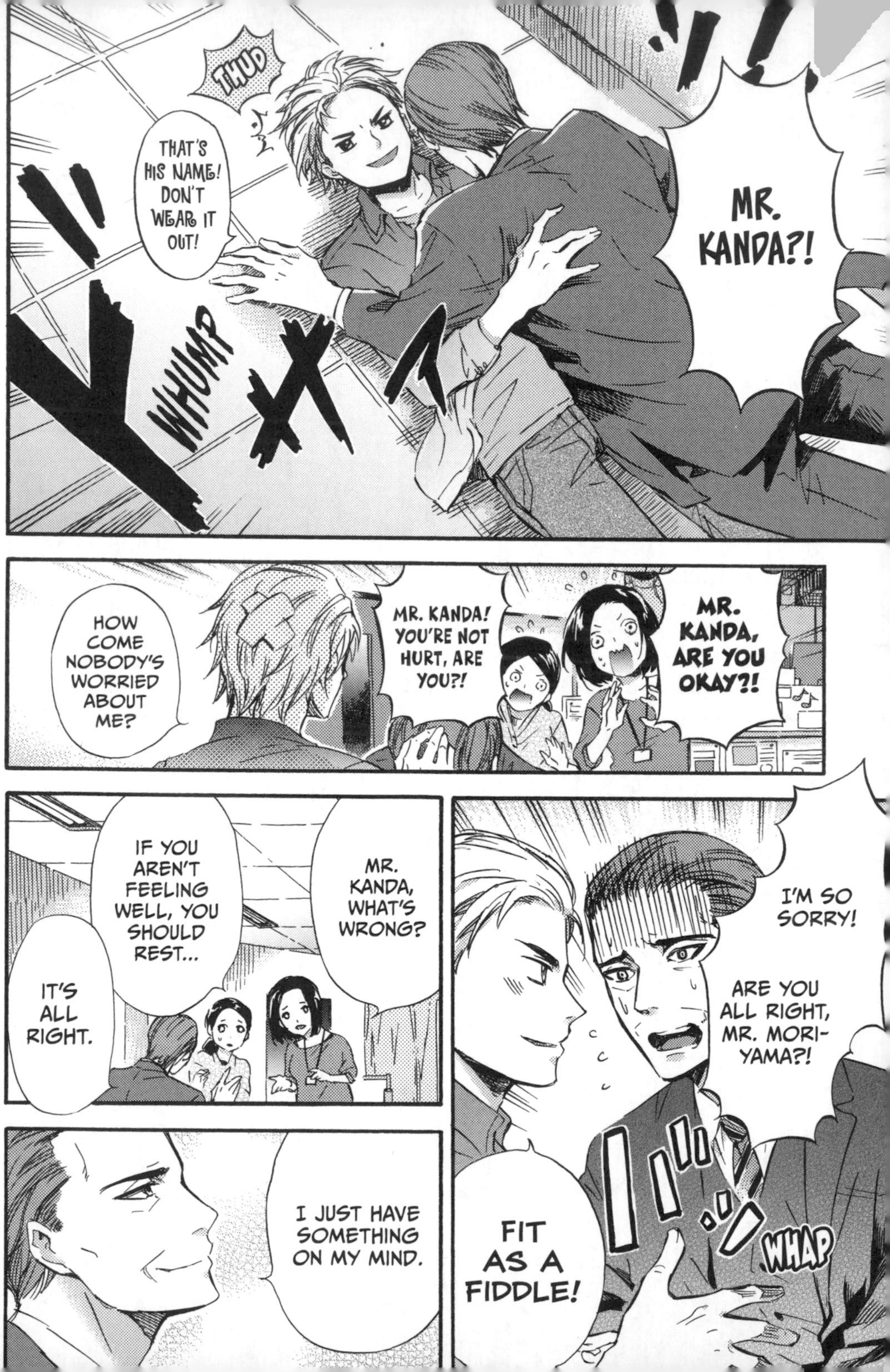
MR. KANDA?!
THUD
THAT'S HIS NAME! DON'T WEAR IT OUT!
WHUMP
MR. KANDA, ARE YOU OKAY?!
MR. KANDA! YOU'RE NOT HURT, ARE YOU?!
HOW COME NOBODY'S WORRIED ABOUT ME?
I'M SO SORRY!
ARE YOU ALL RIGHT, MR. MORI-YAMA?!
WHAP
FIT AS A FIDDLE!
MR. KANDA, WHAT'S WRONG?
IF YOU AREN'T FEELING WELL, YOU SHOULD REST...
IT'S ALL RIGHT.
I JUST HAVE SOMETHING ON MY MIND.

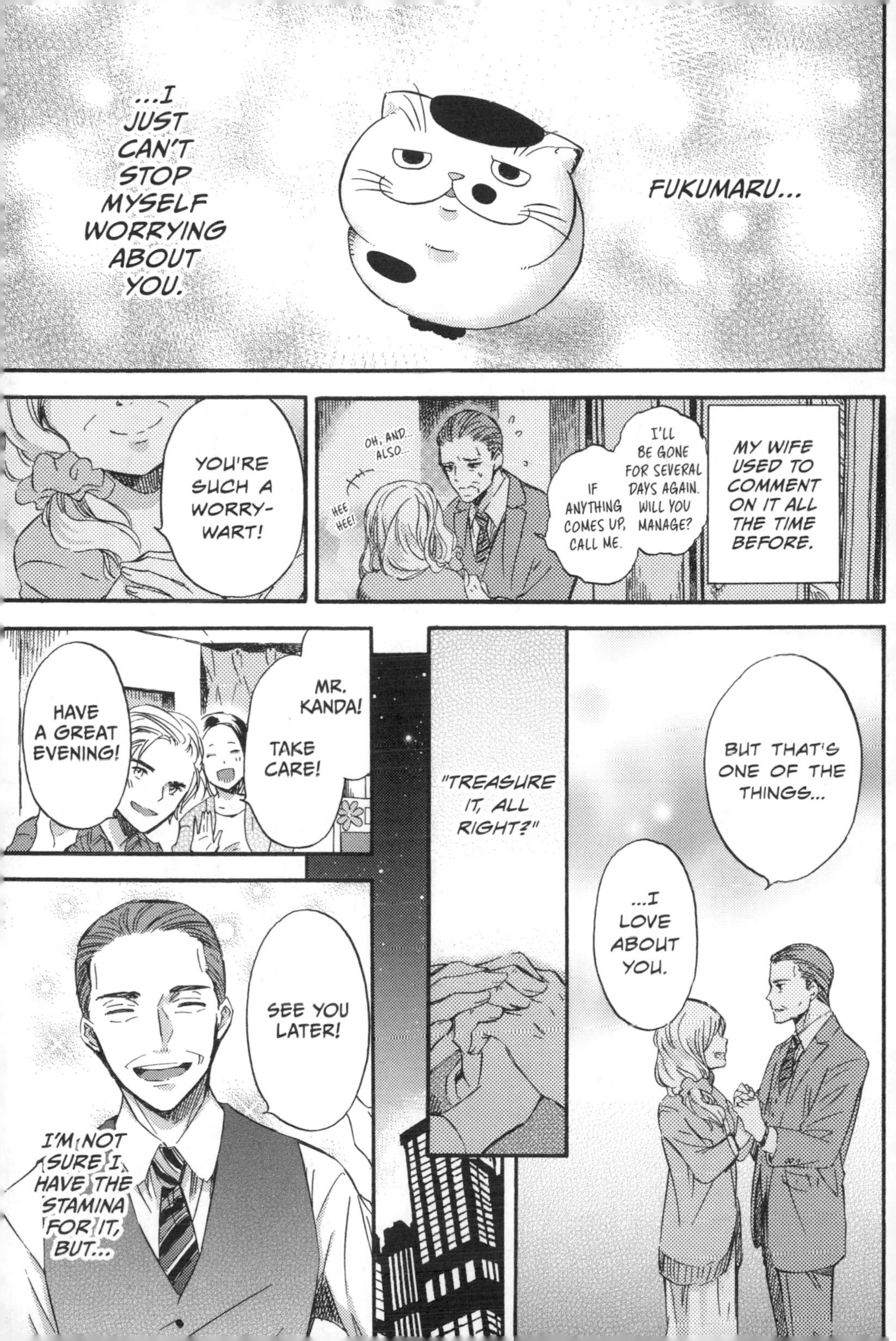
FUKUMARU...
...I JUST CAN'T STOP MYSELF WORRYING ABOUT YOU.
MY WIFE USED TO COMMENT ON IT ALL THE TIME BEFORE.
I'LL BE GONE FOR SEVERAL DAYS AGAIN. WILL YOU MANAGE?
IF ANYTHING COMES UP, CALL ME.
OH, AND... ALSO...
HEE HEE!
YOU'RE SUCH A WORRY-WART!
BUT THAT'S ONE OF THE THINGS...
...I LOVE ABOUT YOU.
"TREASURE IT, ALL RIGHT?"
MR. KANDA!
TAKE CARE!
HAVE A GREAT EVENING!
SEE YOU LATER!
I'M NOT SURE I HAVE THE STAMINA FOR IT, BUT...

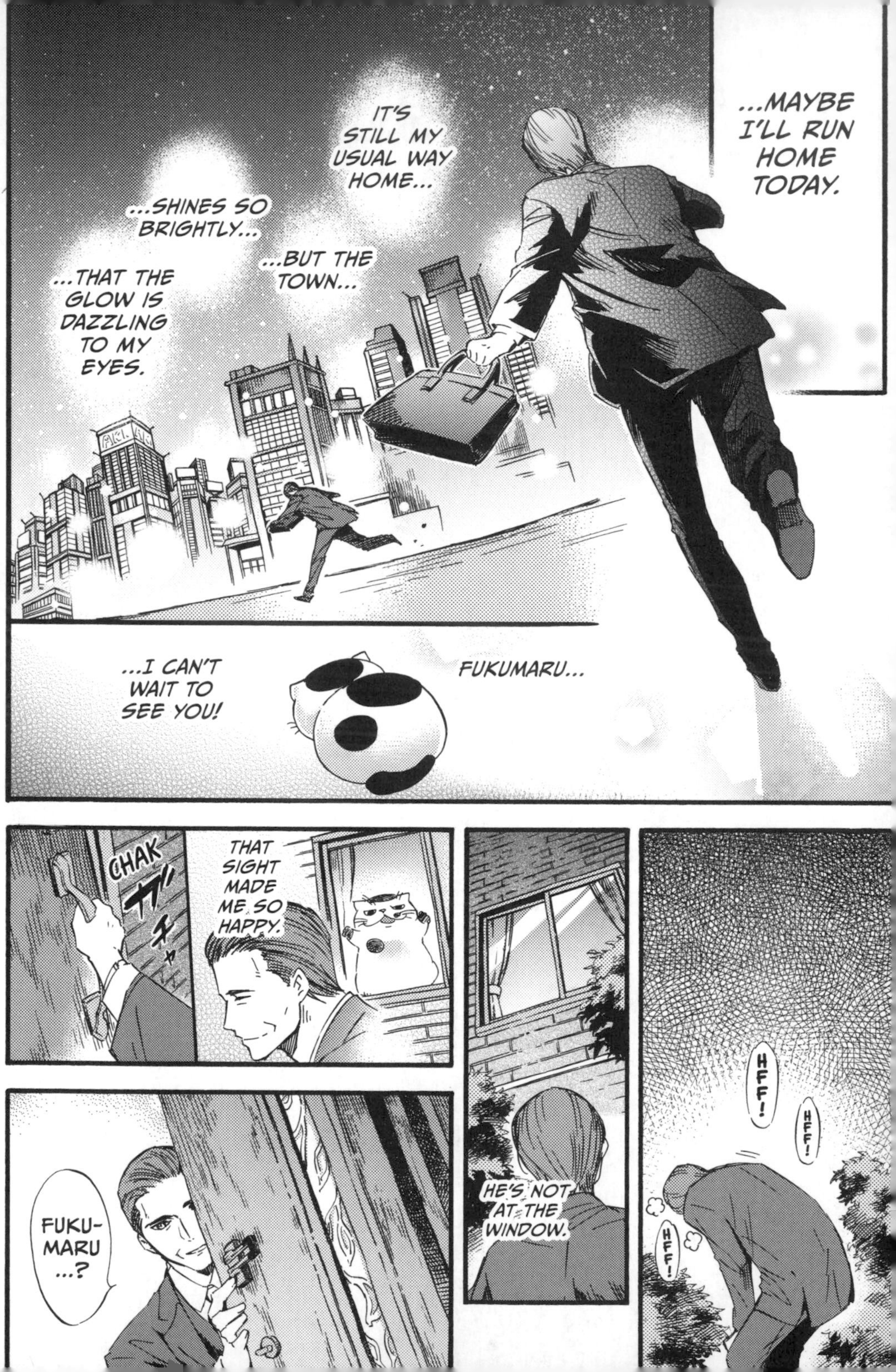
...MAYBE I'LL RUN HOME TODAY.
IT'S STILL MY USUAL WAY HOME...
...BUT THE TOWN...
...SHINES SO BRIGHTLY...
...THAT THE GLOW IS DAZZLING TO MY EYES.
FUKUMARU...
...I CAN'T WAIT TO SEE YOU!
HFF!
HFF!
HFF!
HE'S NOT AT THE WINDOW.
THAT SIGHT MADE ME SO HAPPY.
CHAK
FUKU-MARU ...?

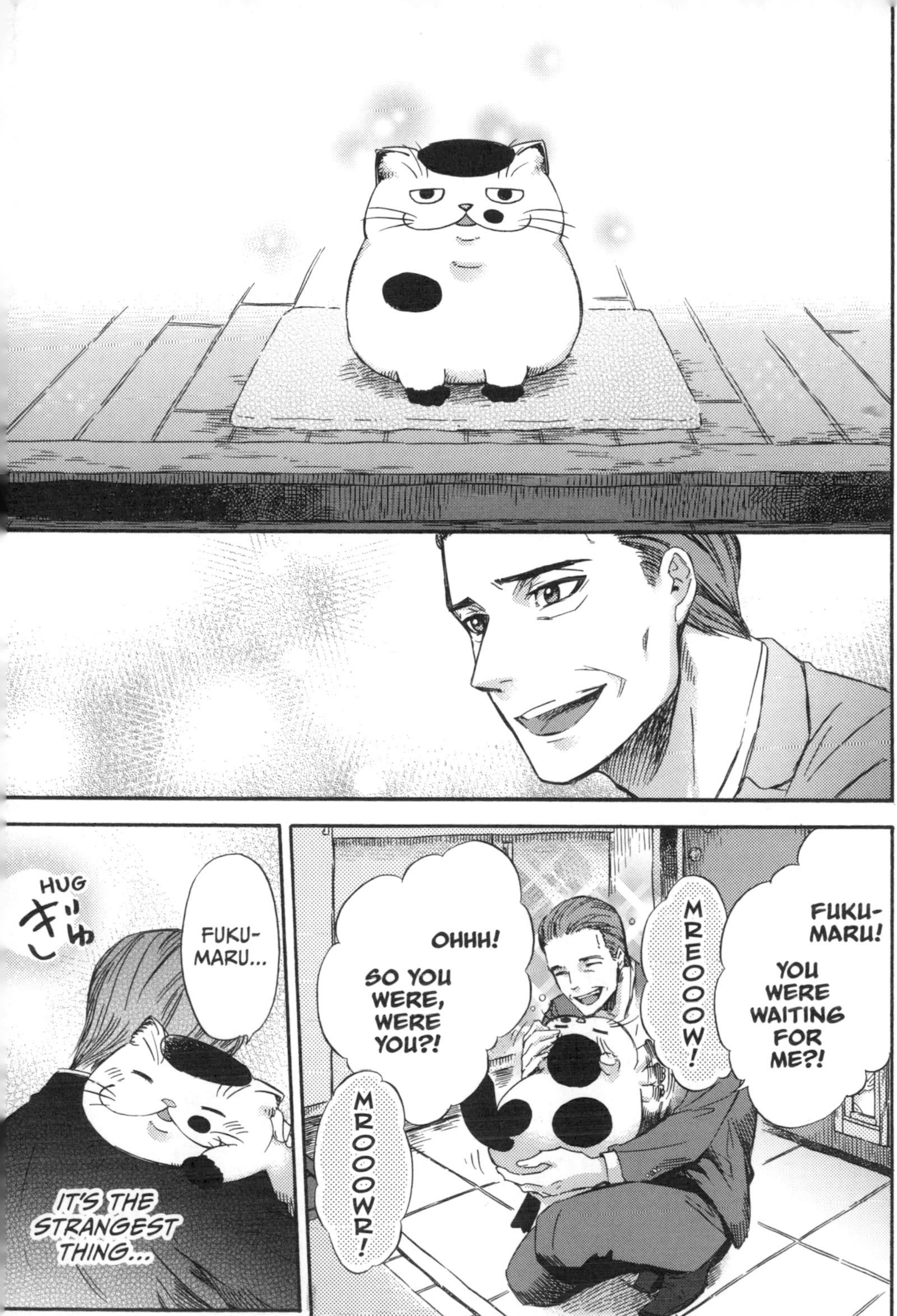
FUKU-MARU!
YOU WERE WAITING FOR ME?!
MREOOOOW!
OHHH!
SO YOU WERE, WERE YOU?!
MROOOOWR!
FUKU-MARU...
HUG
ぎゅ
IT'S THE STRANGEST THING...

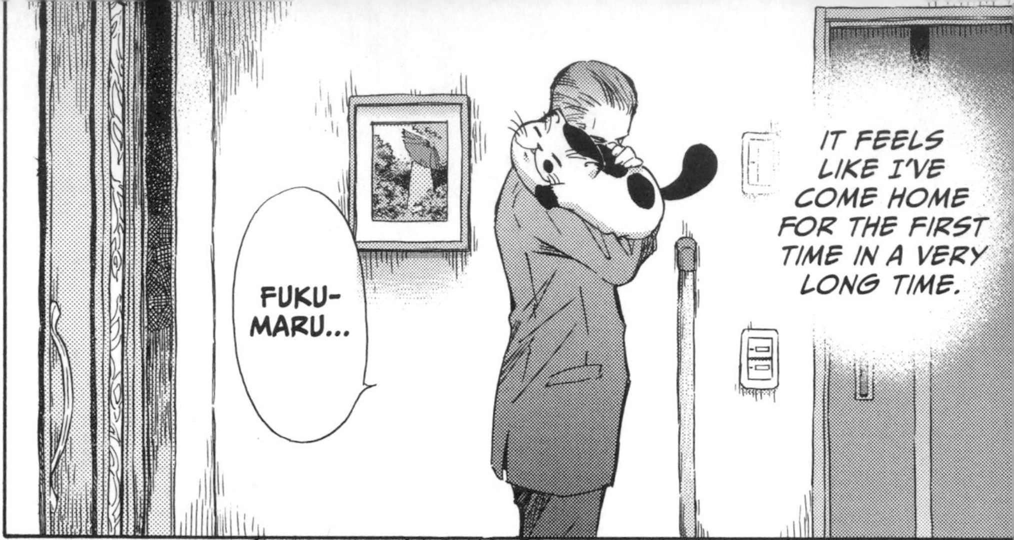
IT FEELS LIKE I'VE COME HOME FOR THE FIRST TIME IN A VERY LONG TIME.
FUKU-MARU...
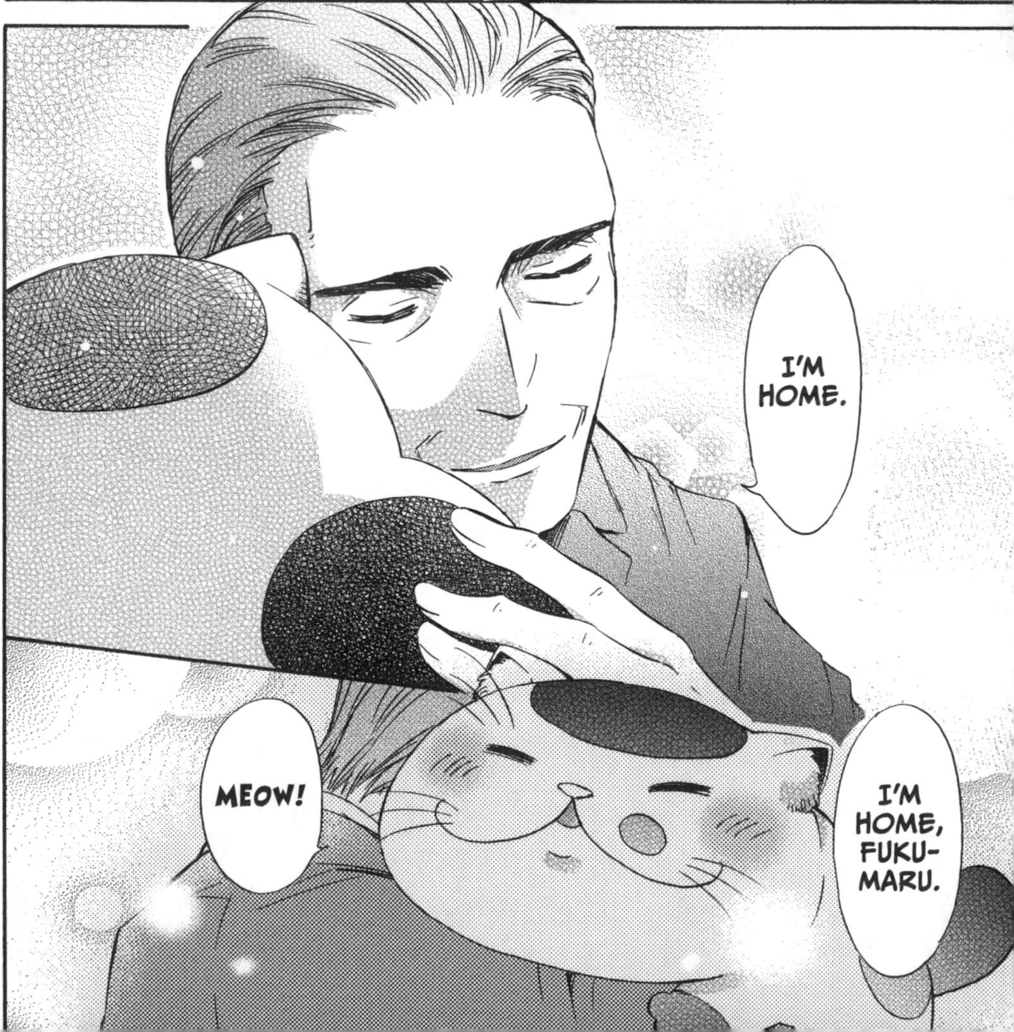
I'M HOME.
I'M HOME, FUKU-MARU.
MEOW!

# Chapter 13 Loyal Kitty Fukumaru

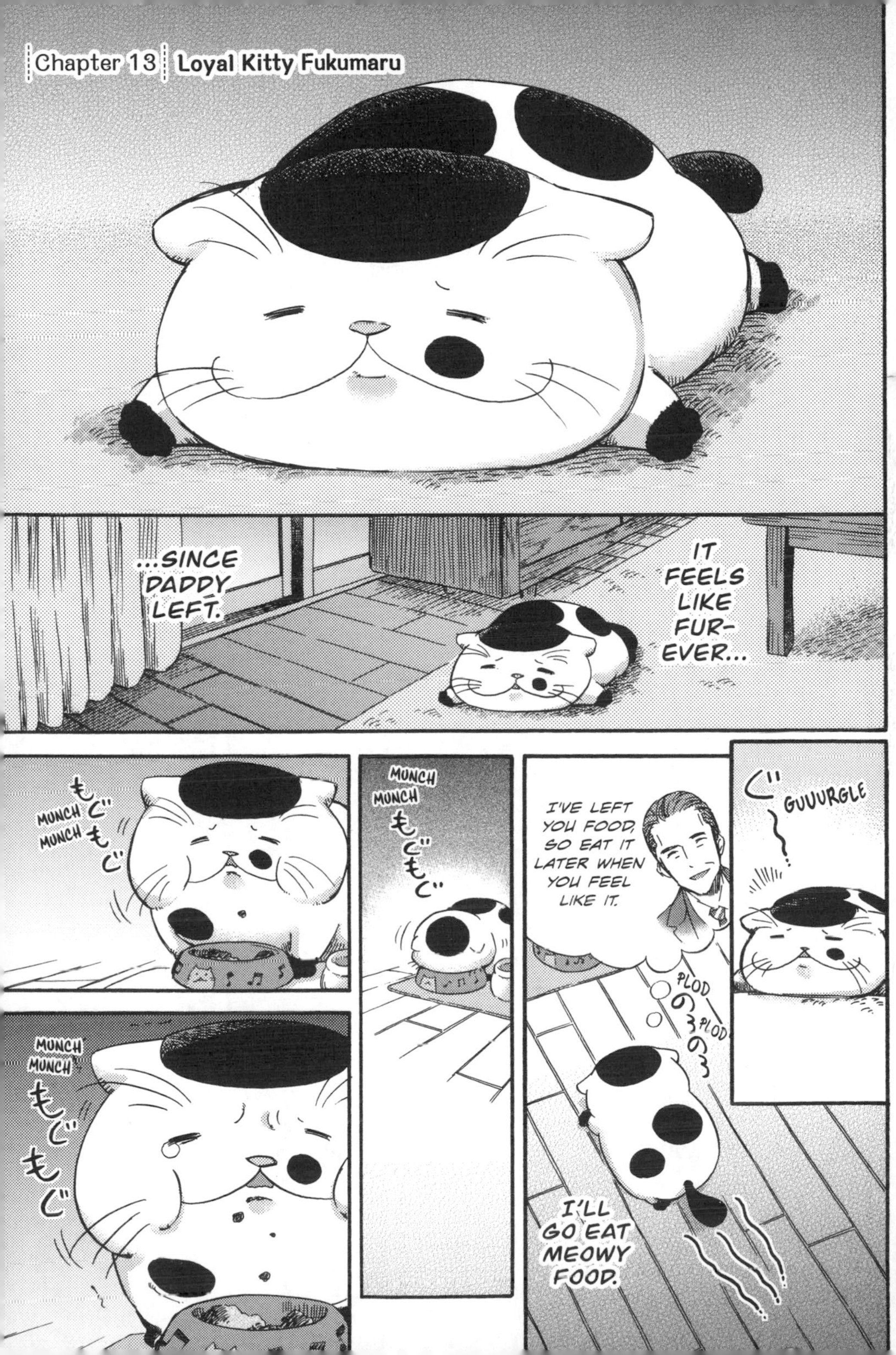
IT FEELS LIKE FUR-EVER...
...SINCE DADDY LEFT.
ぐ～
GUUURGLE
I'VE LEFT YOU FOOD, SO EAT IT LATER WHEN YOU FEEL LIKE IT.
PLOD のろ
PLOD のろ
I'LL GO EAT MEOWY FOOD.
MUNCH MUNCH もぐもぐ
MUNCH MUNCH もぐもぐ
MUNCH MUNCH もぐもぐ

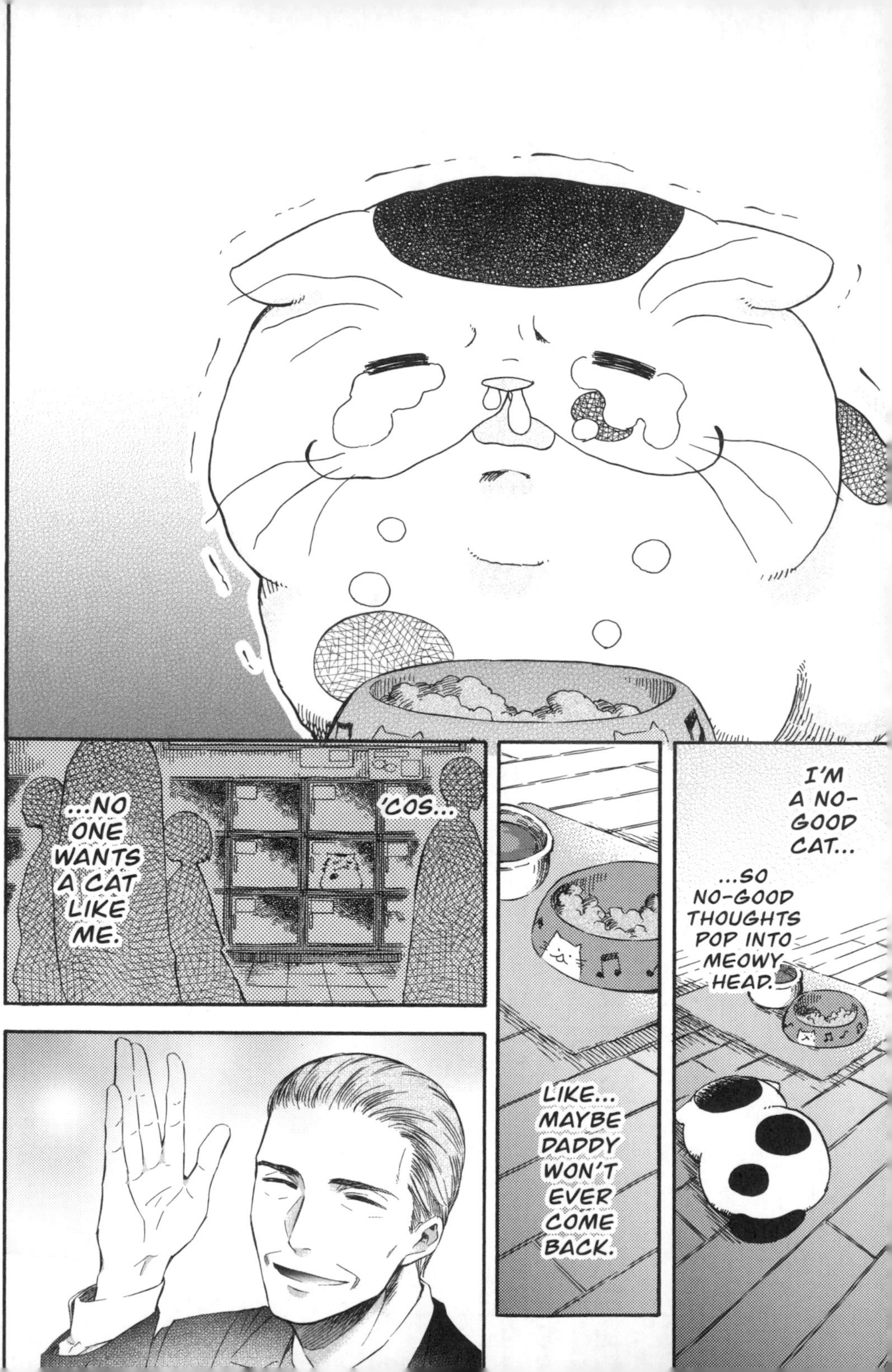
I'M A NO-GOOD CAT...
...SO NO-GOOD THOUGHTS POP INTO MEOWY HEAD.
LIKE... MAYBE DADDY WON'T EVER COME BACK.
'COS...
...NO ONE WANTS A CAT LIKE ME.

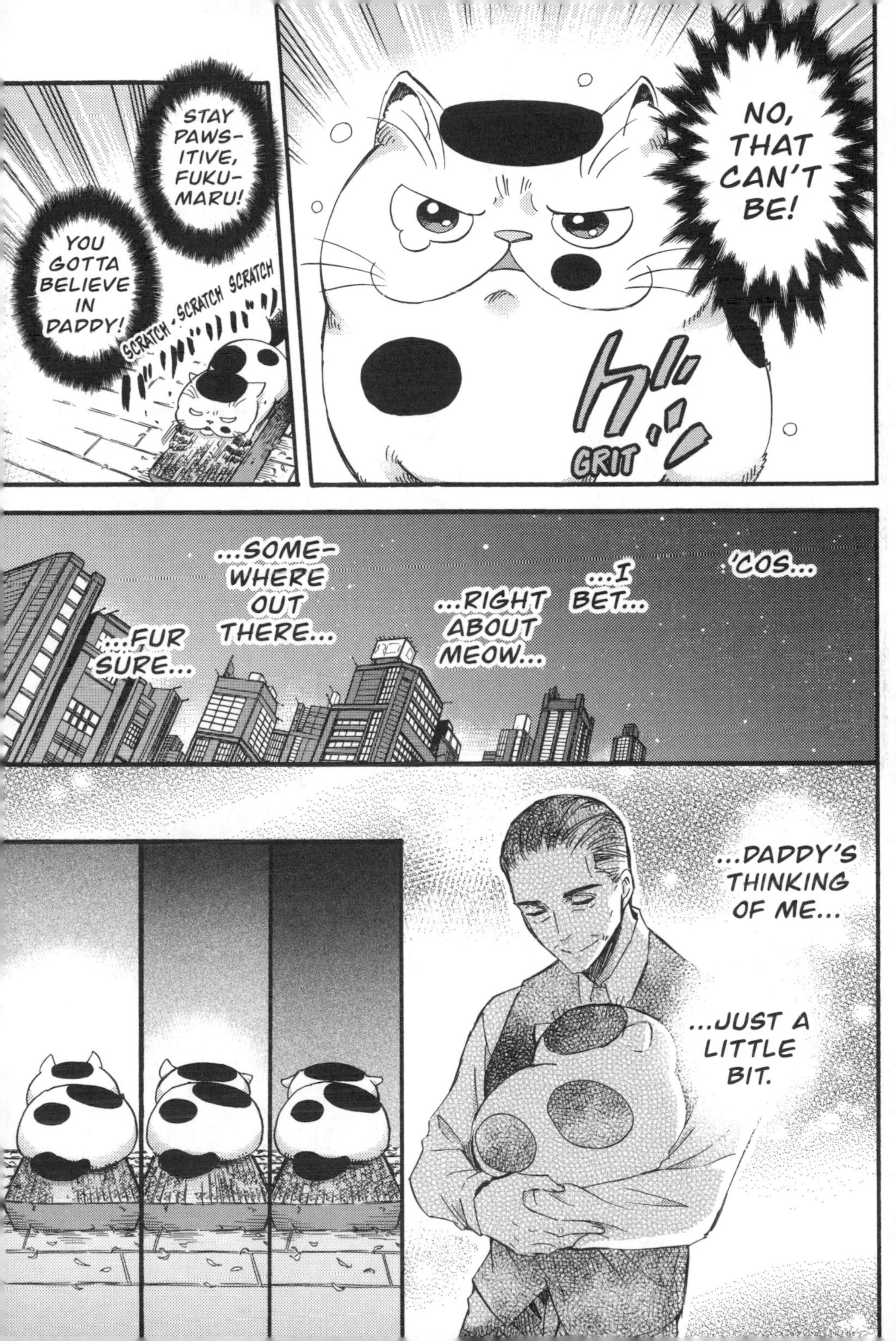
NO, THAT CAN'T BE!
GRIT
STAY PAWS-ITIVE, FUKU-MARU!
YOU GOTTA BELIEVE IN DADDY!
SCRATCH SCRATCH SCRATCH
'COS...
...I BET...
...RIGHT ABOUT MEOW...
...SOME-WHERE OUT THERE...
...FUR SURE...
...DADDY'S THINKING OF ME...
...JUST A LITTLE BIT.

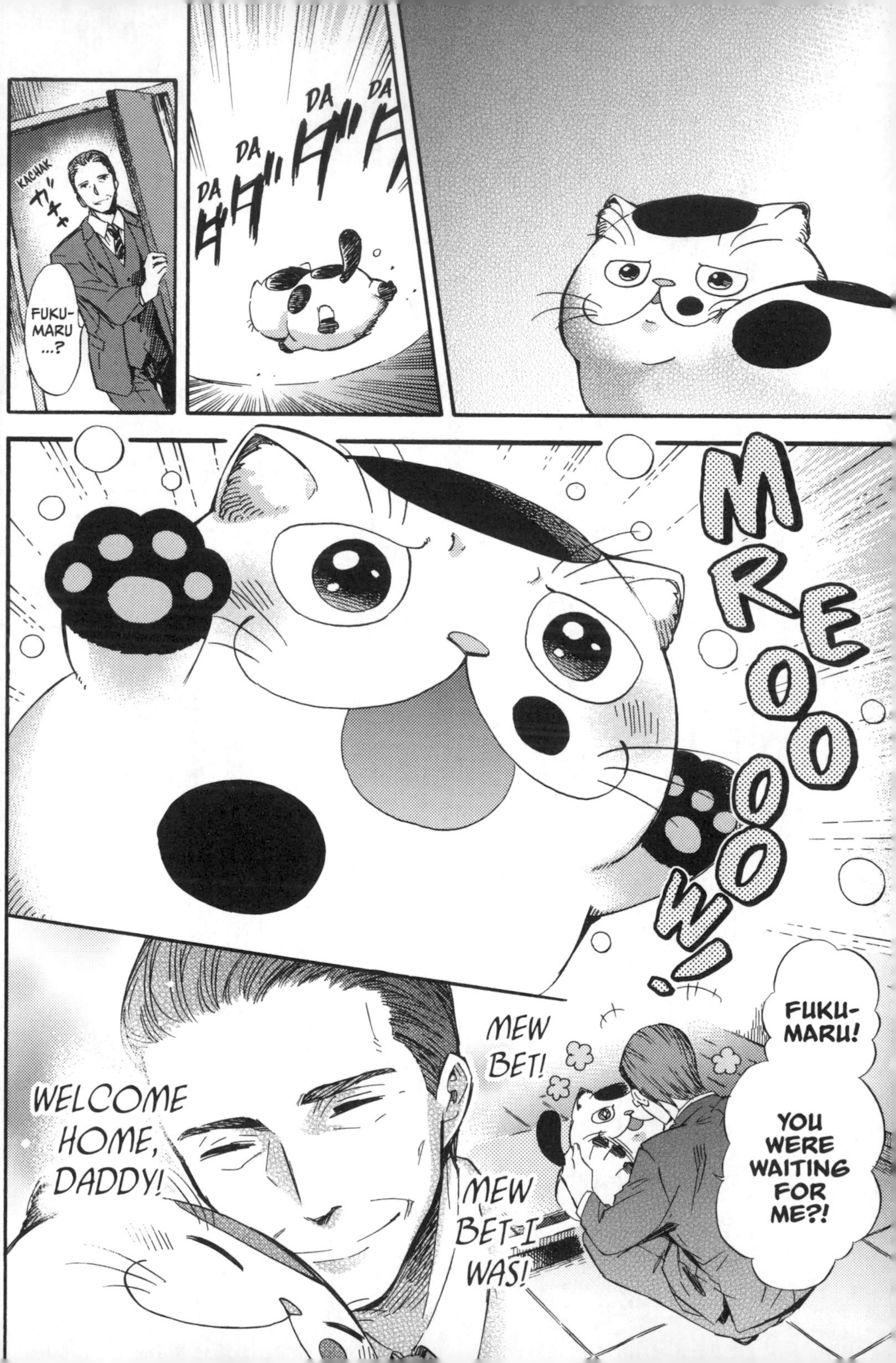
DA DA DA DA
ダダダダ
KACHAK
ガチャ
FUKU-MARU ...?
MREOOOOW!
FUKU-MARU!
YOU WERE WAITING FOR ME?!
MEW BET!
MEW BET I WAS!
WELCOME HOME, DADDY!

WANTED: SELFIES WITH FUKUMARU

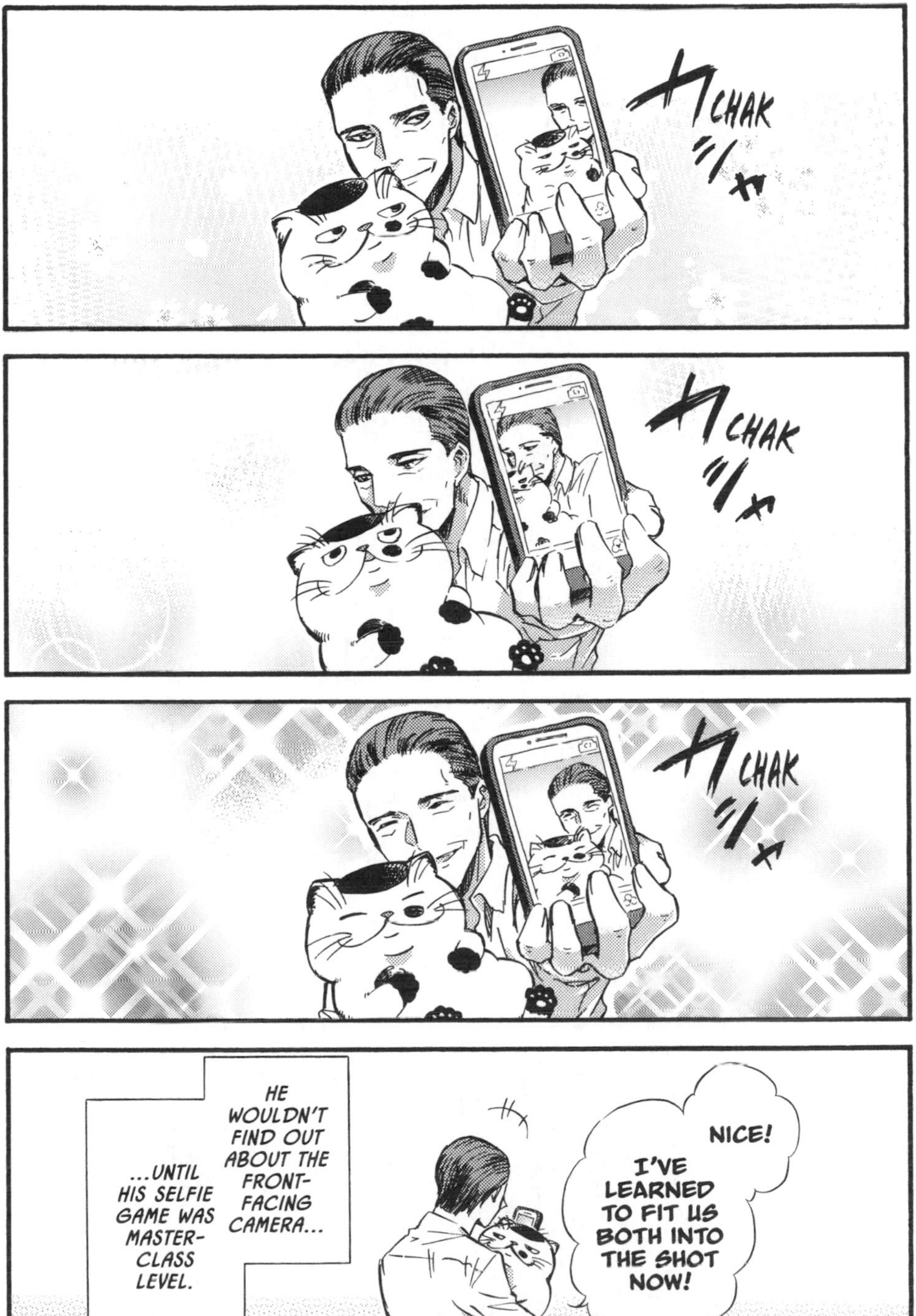
CHAK
CHAK
CHAK
NICE! I'VE LEARNED TO FIT US BOTH INTO THE SHOT NOW!
HE WOULDN'T FIND OUT ABOUT THE FRONT-FACING CAMERA...
...UNTIL HIS SELFIE GAME WAS MASTER-CLASS LEVEL.

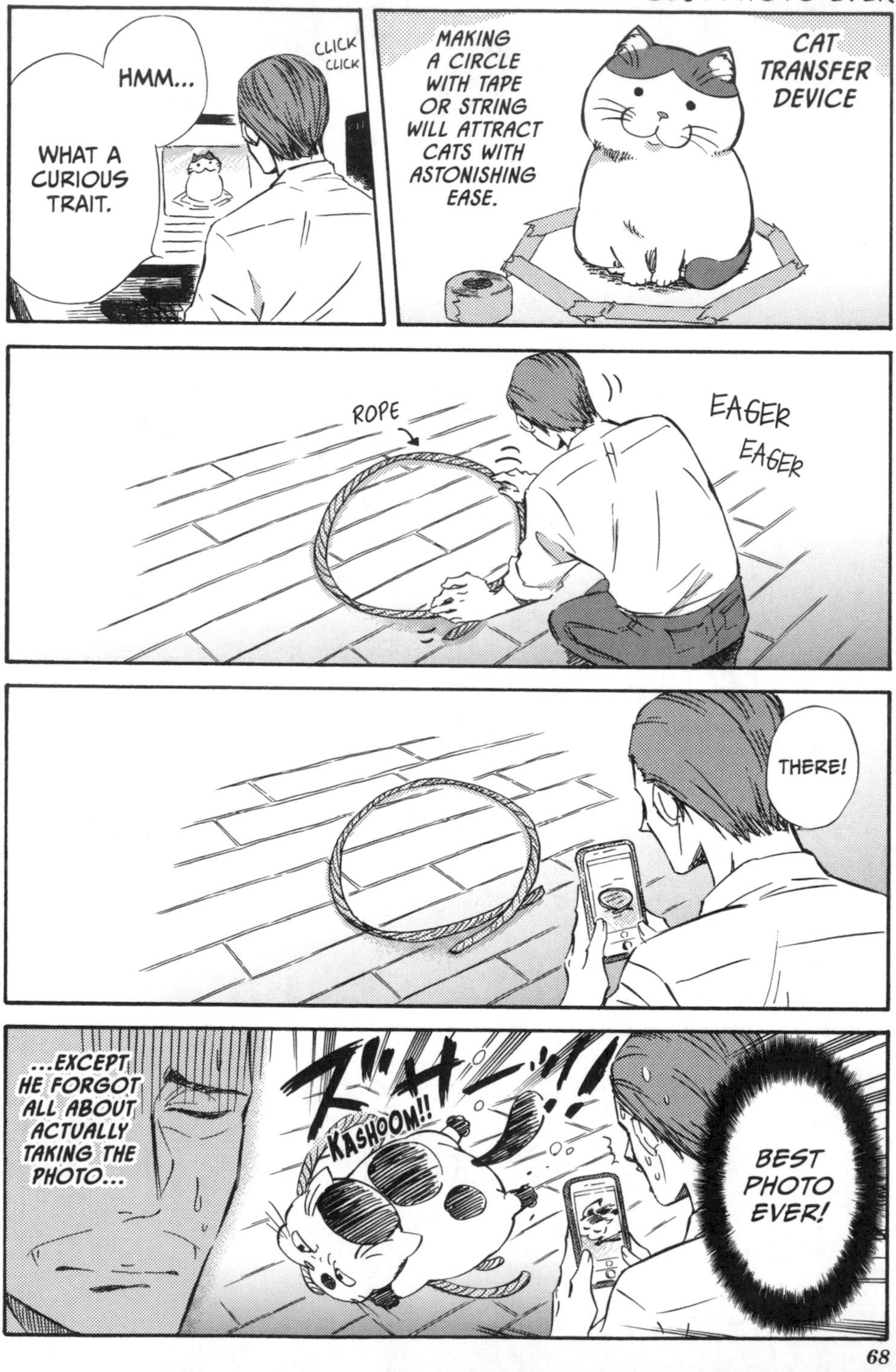
CAT TRANSFER DEVICE
MAKING A CIRCLE WITH TAPE OR STRING WILL ATTRACT CATS WITH ASTONISHING EASE.
CLICK CLICK
HMM...
WHAT A CURIOUS TRAIT.
EAGER EAGER
ROPE
THERE!
BEST PHOTO EVER!
KASHOOM!!
...EXCEPT HE FORGOT ALL ABOUT ACTUALLY TAKING THE PHOTO...

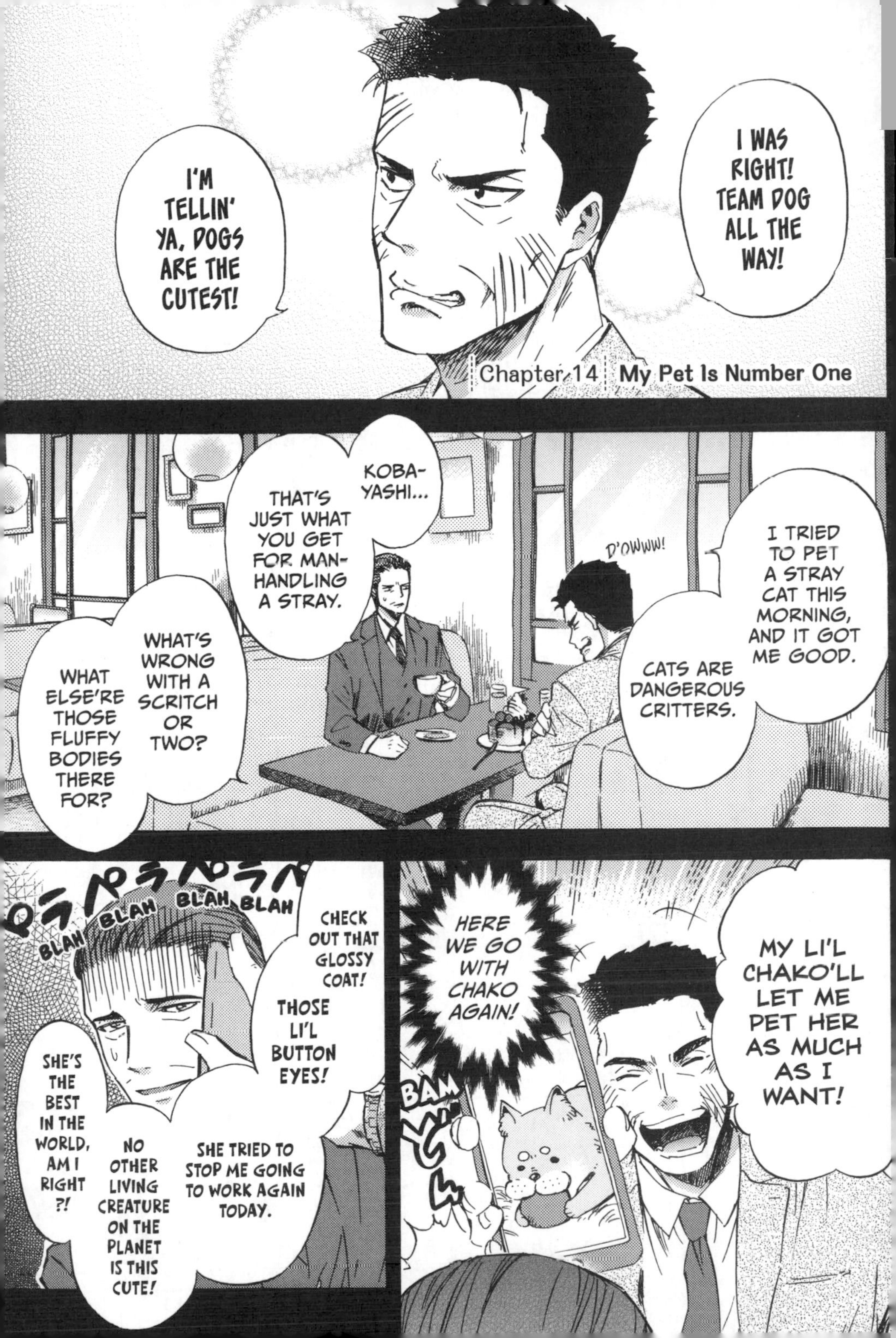
I WAS RIGHT! TEAM DOG ALL THE WAY!
I'M TELLIN' YA, DOGS ARE THE CUTEST!
Chapter 14 My Pet Is Number One
I TRIED TO PET A STRAY CAT THIS MORNING, AND IT GOT ME GOOD.
CATS ARE DANGEROUS CRITTERS.
D'OWWW!
KOBA-YASHI...
THAT'S JUST WHAT YOU GET FOR MAN-HANDLING A STRAY.
WHAT'S WRONG WITH A SCRITCH OR TWO?
WHAT ELSE'RE THOSE FLUFFY BODIES THERE FOR?
MY LI'L CHAKO'LL LET ME PET HER AS MUCH AS I WANT!
HERE WE GO WITH CHAKO AGAIN!
BLAH BLAH BLAH BLAH
CHECK OUT THAT GLOSSY COAT!
THOSE LI'L BUTTON EYES!
SHE TRIED TO STOP ME GOING TO WORK AGAIN TODAY.
NO OTHER LIVING CREATURE ON THE PLANET IS THIS CUTE!
SHE'S THE BEST IN THE WORLD, AM I RIGHT?!

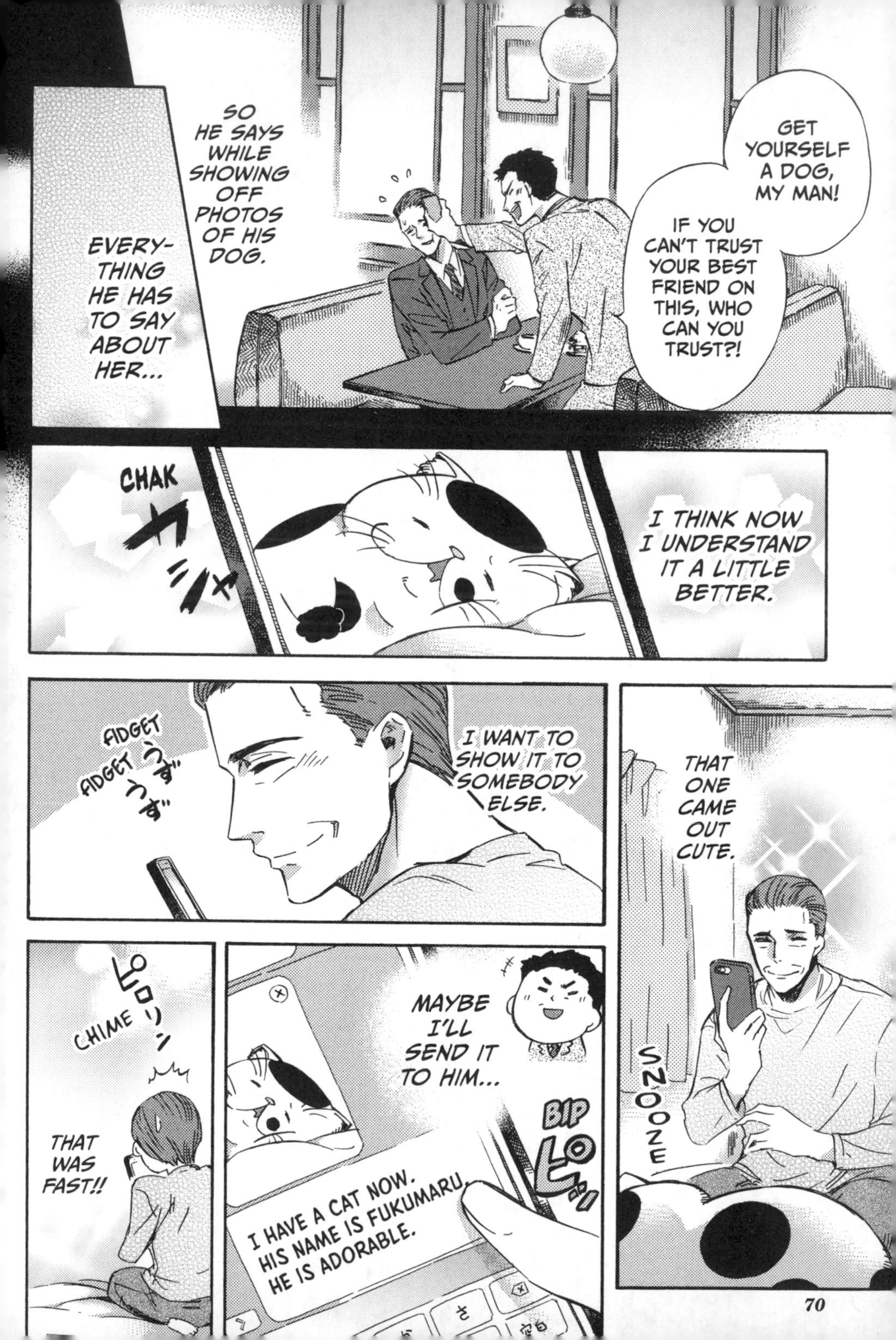
GET YOURSELF A DOG, MY MAN!
IF YOU CAN'T TRUST YOUR BEST FRIEND ON THIS, WHO CAN YOU TRUST?!
SO HE SAYS WHILE SHOWING OFF PHOTOS OF HIS DOG.
EVERY-THING HE HAS TO SAY ABOUT HER...
I THINK NOW I UNDERSTAND IT A LITTLE BETTER.
CHAK
THAT ONE CAME OUT CUTE.
SNOOZE
I WANT TO SHOW IT TO SOMEBODY ELSE.
FIDGET FIDGET
うず うず
MAYBE I'LL SEND IT TO HIM...
I HAVE A CAT NOW. HIS NAME IS FUKUMARU. HE IS ADORABLE.
BIP
CHIME
THAT WAS FAST!!

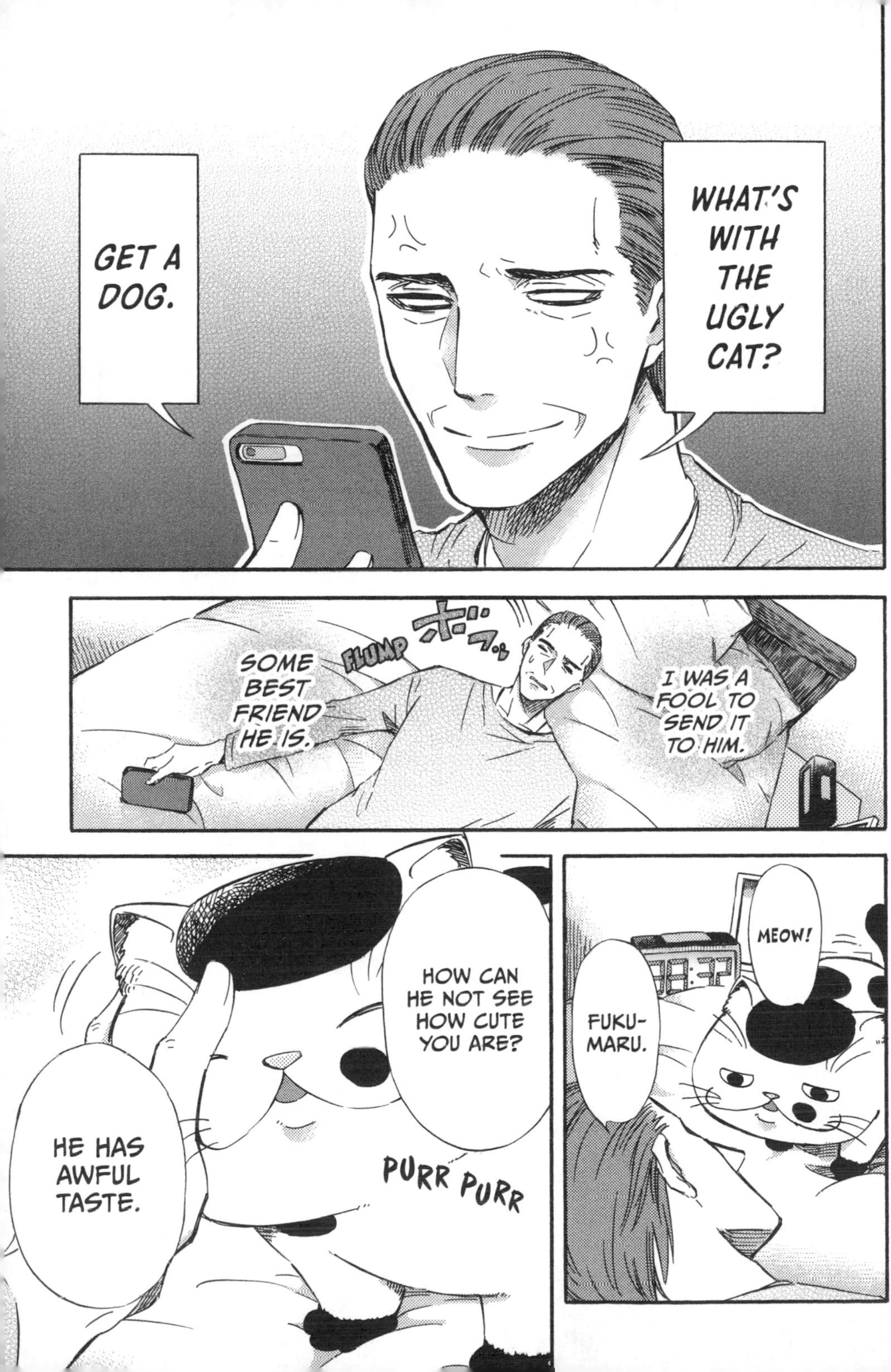
WHAT'S WITH THE UGLY CAT?
GET A DOG.
FLUMP
I WAS A FOOL TO SEND IT TO HIM.
SOME BEST FRIEND HE IS.
MEOW!
FUKU-MARU.
HOW CAN HE NOT SEE HOW CUTE YOU ARE?
PURR PURR
HE HAS AWFUL TASTE.

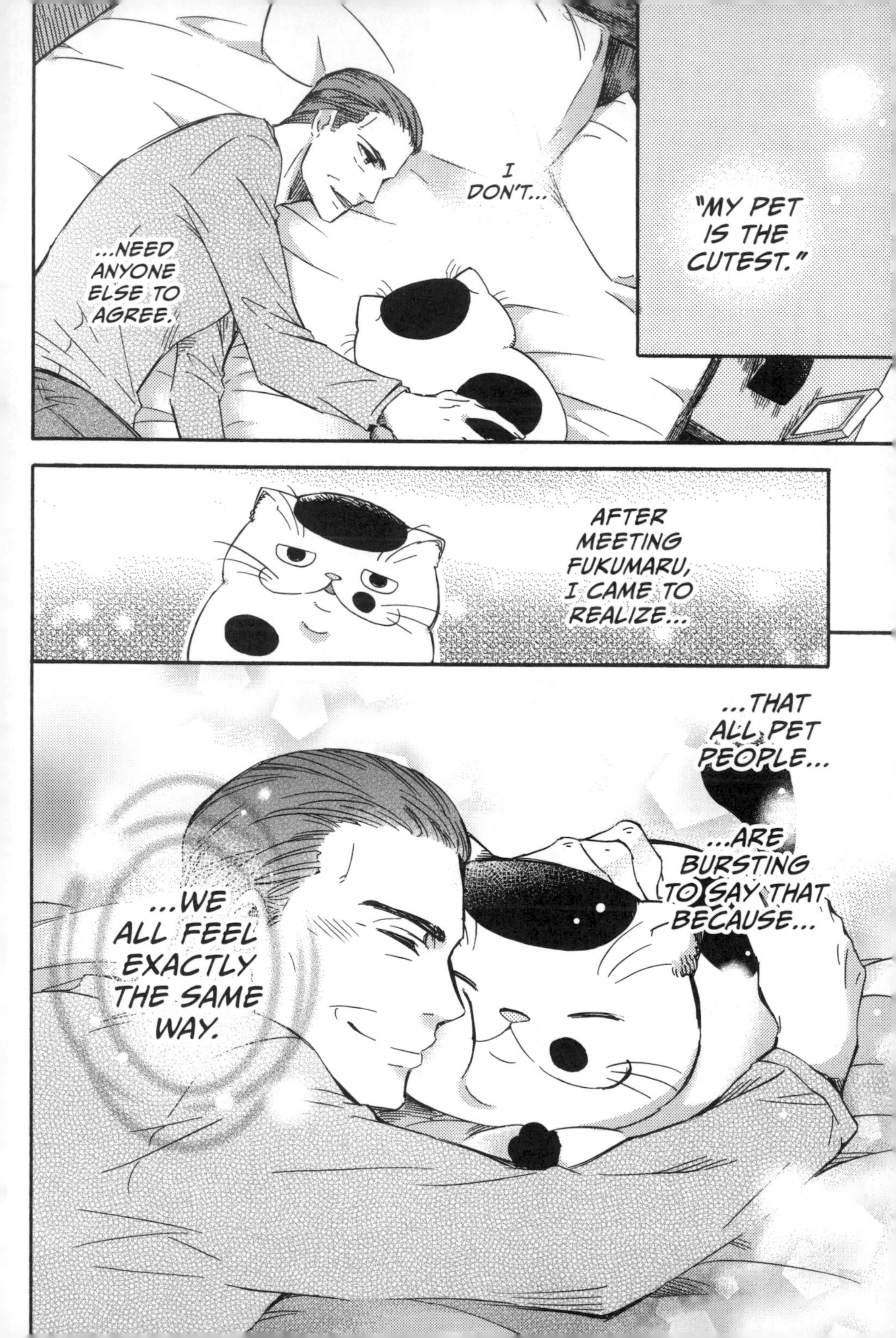
"MY PET IS THE CUTEST."
I DON'T...
...NEED ANYONE ELSE TO AGREE.
AFTER MEETING FUKUMARU, I CAME TO REALIZE...
...THAT ALL PET PEOPLE...
...ARE BURSTING TO SAY THAT BECAUSE...
...WE ALL FEEL EXACTLY THE SAME WAY.

## Chapter 15 Fukumaru and the Black Thing

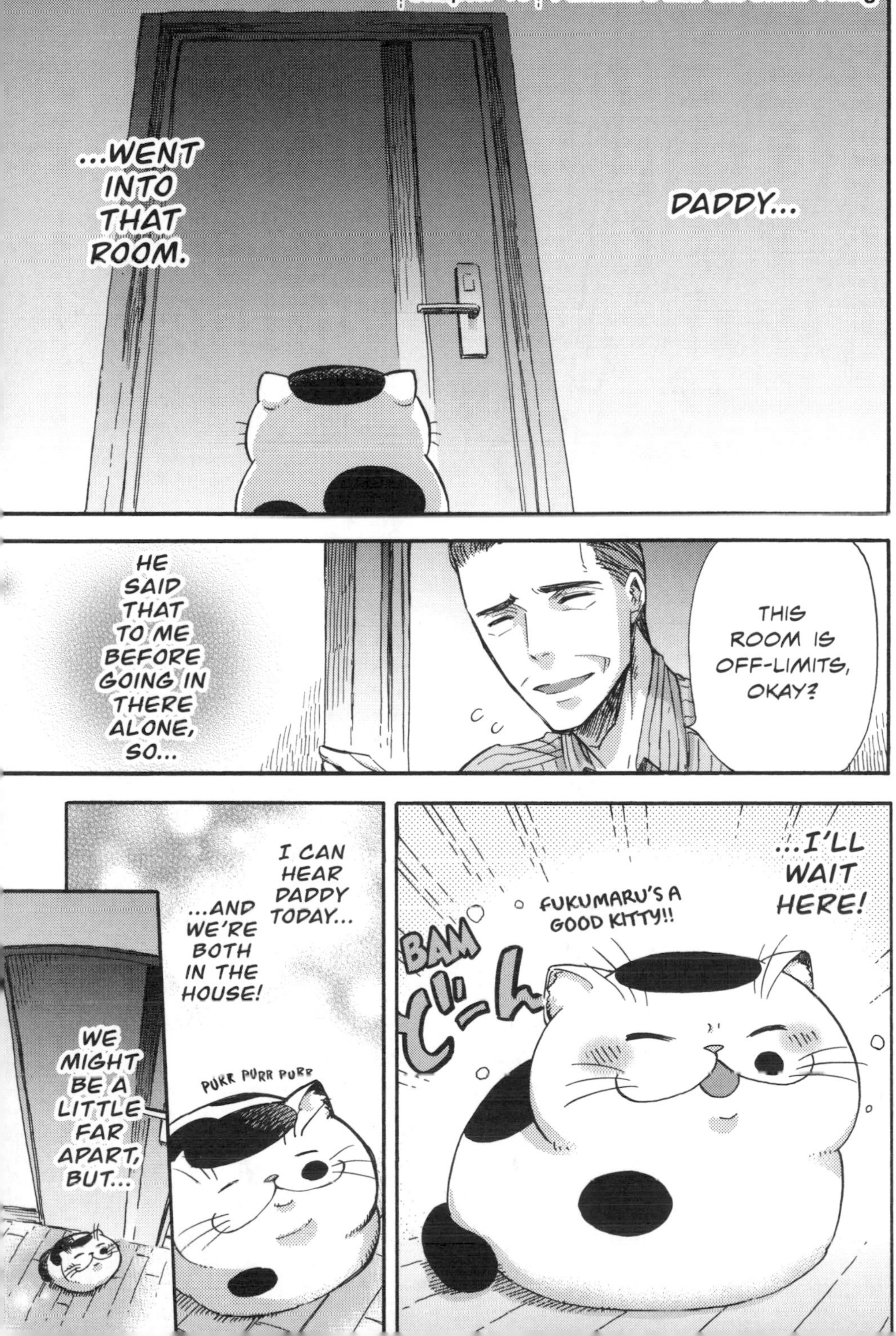
DADDY...
...WENT INTO THAT ROOM.
THIS ROOM IS OFF-LIMITS, OKAY?
HE SAID THAT TO ME BEFORE GOING IN THERE ALONE, SO...
...I'LL WAIT HERE!
FUKUMARU'S A GOOD KITTY!!
BAM
I CAN HEAR DADDY TODAY...
...AND WE'RE BOTH IN THE HOUSE!
WE MIGHT BE A LITTLE FAR APART, BUT...
PURR PURR PURR

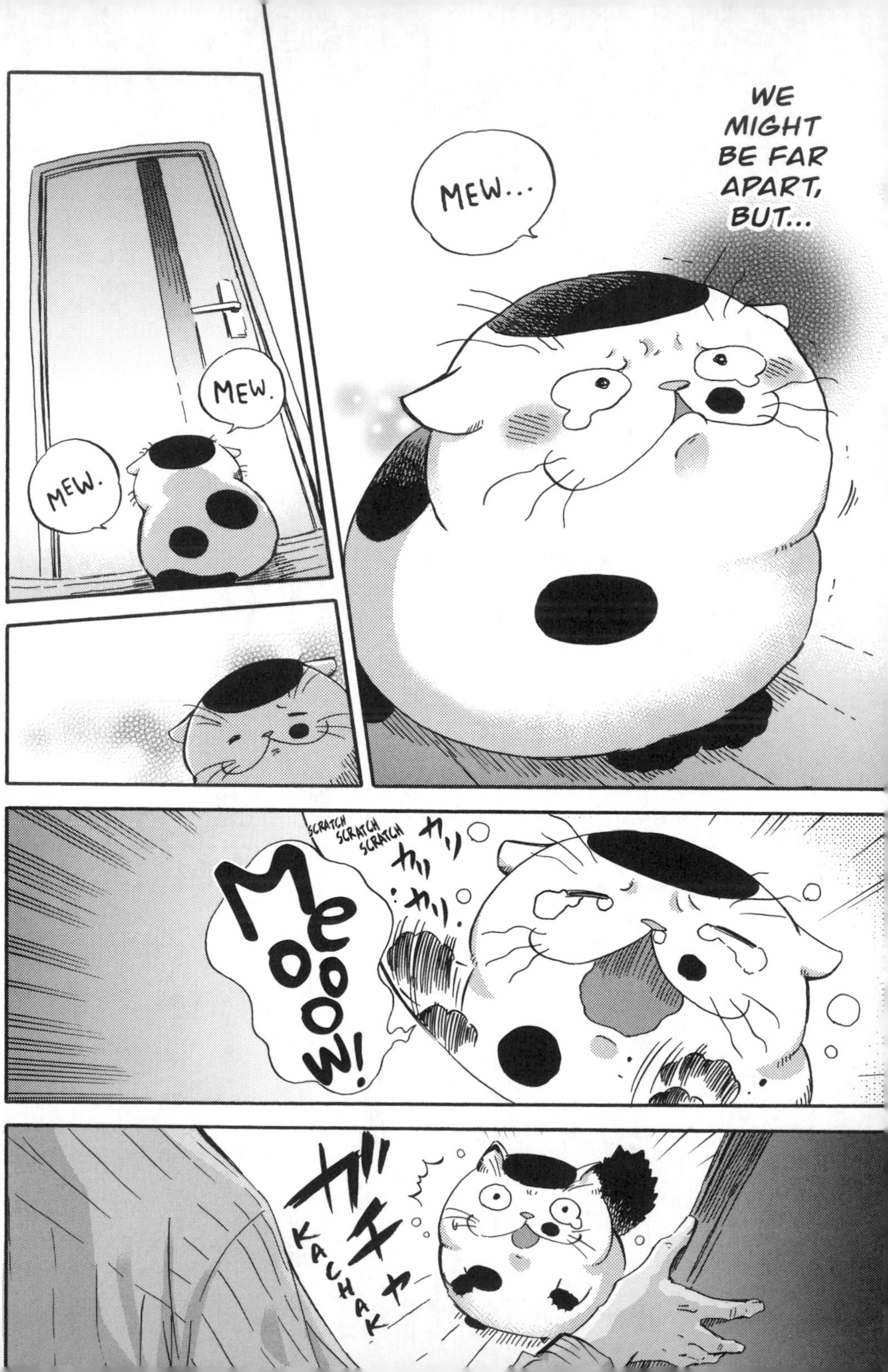
WE MIGHT BE FAR APART, BUT...
MEW...
MEW.
MEW.
SCRATCH SCRATCH SCRATCH
Meooow!
KACHAK

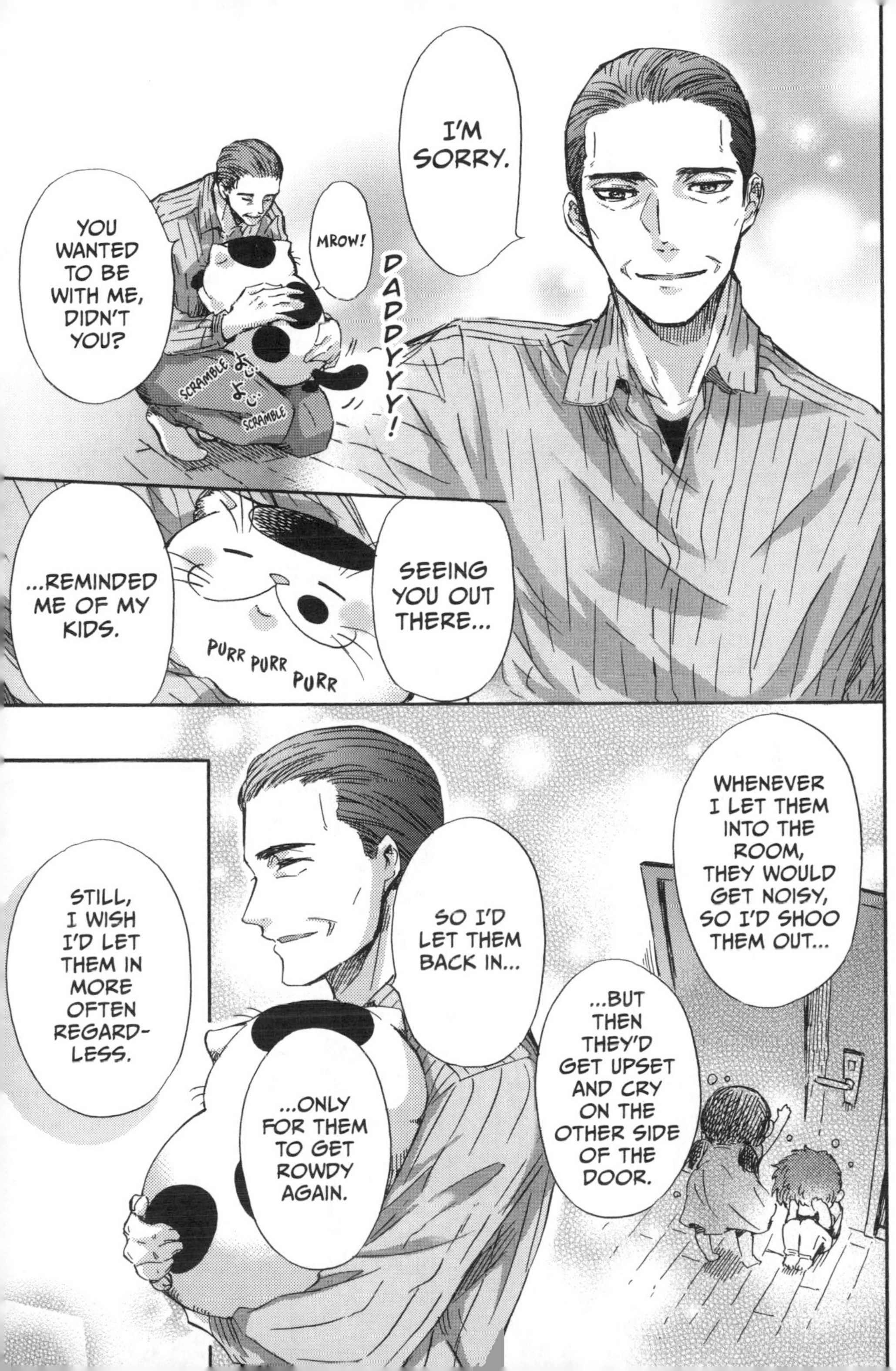
I'M SORRY.
MROW!
DADDYYY!
YOU WANTED TO BE WITH ME, DIDN'T YOU?
SCRAMBLE よじ
よじ SCRAMBLE
SEEING YOU OUT THERE...
...REMINDED ME OF MY KIDS.
PURR PURR PURR
WHENEVER I LET THEM INTO THE ROOM, THEY WOULD GET NOISY, SO I'D SHOO THEM OUT...
SO I'D LET THEM BACK IN...
...BUT THEN THEY'D GET UPSET AND CRY ON THE OTHER SIDE OF THE DOOR.
...ONLY FOR THEM TO GET ROWDY AGAIN.
STILL, I WISH I'D LET THEM IN MORE OFTEN REGARDLESS.

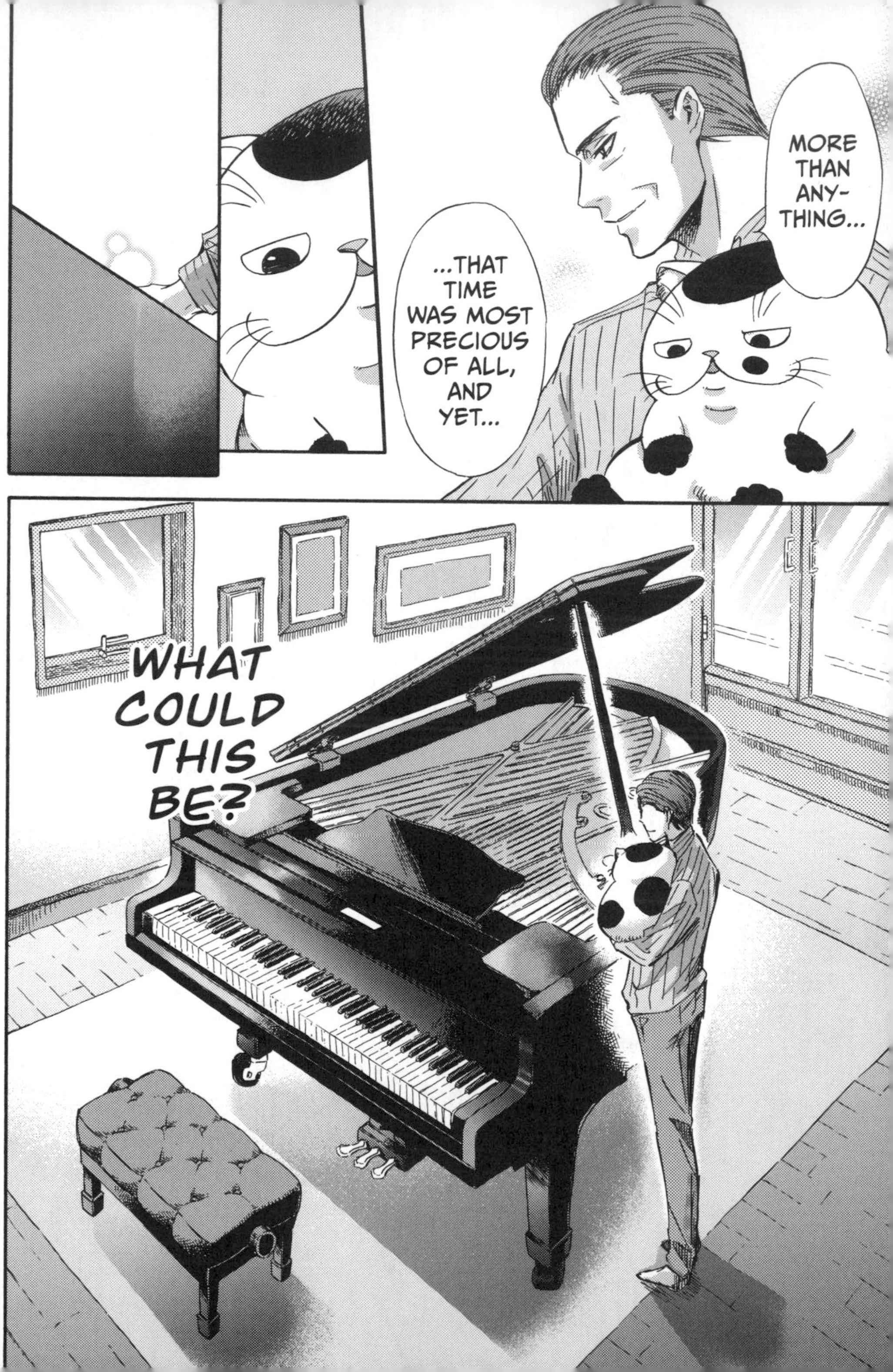
MORE THAN ANY-THING...
...THAT TIME WAS MOST PRECIOUS OF ALL, AND YET...
WHAT COULD THIS BE?

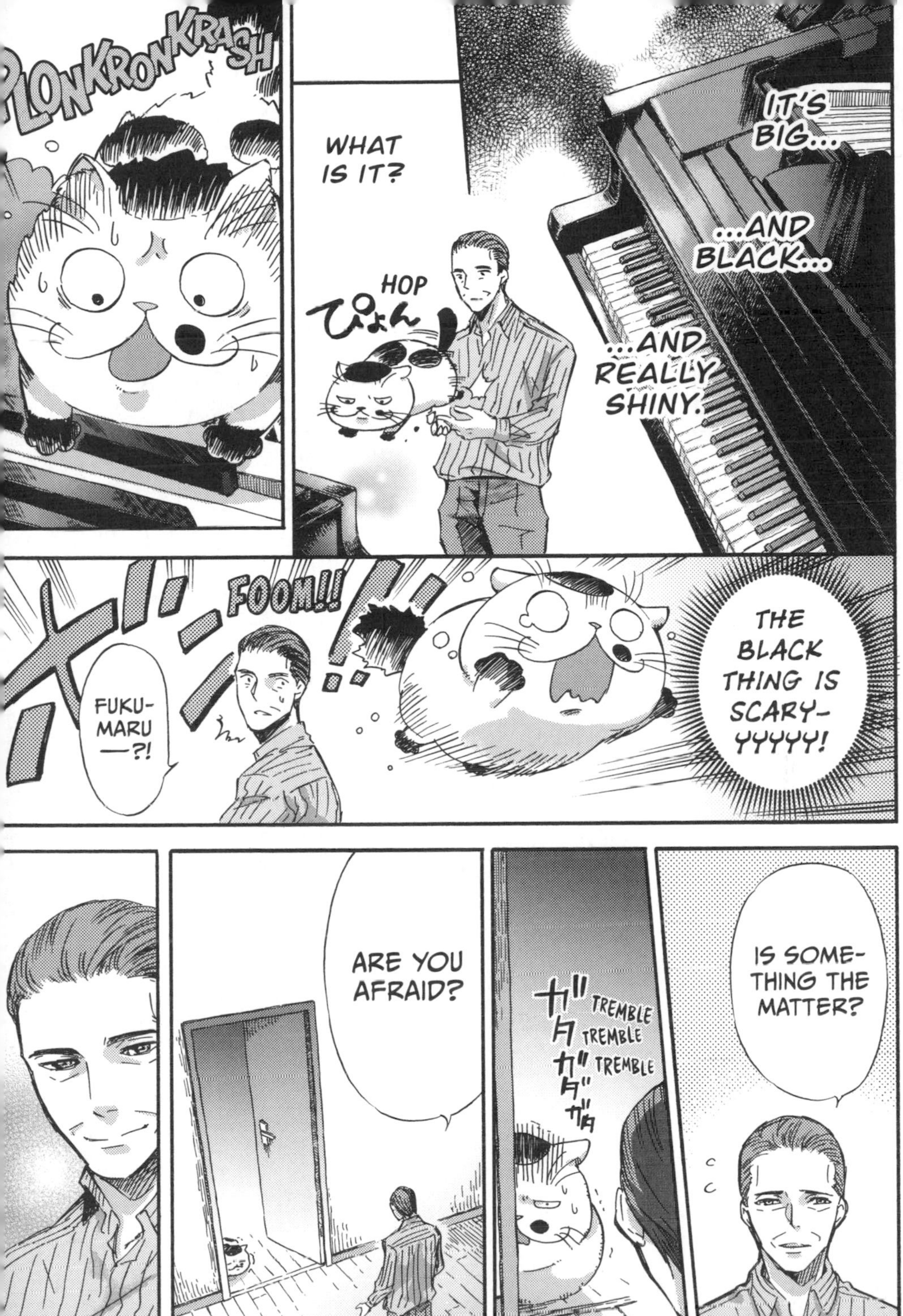
IT'S BIG...
...AND BLACK...
...AND REALLY SHINY.
WHAT IS IT?
HOP
ぴょん
PLONKRONKRASH
THE BLACK THING IS SCARY-YYYYY!
FOOM!!
FUKU-MARU—?!
IS SOME-THING THE MATTER?
ガタガタガタ
TREMBLE TREMBLE TREMBLE
ARE YOU AFRAID?

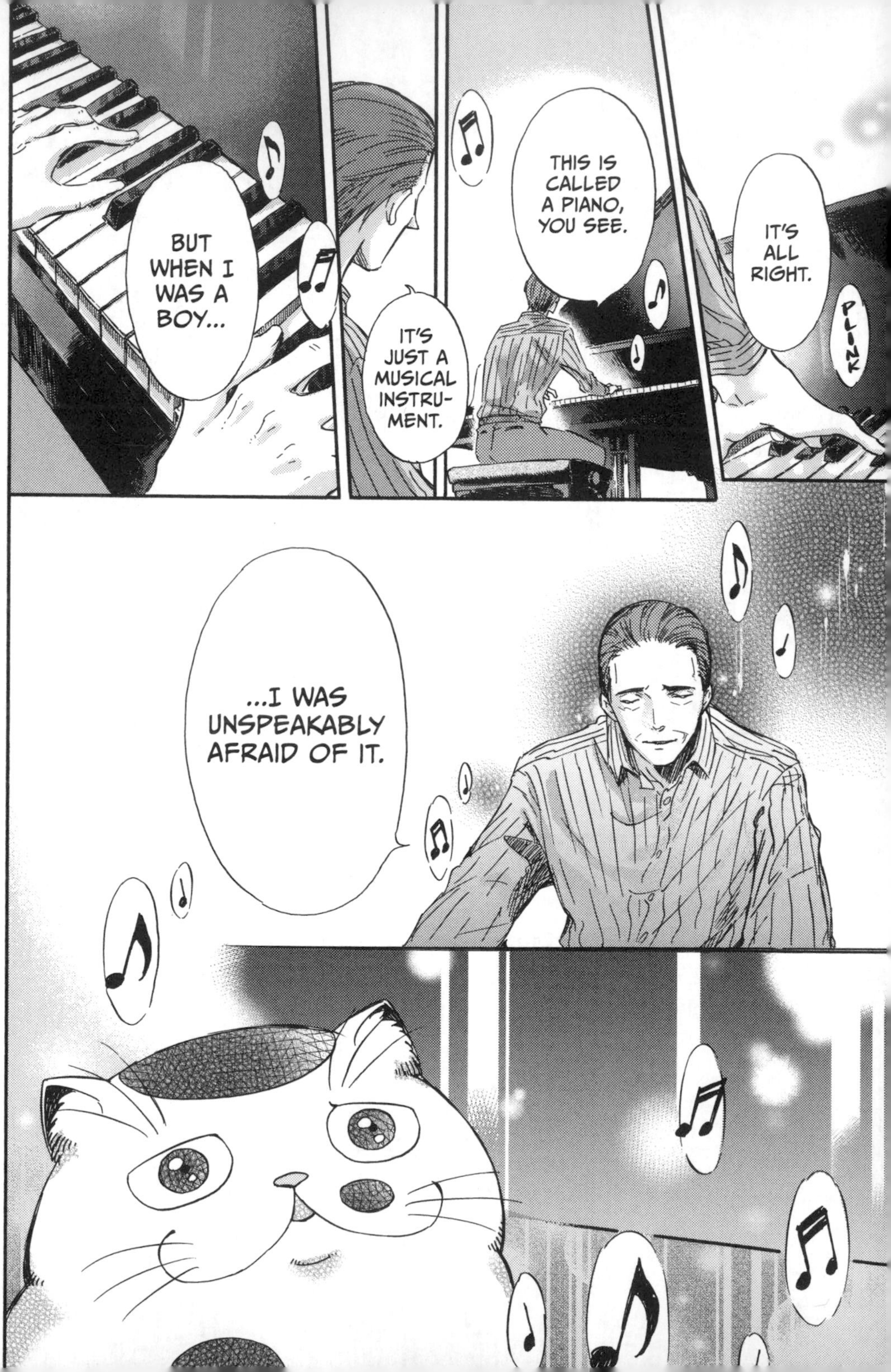
IT'S ALL RIGHT.
PLINK
THIS IS CALLED A PIANO, YOU SEE.
IT'S JUST A MUSICAL INSTRU- MENT.
BUT WHEN I WAS A BOY...
...I WAS UNSPEAKABLY AFRAID OF IT.

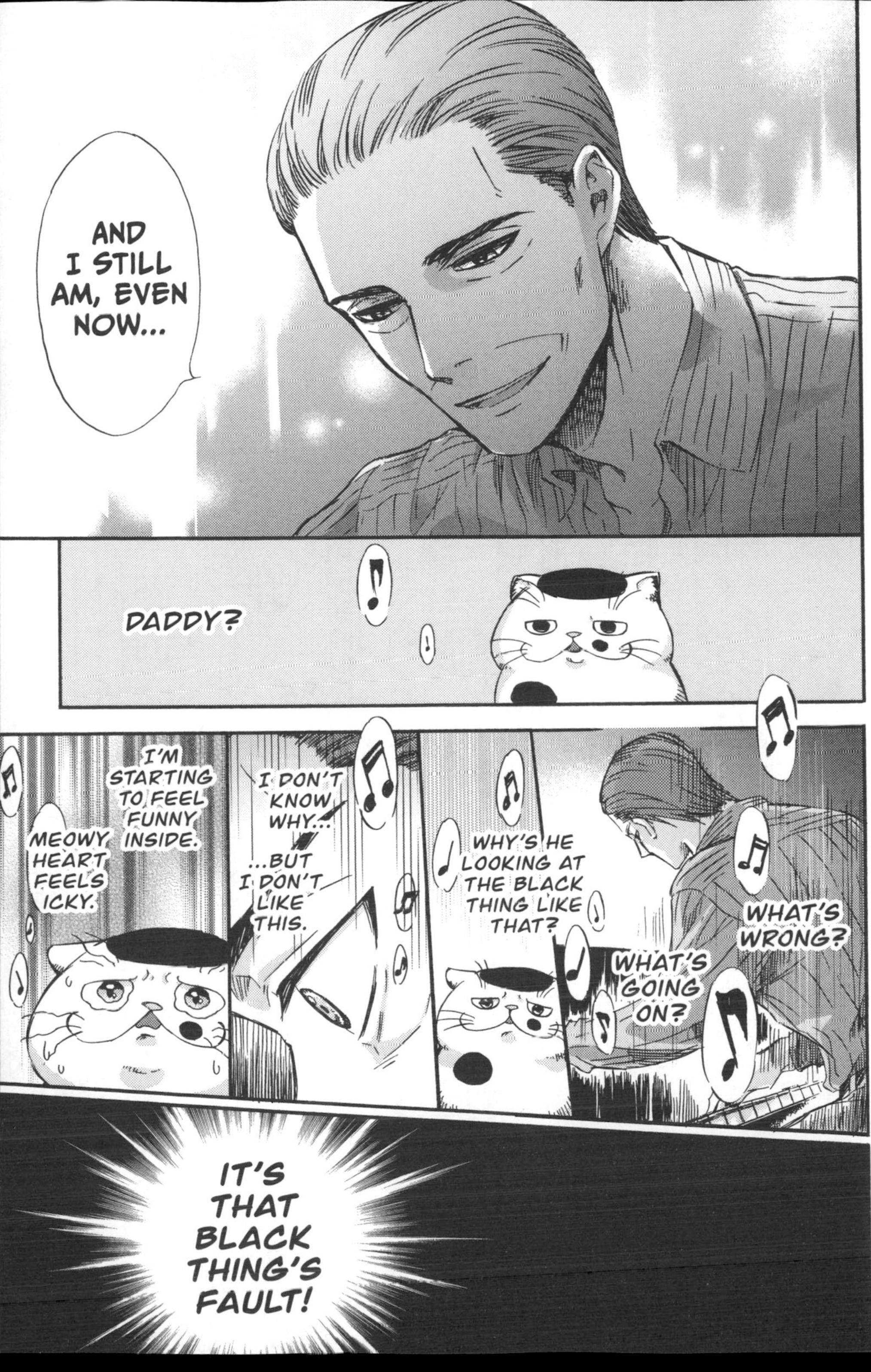
AND I STILL AM, EVEN NOW...
DADDY?
WHAT'S WRONG?
WHAT'S GOING ON?
WHY'S HE LOOKING AT THE BLACK THING LIKE THAT?
I DON'T KNOW WHY...
...BUT I DON'T LIKE THIS.
I'M STARTING TO FEEL FUNNY INSIDE.
MEOWY HEART FEELS ICKY.
IT'S THAT BLACK THING'S FAULT!

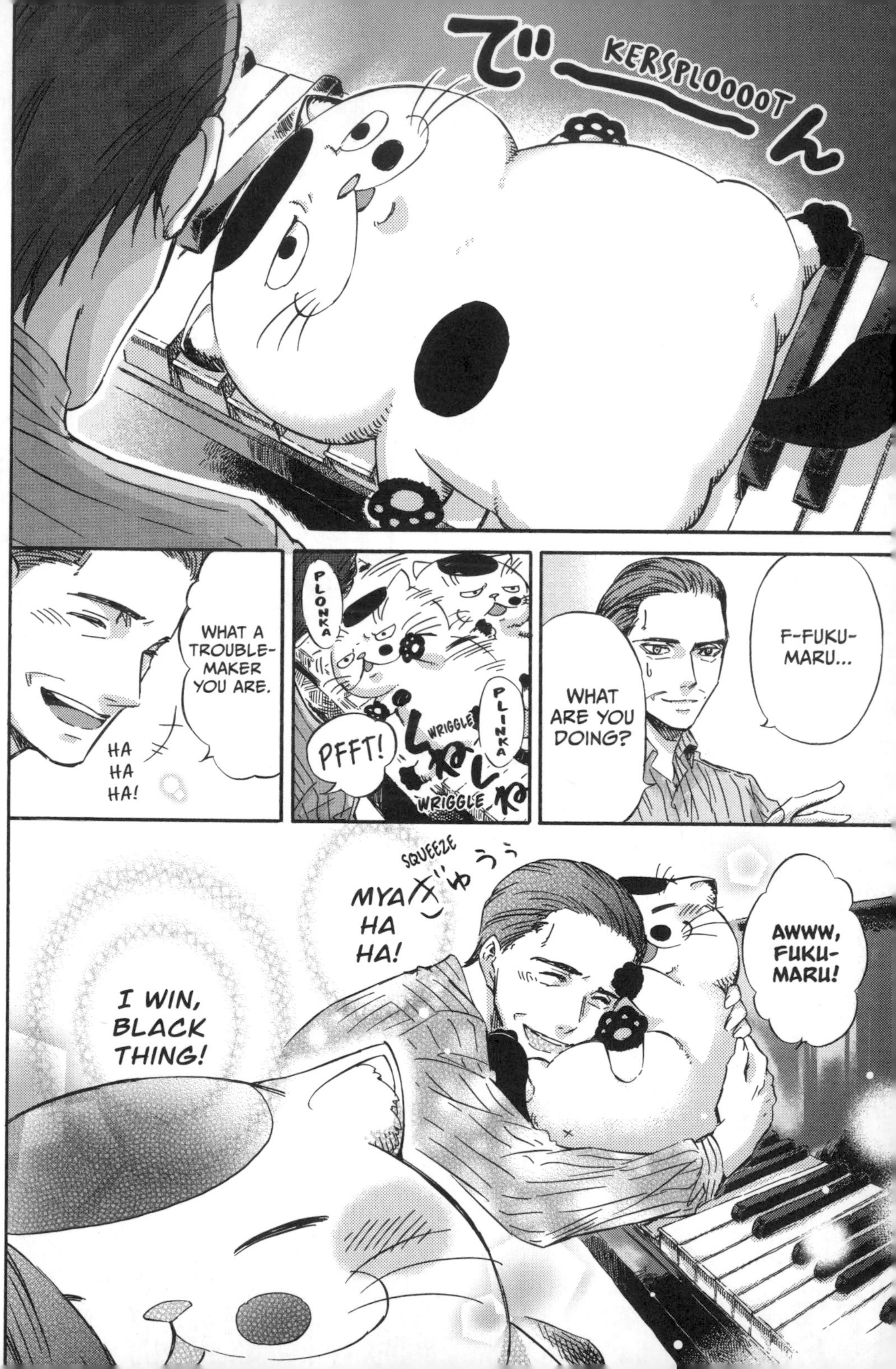
KERSPLOOOOT
F-FUKU-MARU...
WHAT ARE YOU DOING?
PLONKA
PLINKA
WRIGGLE
PFFT!
WRIGGLE
WHAT A TROUBLE-MAKER YOU ARE.
HA HA HA!
AWWW, FUKU-MARU!
SQUEEZE
MYA HA HA!
I WIN, BLACK THING!

UNMOVING, LIKE A MOUNTAIN

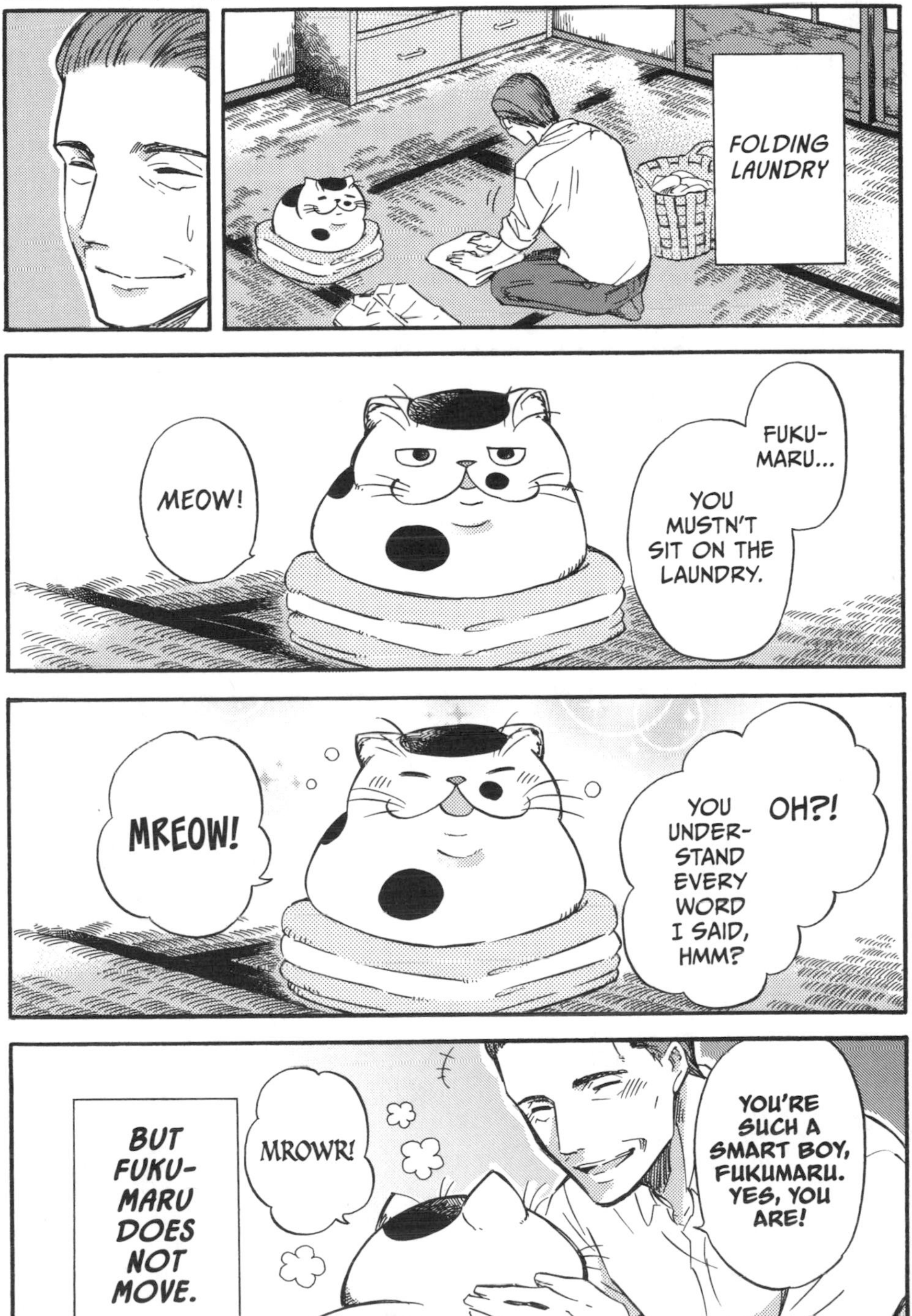
FOLDING LAUNDRY
FUKU-MARU... YOU MUSTN'T SIT ON THE LAUNDRY.
MEOW!
OH?!
YOU UNDER-STAND EVERY WORD I SAID, HMM?
MREOW!
YOU'RE SUCH A SMART BOY, FUKUMARU. YES, YOU ARE!
MROWR!
BUT FUKU-MARU DOES NOT MOVE.

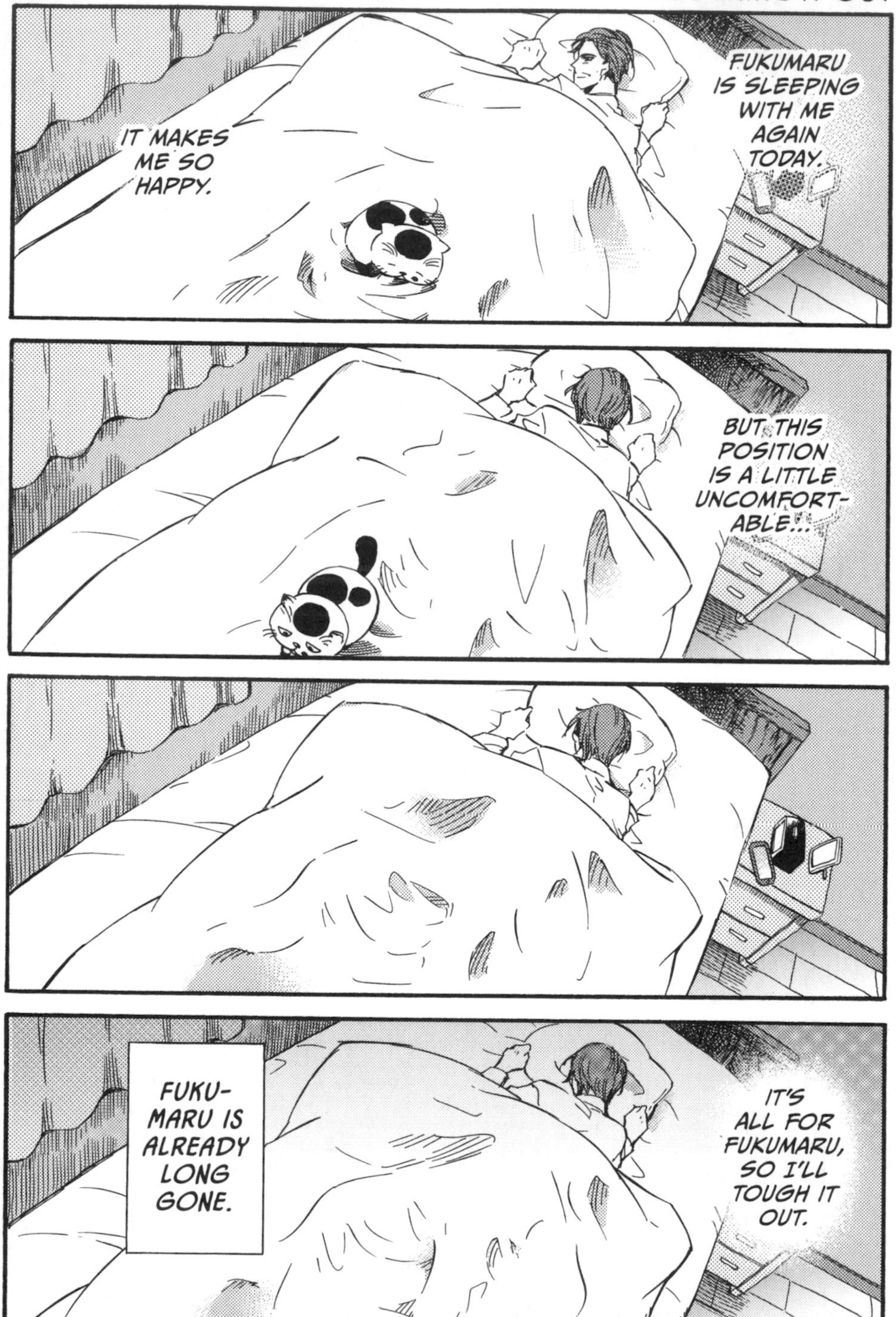
FUKUMARU IS SLEEPING WITH ME AGAIN TODAY.
IT MAKES ME SO HAPPY.
BUT THIS POSITION IS A LITTLE UNCOMFORT-ABLE...
IT'S ALL FOR FUKUMARU, SO I'LL TOUGH IT OUT.
FUKU-MARU IS ALREADY LONG GONE.

## Safe, Worry-Free Design

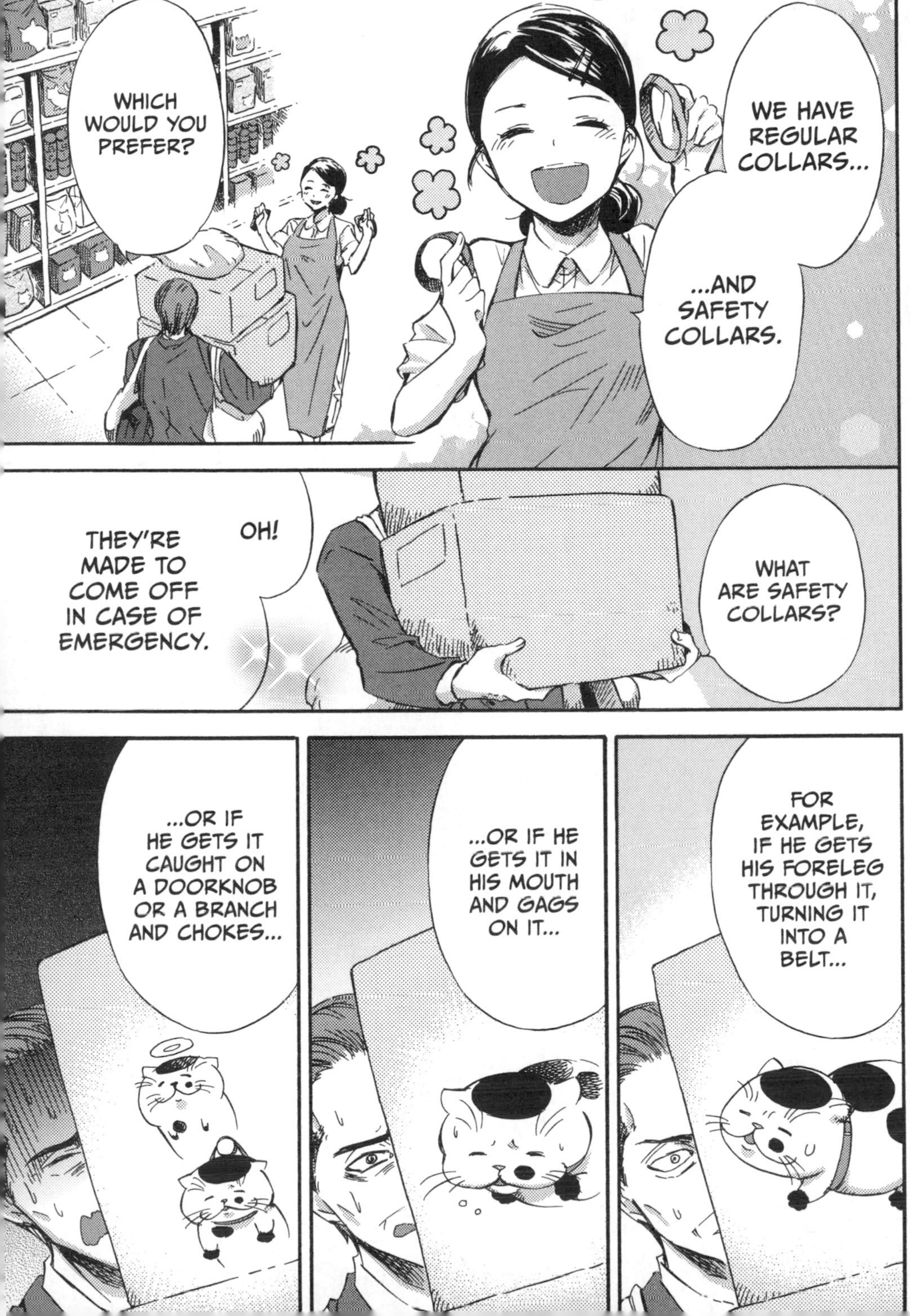
WE HAVE REGULAR COLLARS...
...AND SAFETY COLLARS.
WHICH WOULD YOU PREFER?
WHAT ARE SAFETY COLLARS?
OH!
THEY'RE MADE TO COME OFF IN CASE OF EMERGENCY.
FOR EXAMPLE, IF HE GETS HIS FORELEG THROUGH IT, TURNING IT INTO A BELT...
...OR IF HE GETS IT IN HIS MOUTH AND GAGS ON IT...
...OR IF HE GETS IT CAUGHT ON A DOORKNOB OR A BRANCH AND CHOKES...

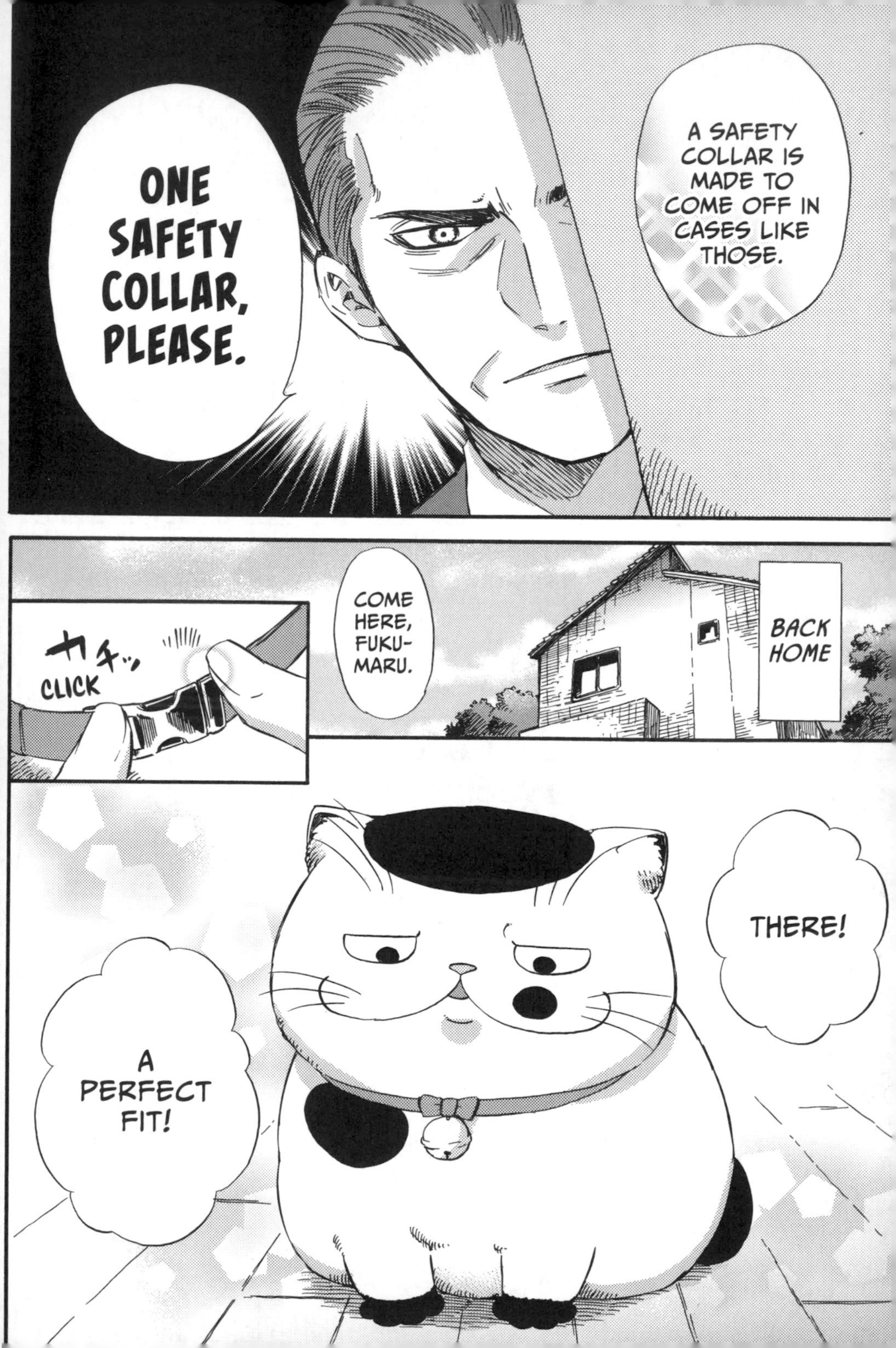
A SAFETY COLLAR IS MADE TO COME OFF IN CASES LIKE THOSE.
ONE SAFETY COLLAR, PLEASE.
BACK HOME
COME HERE, FUKU-MARU.
カチッ
CLICK
THERE!
A PERFECT FIT!

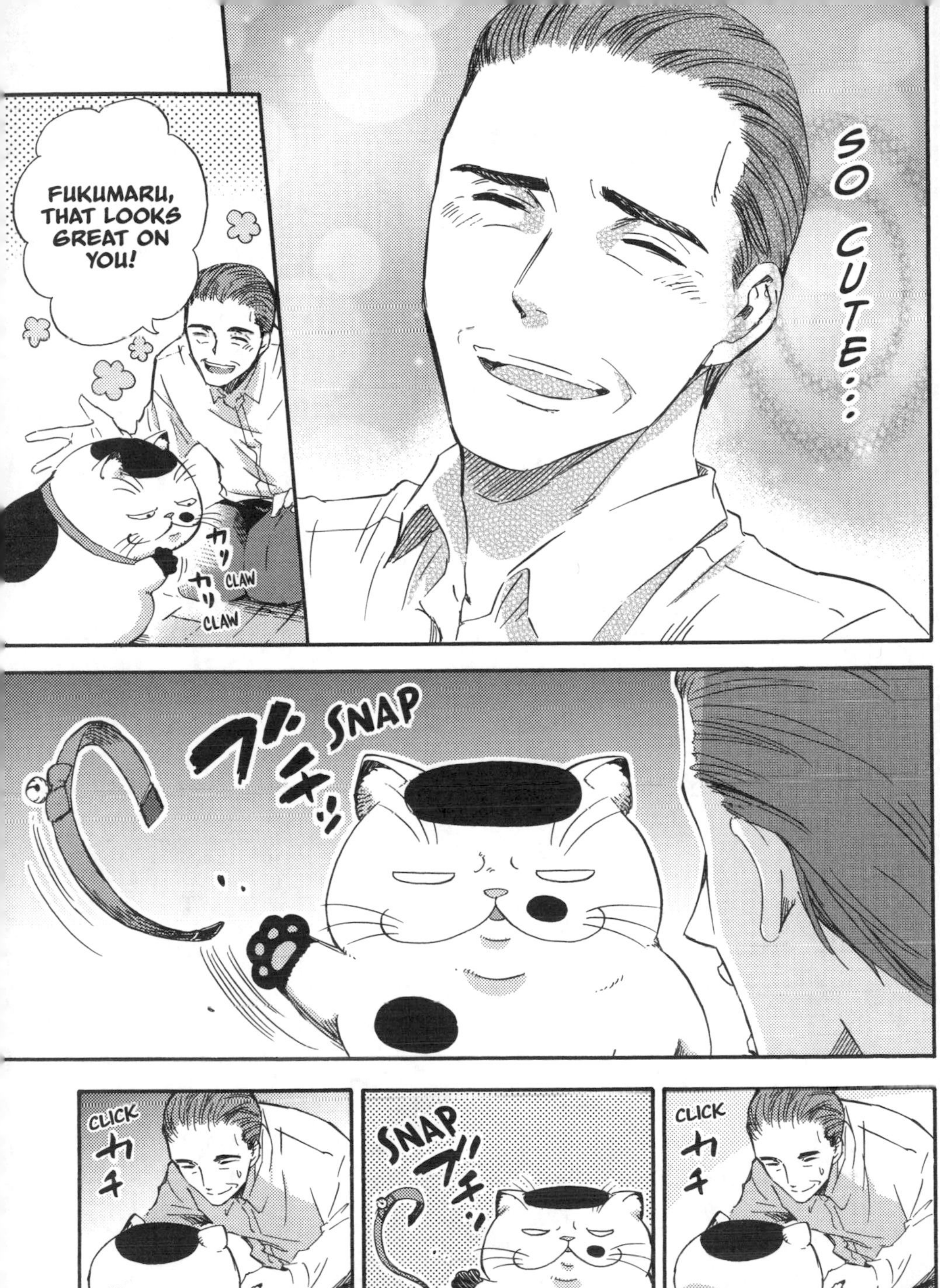
SO CUTE...
FUKUMARU, THAT LOOKS GREAT ON YOU!
カッ
CLAW
カリ
CLAW
ブチッ
SNAP
CLICK
カチ
SNAP
ブチッ
CLICK
カチ

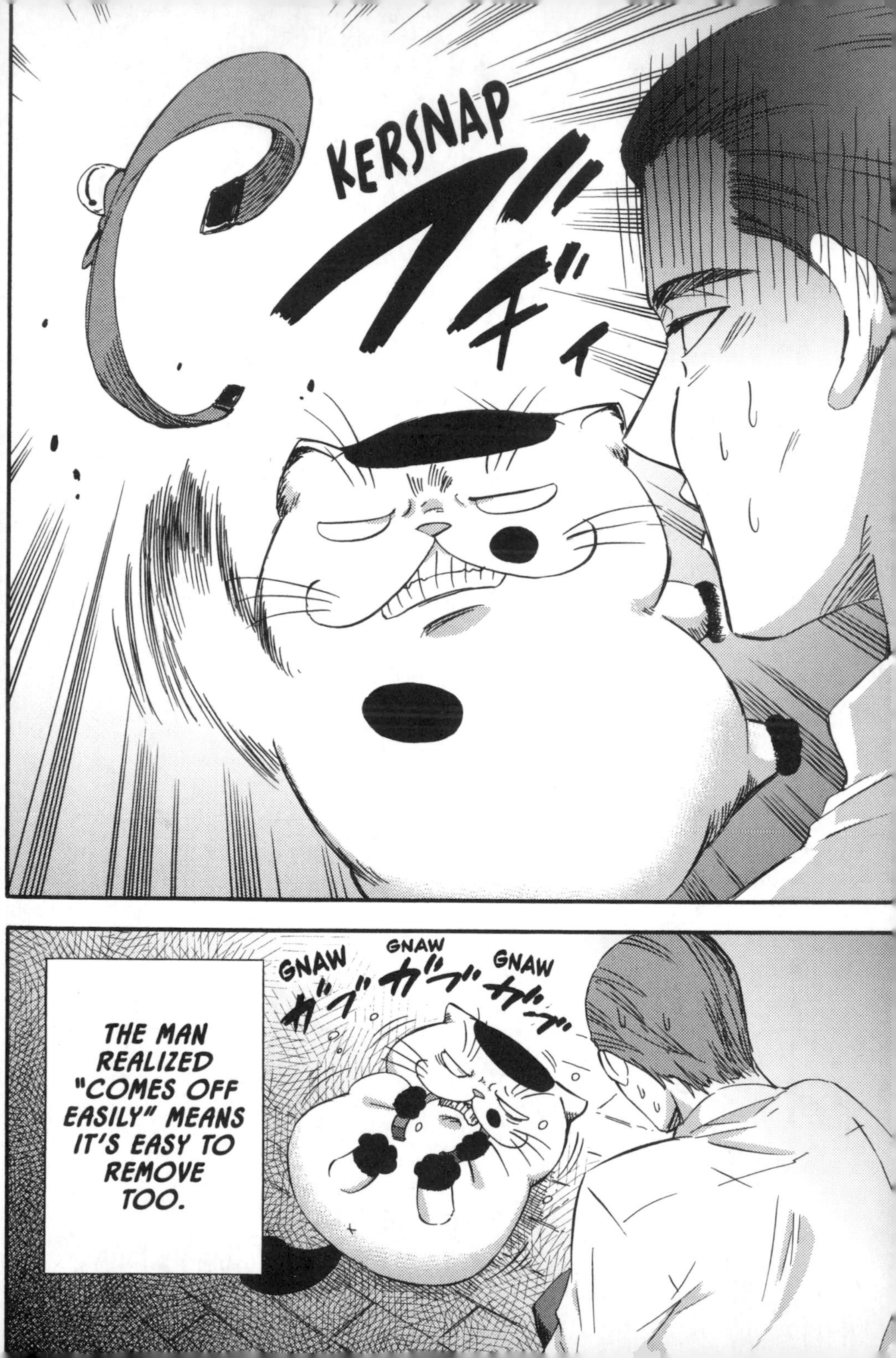
KERSNAP
GNAW
GNAW
GNAW
ガブガブガブ
THE MAN REALIZED "COMES OFF EASILY" MEANS IT'S EASY TO REMOVE TOO.

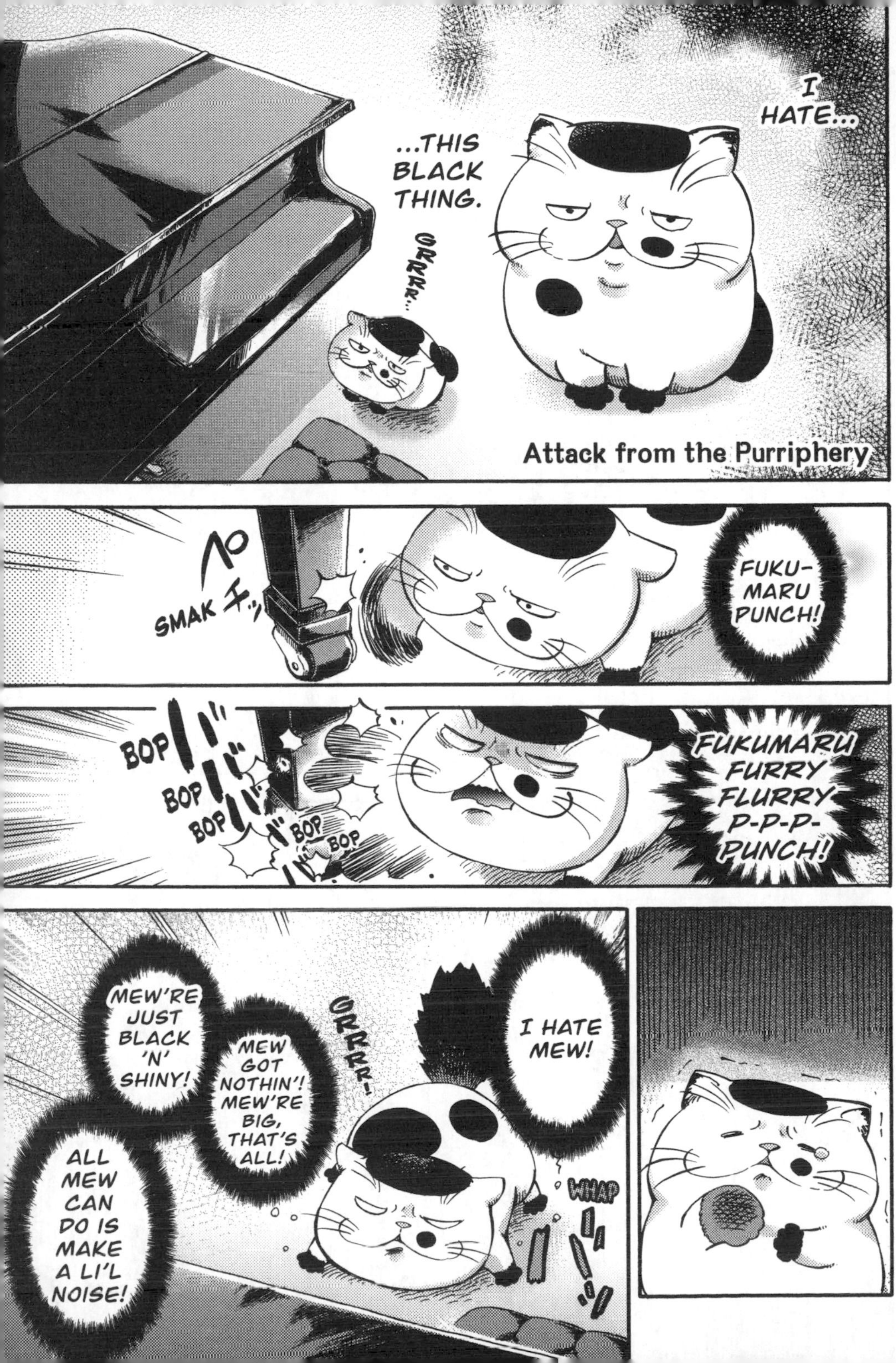
Attack from the Purriphery
I HATE...
...THIS BLACK THING.
GRRRR...
FUKU-MARU PUNCH!
SMAK チッ
FUKUMARU FURRY FLURRY P-P-P-PUNCH!
BOP BOP BOP BOP BOP
I HATE MEW!
GRRRR!
MEW GOT NOTHIN'! MEW'RE BIG, THAT'S ALL!
MEW'RE JUST BLACK 'N' SHINY!
ALL MEW CAN DO IS MAKE A LI'L NOISE!
WHAP

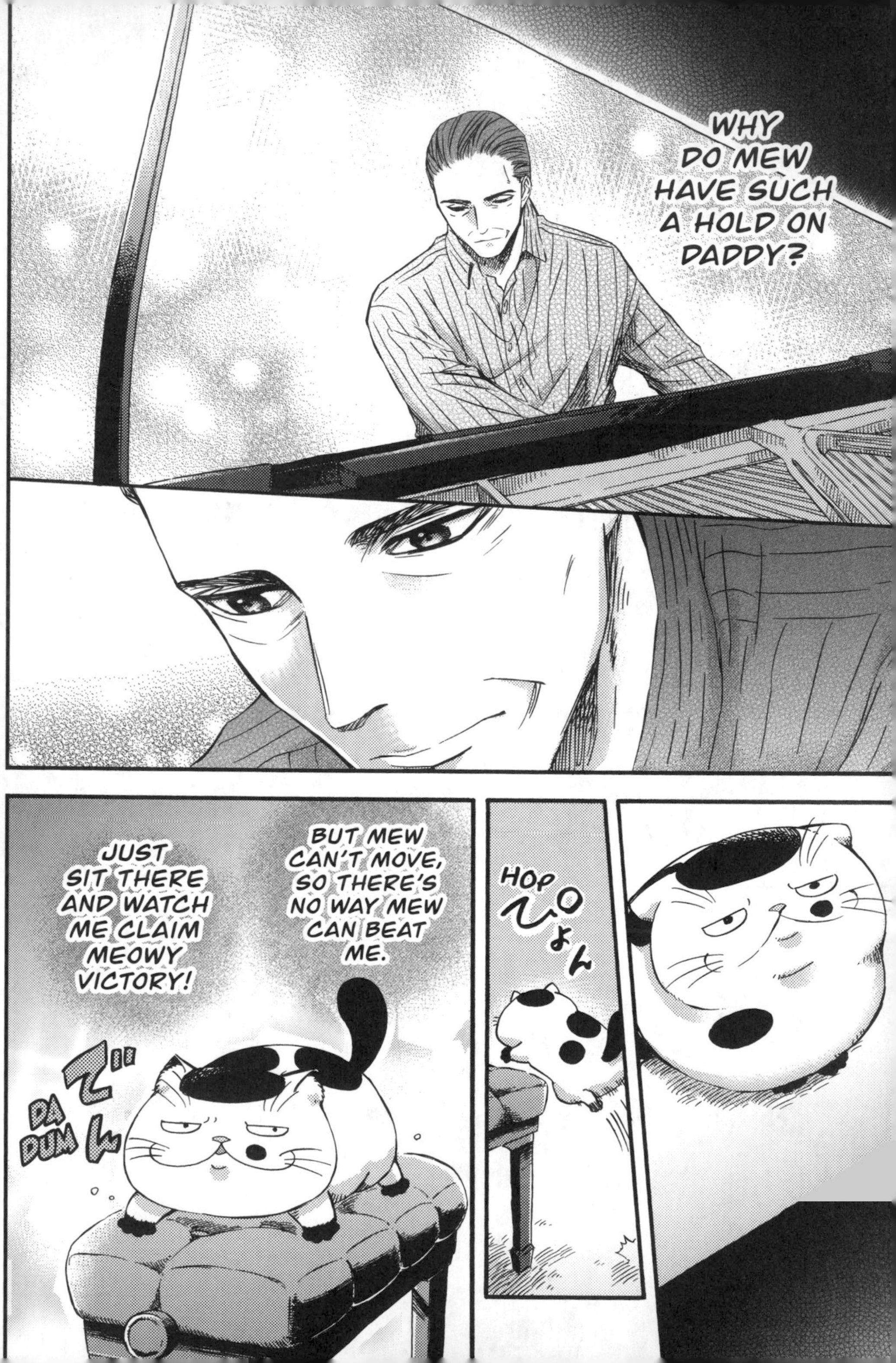
WHY DO MEW HAVE SUCH A HOLD ON DADDY?
HOP
ぴょん
BUT MEW CAN'T MOVE, SO THERE'S NO WAY MEW CAN BEAT ME.
JUST SIT THERE AND WATCH ME CLAIM MEOWY VICTORY!
DA DUM
でん

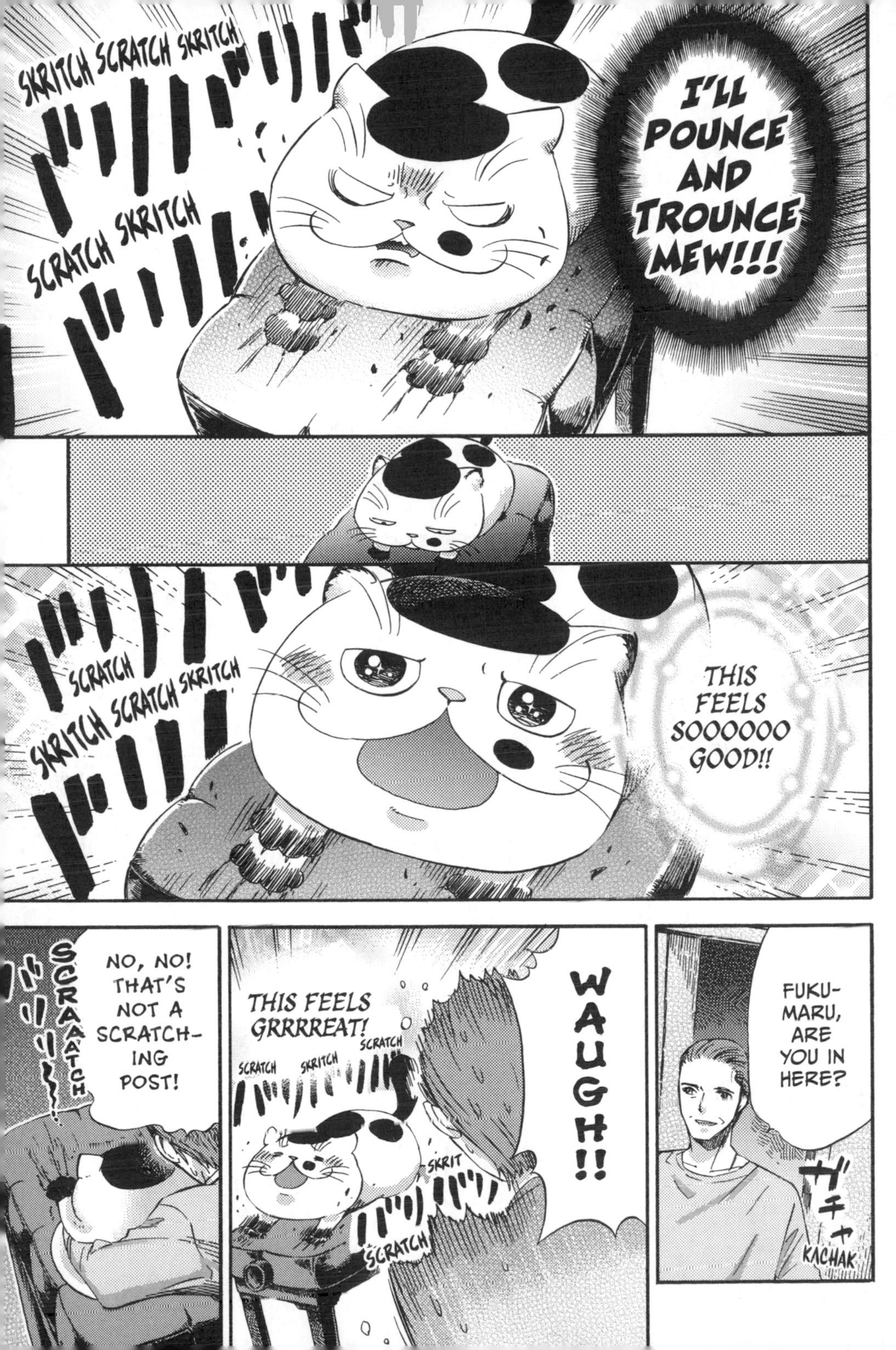
I'LL POUNCE AND TROUNCE MEW!!!
SKRITCH SCRATCH SKRITCH
SCRATCH SKRITCH
THIS FEELS SOOOOOO GOOD!!
SCRATCH
SKRITCH SCRATCH SKRITCH
FUKU-MARU, ARE YOU IN HERE?
KACHAK
WAUGH!!
THIS FEELS GRRRREAT!
SCRATCH
SKRITCH
SCRATCH
SKRIT
SCRATCH
NO, NO! THAT'S NOT A SCRATCH-ING POST!
SCRAAATCH

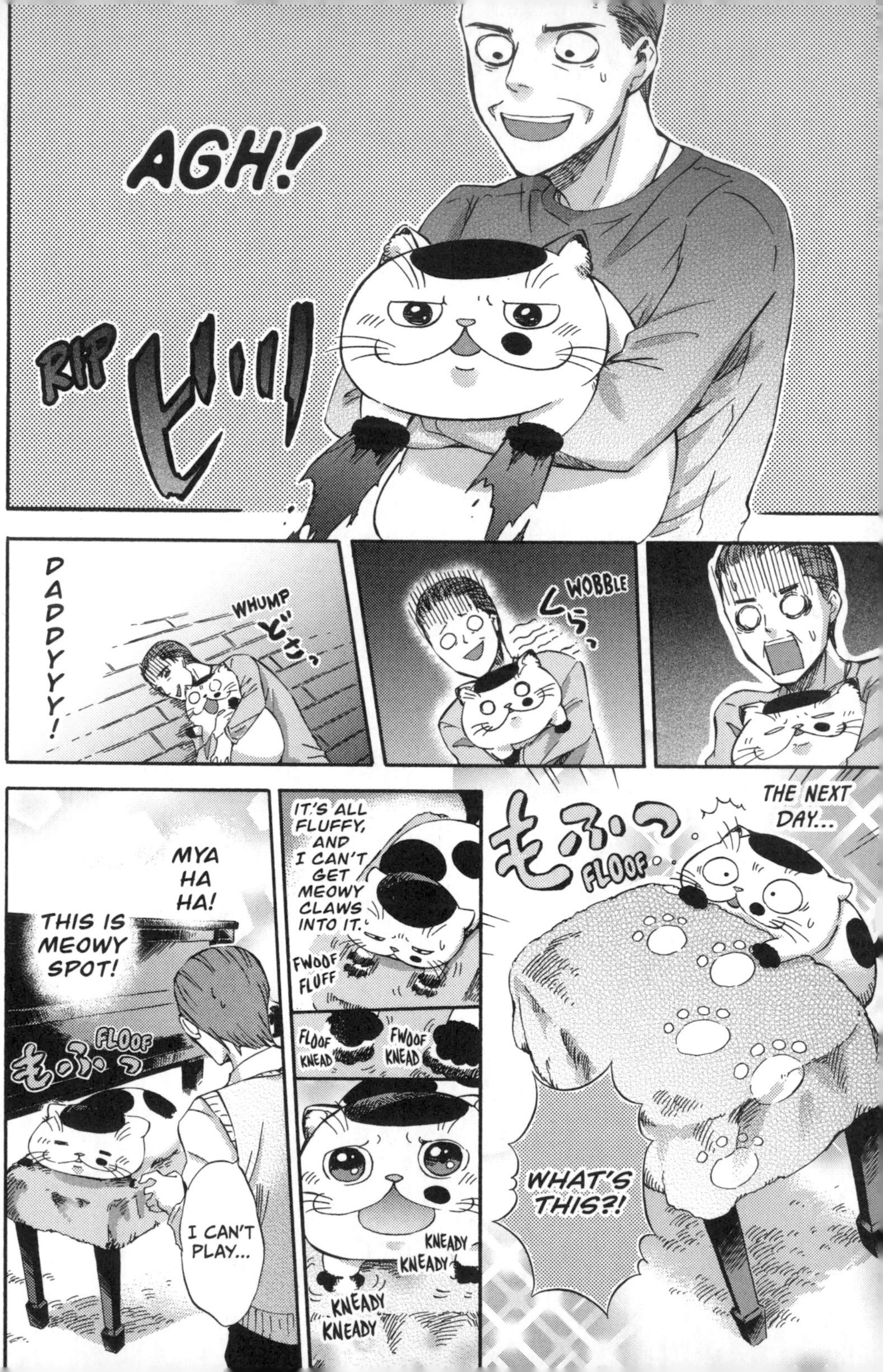
AGH!
RIP
ビリッ
WOBBLE
くらっ
DADDYYY!
WHUMP
どさっ
THE NEXT DAY...
もふっ
FLOOF
WHAT'S THIS?!
IT'S ALL FLUFFY, AND I CAN'T GET MEOWY CLAWS INTO IT.
FWOOF FLUFF
FWOOF KNEAD
FLOOF KNEAD
KNEADY KNEADY
KNEADY KNEADY
MYA HA HA!
THIS IS MEOWY SPOT!
FLOOF
もふっ
I CAN'T PLAY...

## CAT GRASS DIARY

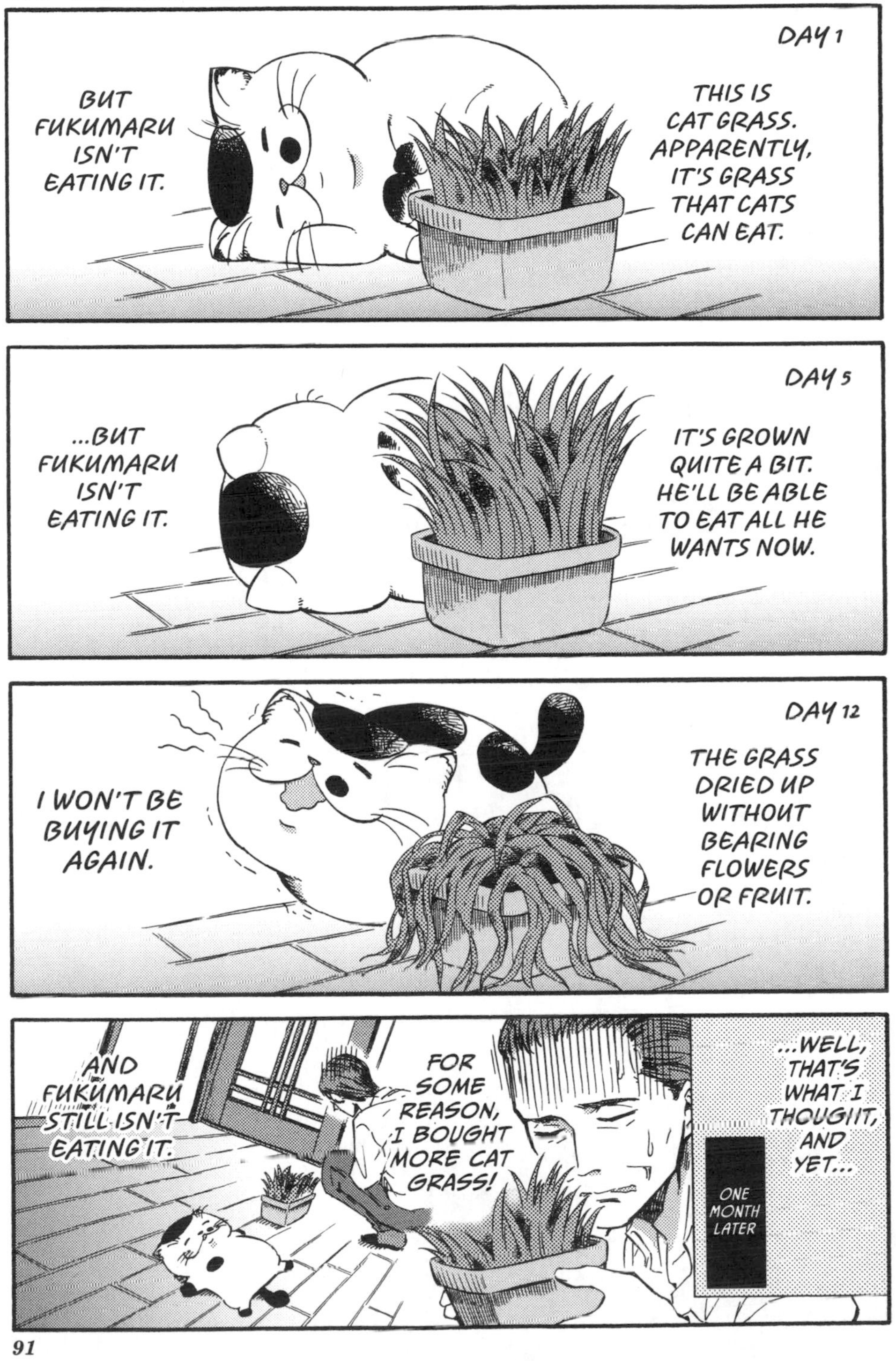

DAY 1
THIS IS CAT GRASS. APPARENTLY, IT'S GRASS THAT CATS CAN EAT.
BUT FUKUMARU ISN'T EATING IT.
DAY 5
IT'S GROWN QUITE A BIT. HE'LL BE ABLE TO EAT ALL HE WANTS NOW.
...BUT FUKUMARU ISN'T EATING IT.
DAY 12
THE GRASS DRIED UP WITHOUT BEARING FLOWERS OR FRUIT.
I WON'T BE BUYING IT AGAIN.
...WELL, THAT'S WHAT I THOUGHT, AND YET...
ONE MONTH LATER
FOR SOME REASON, I BOUGHT MORE CAT GRASS!
AND FUKUMARU STILL ISN'T EATING IT.

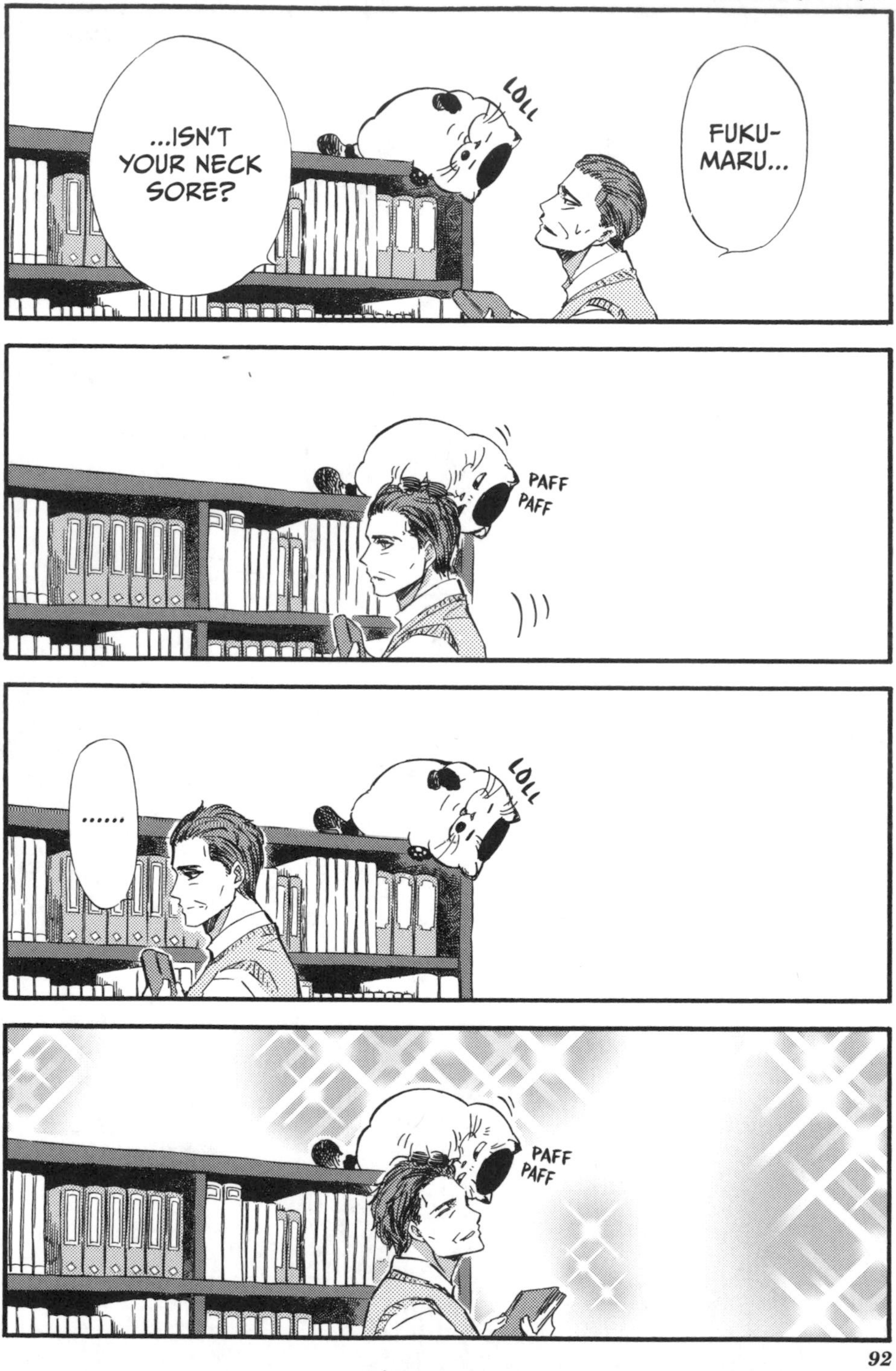
FUKU-MARU...
LOLL
...ISN'T YOUR NECK SORE?
PAFF PAFF
LOLL
......
PAFF PAFF

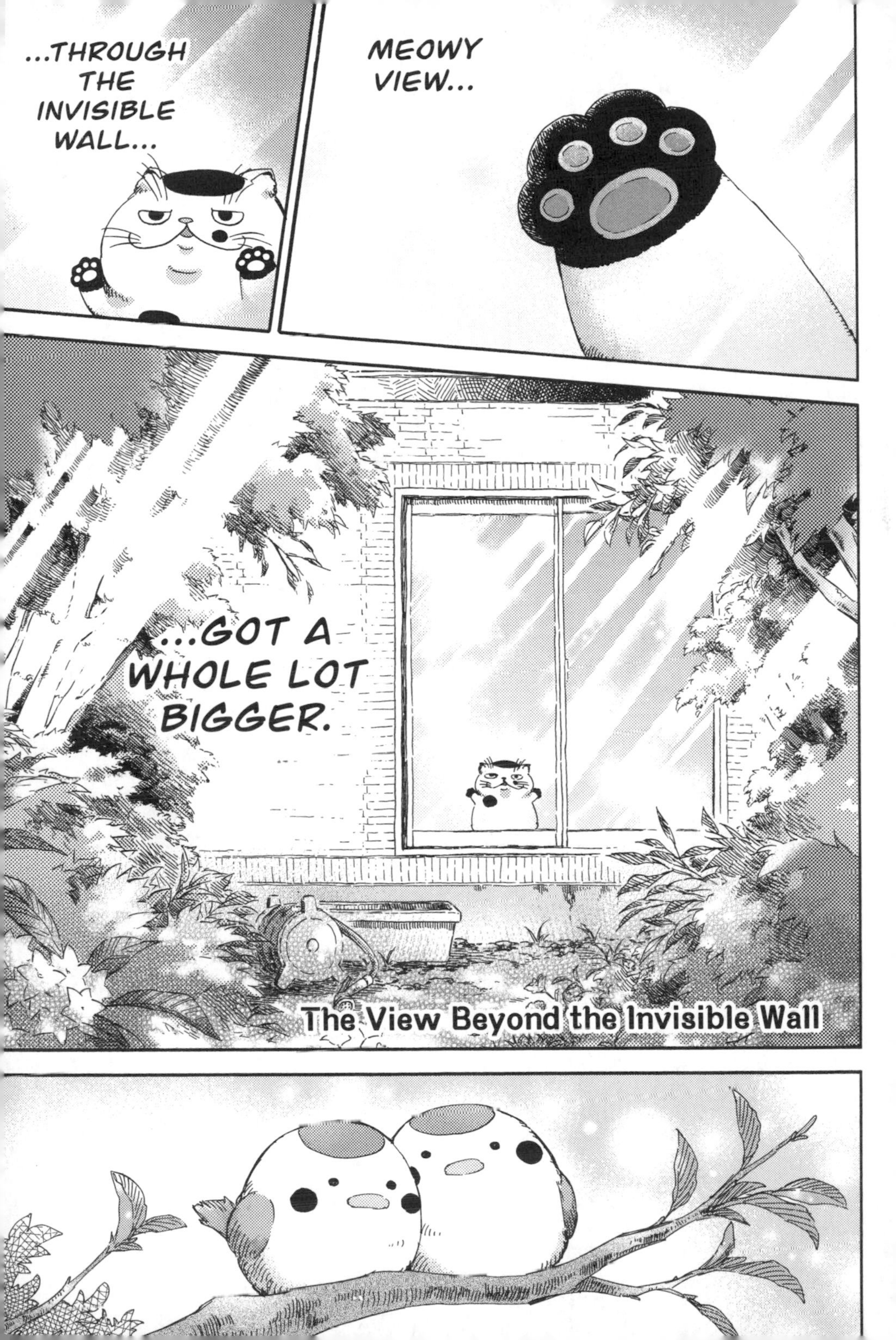
MEOWY VIEW...
...THROUGH THE INVISIBLE WALL...
...GOT A WHOLE LOT BIGGER.
The View Beyond the Invisible Wall

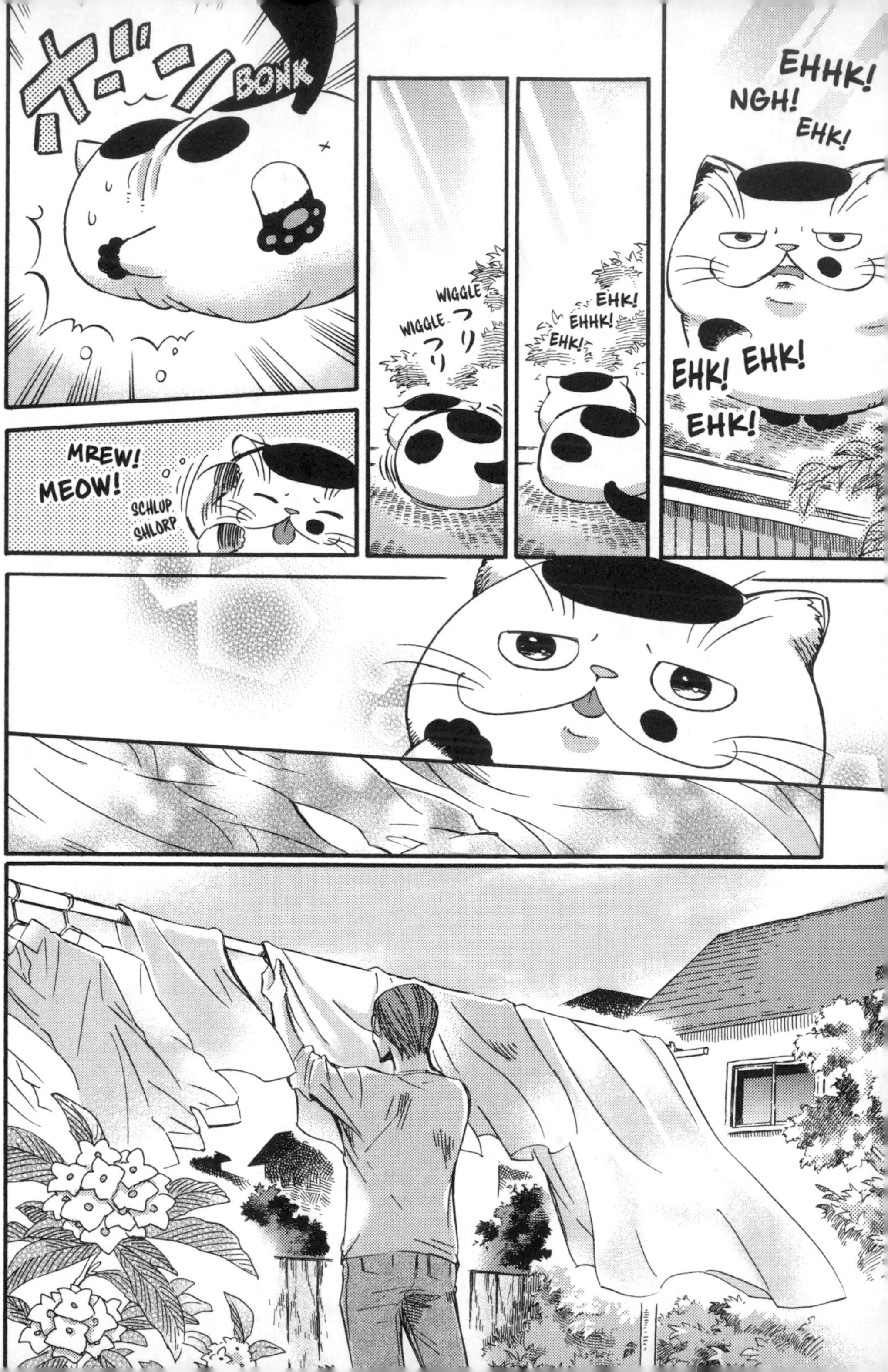
EHHK!
NGH!
EHK!
EHK! EHK!
EHK!
EHK!
EHHK!
EHK!
WIGGLE
WIGGLE
フリフリ
ボーン
BONK
MREW!
MEOW!
SCHLUP
SHLORP

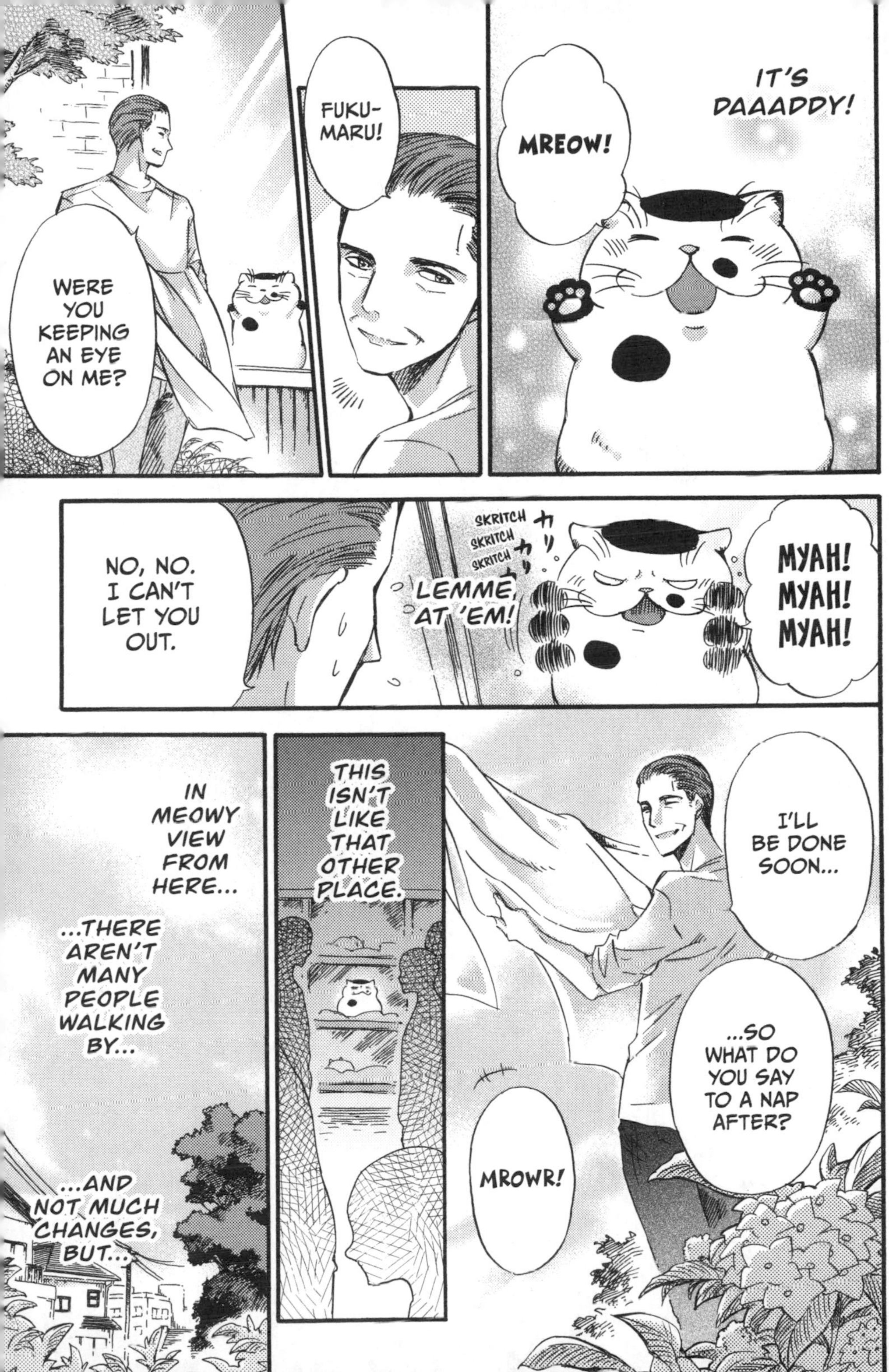
IT'S DAAADDY!
MREOW!
FUKU-MARU!
WERE YOU KEEPING AN EYE ON ME?
MYAH! MYAH! MYAH!
SKRITCH カリ
SKRITCH カリ
SKRITCH カリ
LEMME AT 'EM!
NO, NO. I CAN'T LET YOU OUT.
I'LL BE DONE SOON...
...SO WHAT DO YOU SAY TO A NAP AFTER?
MROWR!
THIS ISN'T LIKE THAT OTHER PLACE.
IN MEOWY VIEW FROM HERE...
...THERE AREN'T MANY PEOPLE WALKING BY...
...AND NOT MUCH CHANGES, BUT...

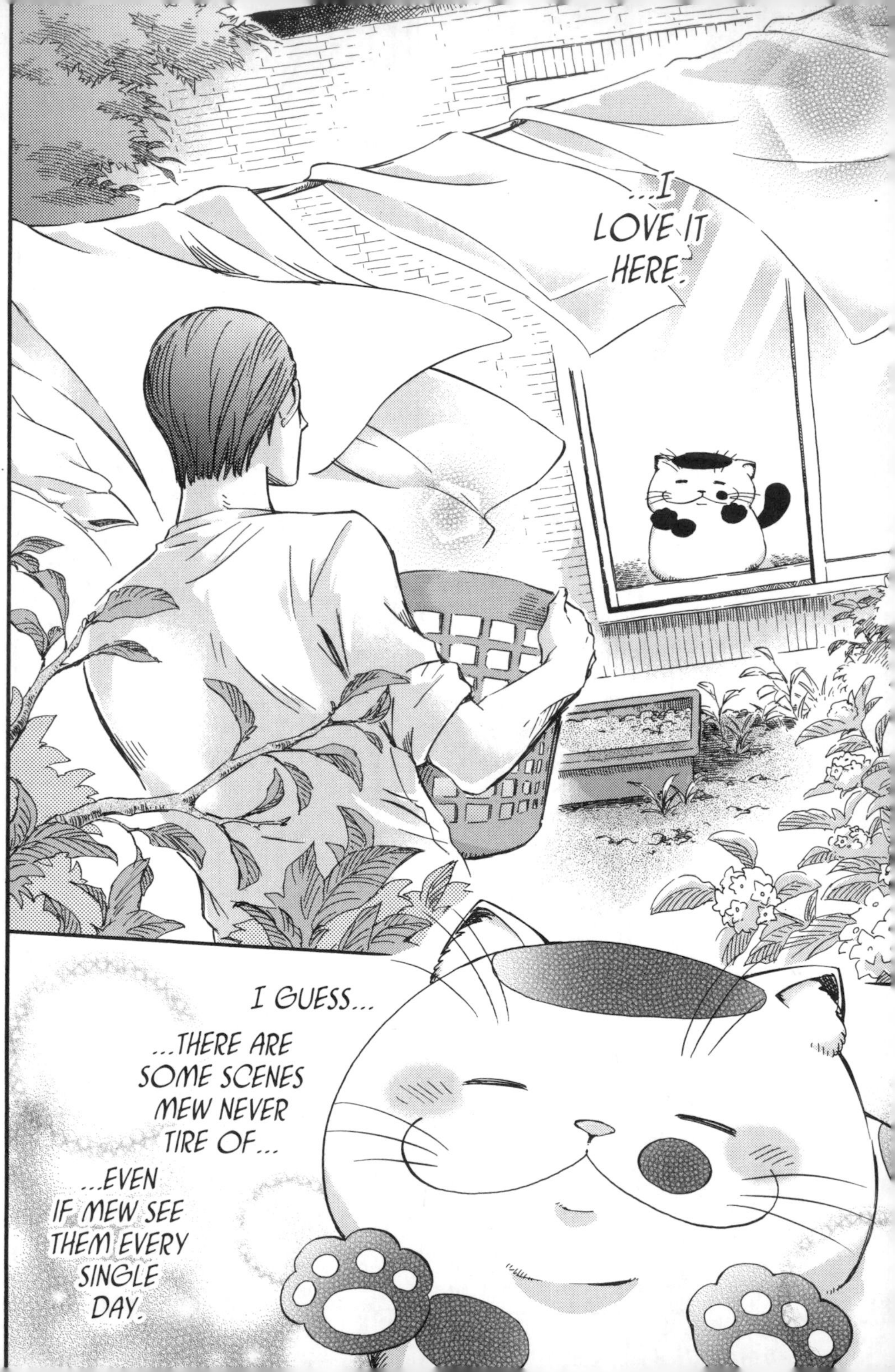
...I LOVE IT HERE.
I GUESS...
...THERE ARE SOME SCENES MEW NEVER TIRE OF...
...EVEN IF MEW SEE THEM EVERY SINGLE DAY.

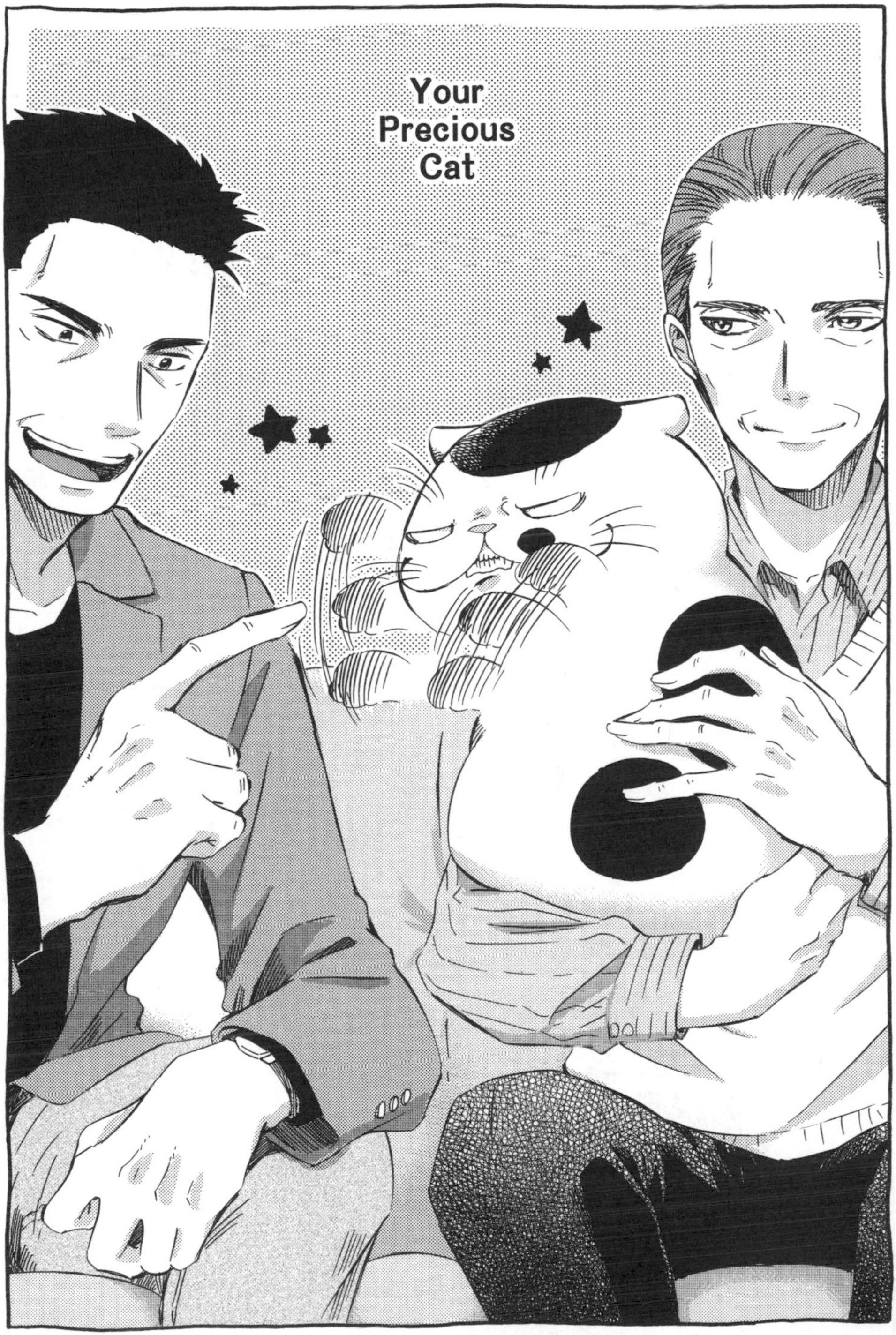
Your Precious Cat

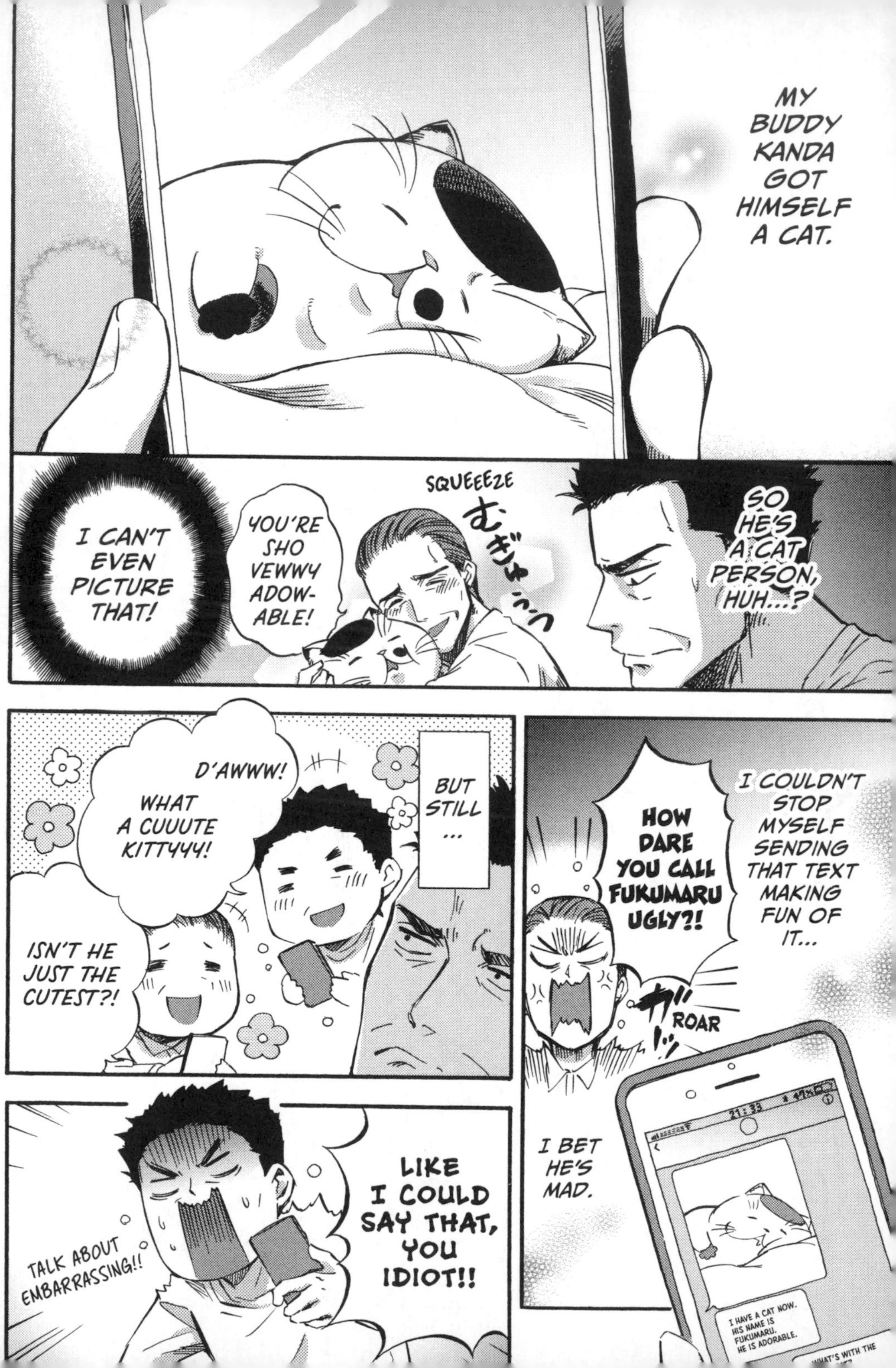
MY BUDDY KANDA GOT HIMSELF A CAT.
SO HE'S A CAT PERSON, HUH...?
SQUEEEZE
YOU'RE SHO VEWWY ADOWABLE!
I CAN'T EVEN PICTURE THAT!
I COULDN'T STOP MYSELF SENDING THAT TEXT MAKING FUN OF IT...
HOW DARE YOU CALL FUKUMARU UGLY?!
ROAR
I BET HE'S MAD.
21:33
I HAVE A CAT NOW. HIS NAME IS FUKUMARU. HE IS ADORABLE.
BUT STILL...
D'AWWW! WHAT A CUUUTE KITTYYY!
ISN'T HE JUST THE CUTEST?!
LIKE I COULD SAY THAT, YOU IDIOT!!
TALK ABOUT EMBARRASSING!!

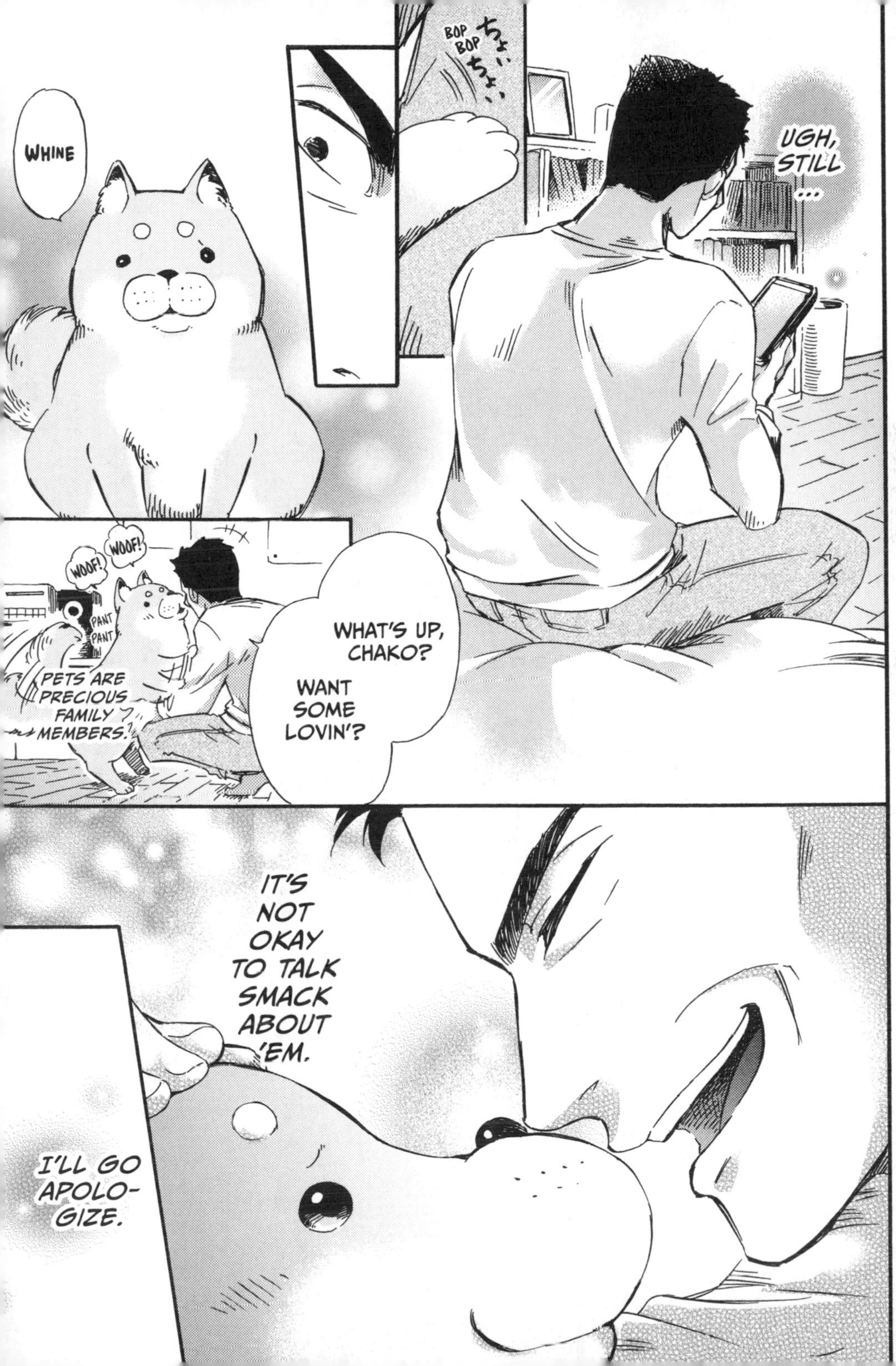
UGH, STILL ...
BOP BOP ちょいちょい
WHINE
WOOF! WOOF!
PANT PANT
PETS ARE PRECIOUS FAMILY MEMBERS.
WHAT'S UP, CHAKO?
WANT SOME LOVIN'?
IT'S NOT OKAY TO TALK SMACK ABOUT 'EM.
I'LL GO APOLOGIZE.

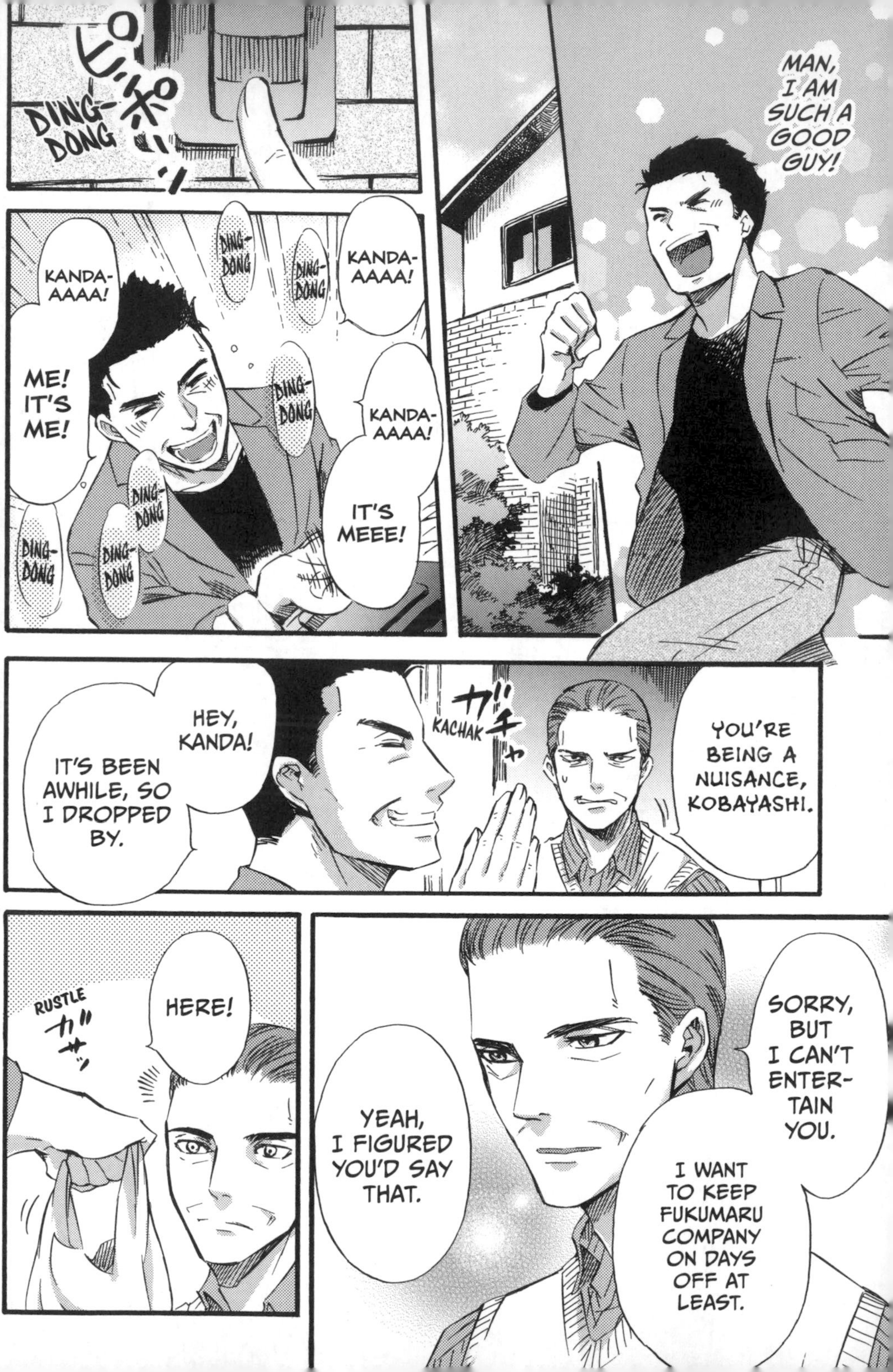
MAN, I AM SUCH A GOOD GUY!
DING-DONG
KANDA-AAAA!
DING-DONG
DING-DONG
KANDA-AAAA!
IT'S MEEE!
DING-DONG
KANDA-AAAA!
ME! IT'S ME!
DING-DONG
DING-DONG
DING-DONG
YOU'RE BEING A NUISANCE, KOBAYASHI.
KACHAK
HEY, KANDA!
IT'S BEEN AWHILE, SO I DROPPED BY.
SORRY, BUT I CAN'T ENTER-TAIN YOU.
I WANT TO KEEP FUKUMARU COMPANY ON DAYS OFF AT LEAST.
YEAH, I FIGURED YOU'D SAY THAT.
HERE!
RUSTLE

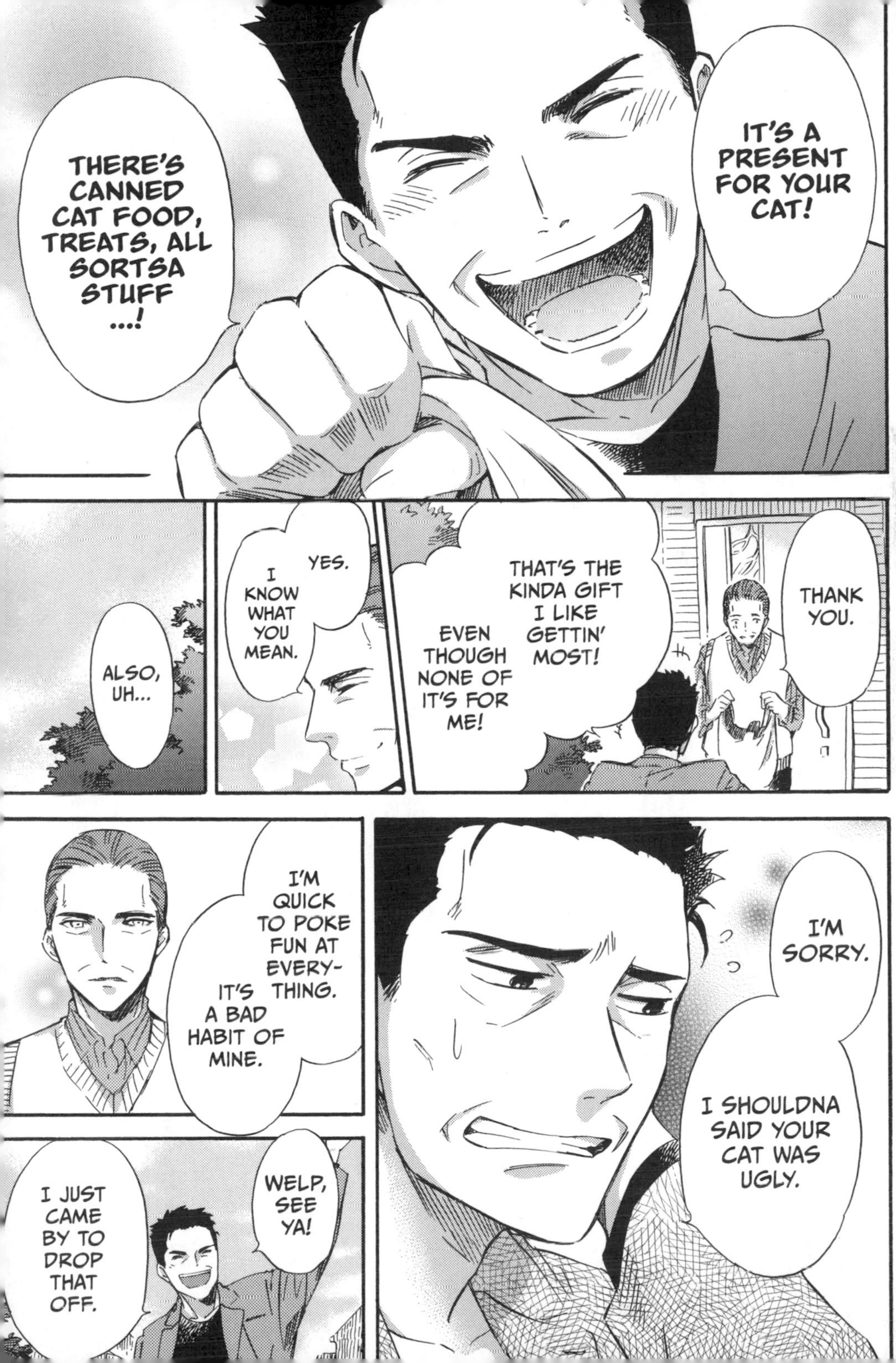
IT'S A PRESENT FOR YOUR CAT!
THERE'S CANNED CAT FOOD, TREATS, ALL SORTSA STUFF ...!
THANK YOU.
THAT'S THE KINDA GIFT I LIKE GETTIN' MOST!
EVEN THOUGH NONE OF IT'S FOR ME!
YES.
I KNOW WHAT YOU MEAN.
ALSO, UH...
I'M SORRY.
I SHOULDNA SAID YOUR CAT WAS UGLY.
I'M QUICK TO POKE FUN AT EVERY-THING.
IT'S A BAD HABIT OF MINE.
WELP, SEE YA!
I JUST CAME BY TO DROP THAT OFF.

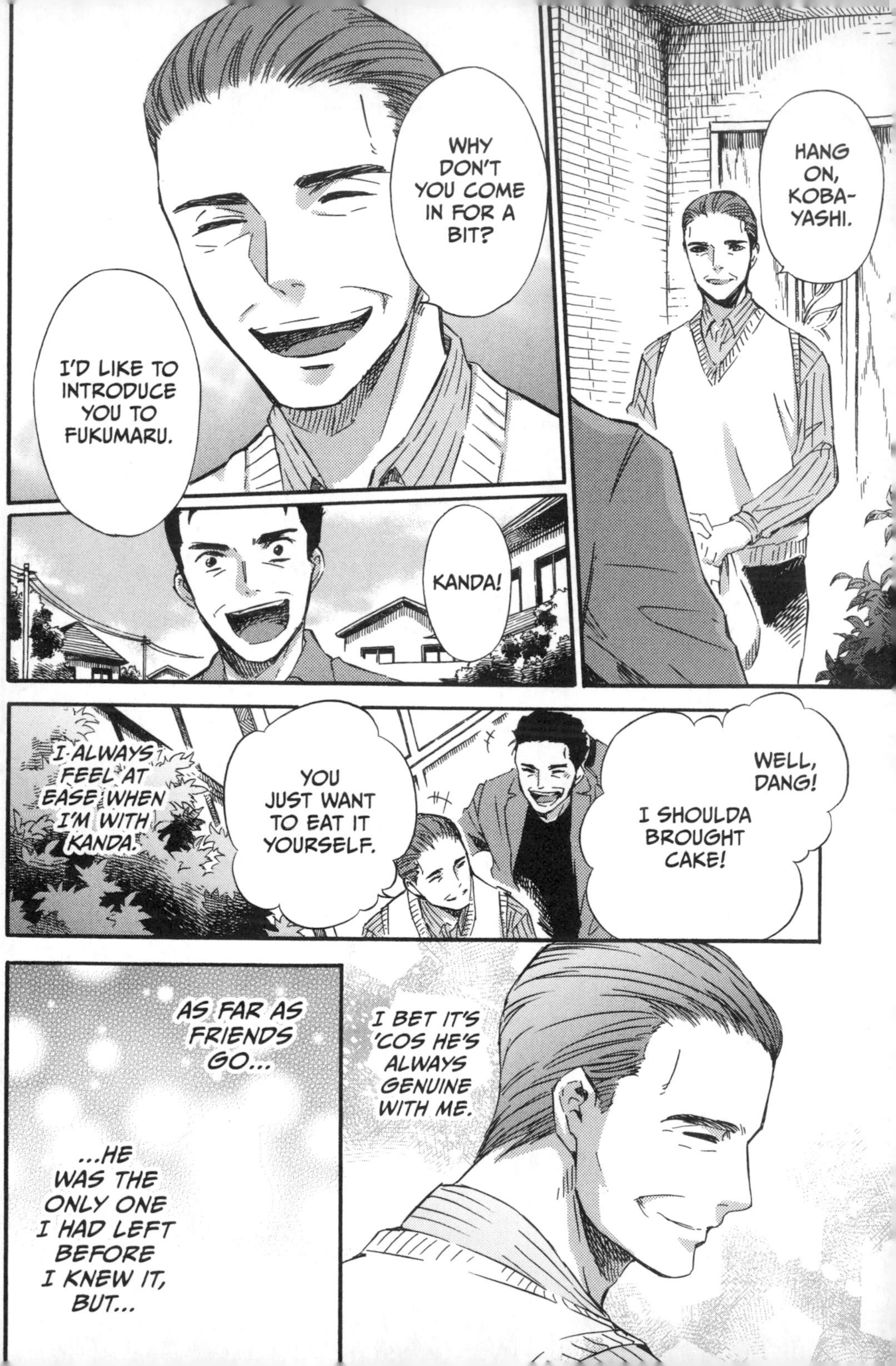
HANG ON, KOBA-YASHI.
WHY DON'T YOU COME IN FOR A BIT?
I'D LIKE TO INTRODUCE YOU TO FUKUMARU.
KANDA!
WELL, DANG!
I SHOULDA BROUGHT CAKE!
YOU JUST WANT TO EAT IT YOURSELF.
I ALWAYS FEEL AT EASE WHEN I'M WITH KANDA.
I BET IT'S 'COS HE'S ALWAYS GENUINE WITH ME.
AS FAR AS FRIENDS GO...
...HE WAS THE ONLY ONE I HAD LEFT BEFORE I KNEW IT, BUT...

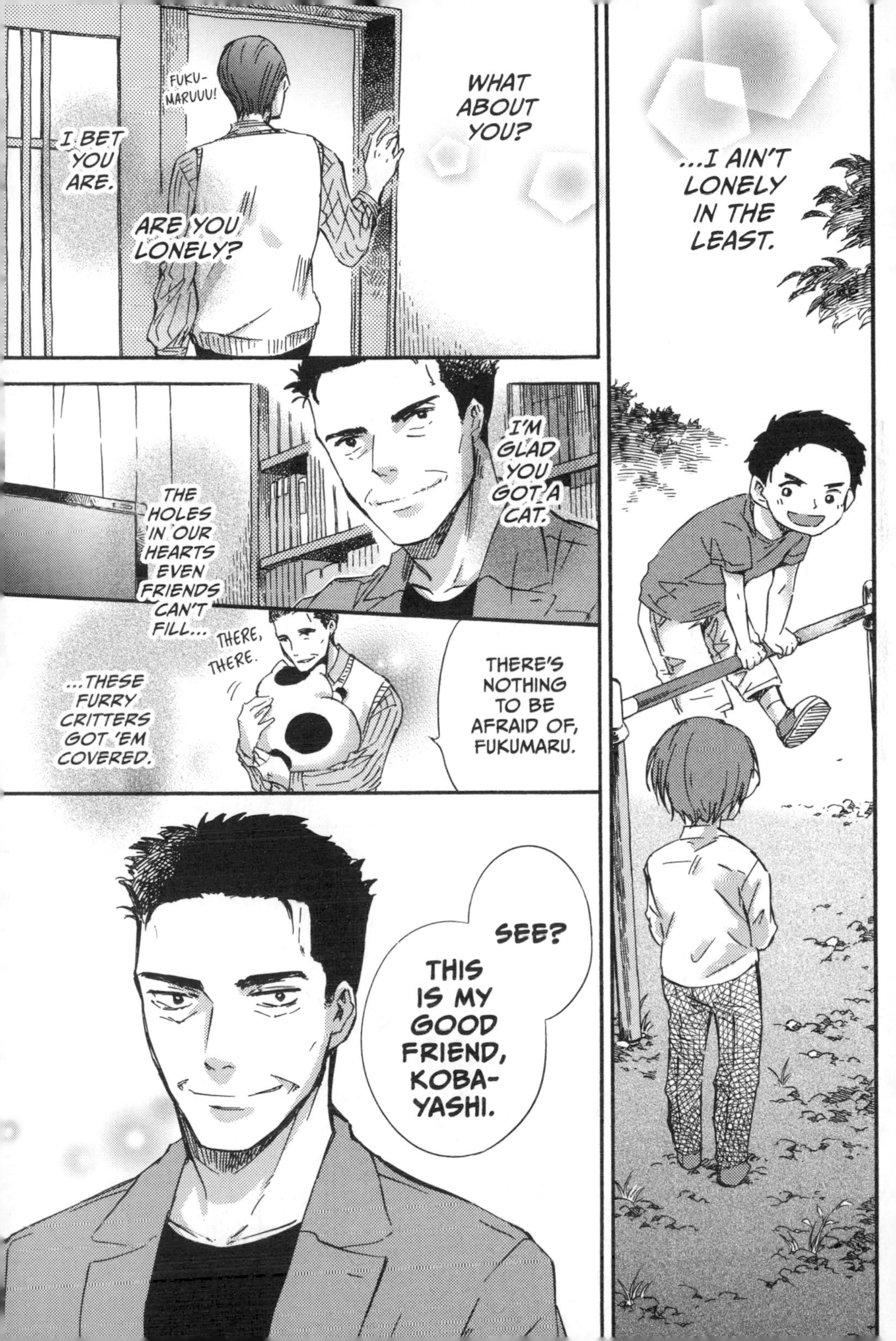
...I AIN'T LONELY IN THE LEAST.
WHAT ABOUT YOU?
FUKU-MARUUU!
I BET YOU ARE.
ARE YOU LONELY?
I'M GLAD YOU GOT A CAT.
THE HOLES IN OUR HEARTS EVEN FRIENDS CAN'T FILL...
THERE'S NOTHING TO BE AFRAID OF, FUKUMARU.
THERE, THERE.
...THESE FURRY CRITTERS GOT 'EM COVERED.
SEE?
THIS IS MY GOOD FRIEND, KOBA-YASHI.

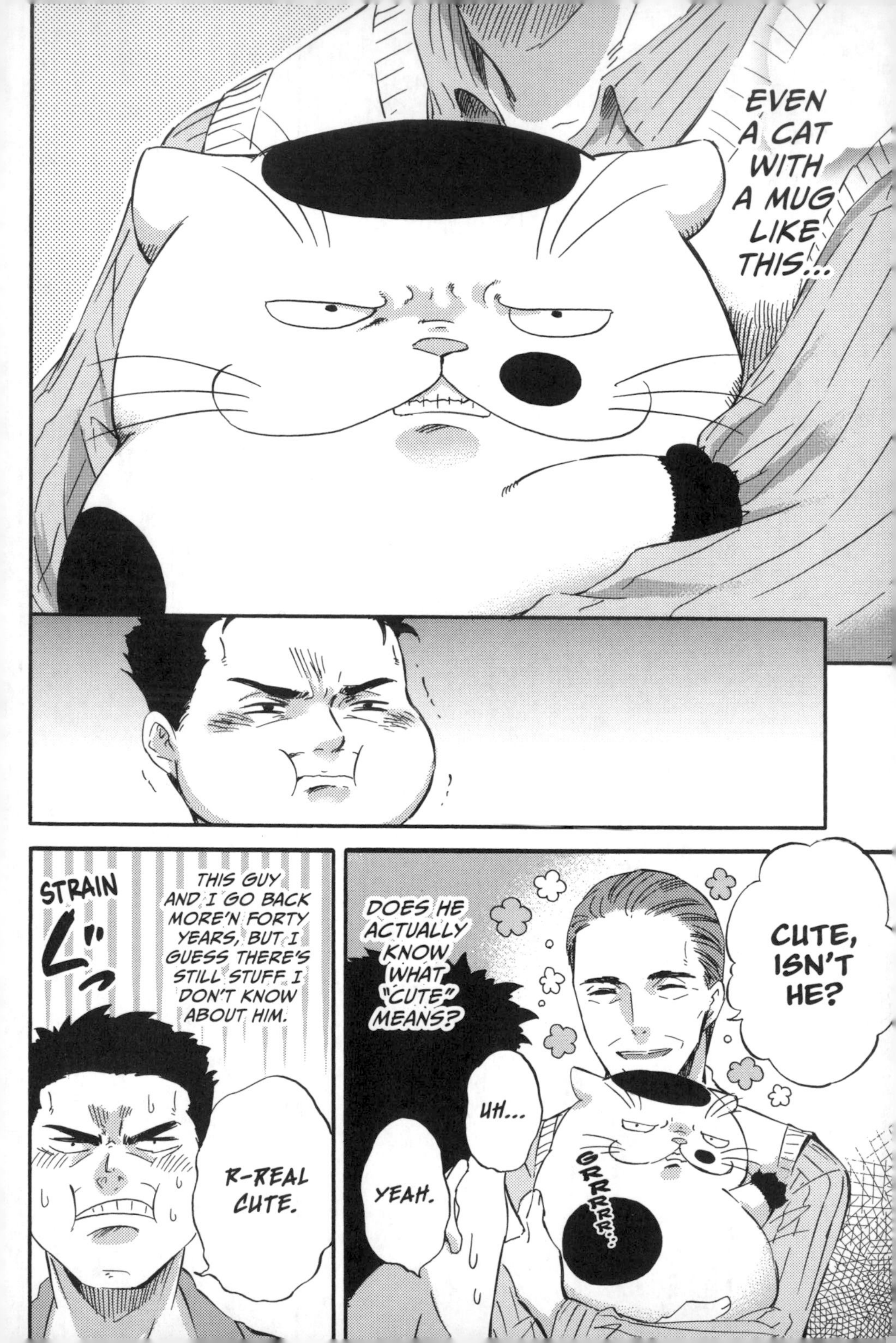
EVEN A CAT WITH A MUG LIKE THIS...
CUTE, ISN'T HE?
DOES HE ACTUALLY KNOW WHAT "CUTE" MEANS?
UH...
YEAH.
GRRRR...
THIS GUY AND I GO BACK MORE'N FORTY YEARS, BUT I GUESS THERE'S STILL STUFF I DON'T KNOW ABOUT HIM.
STRAIN
R-REAL CUTE.

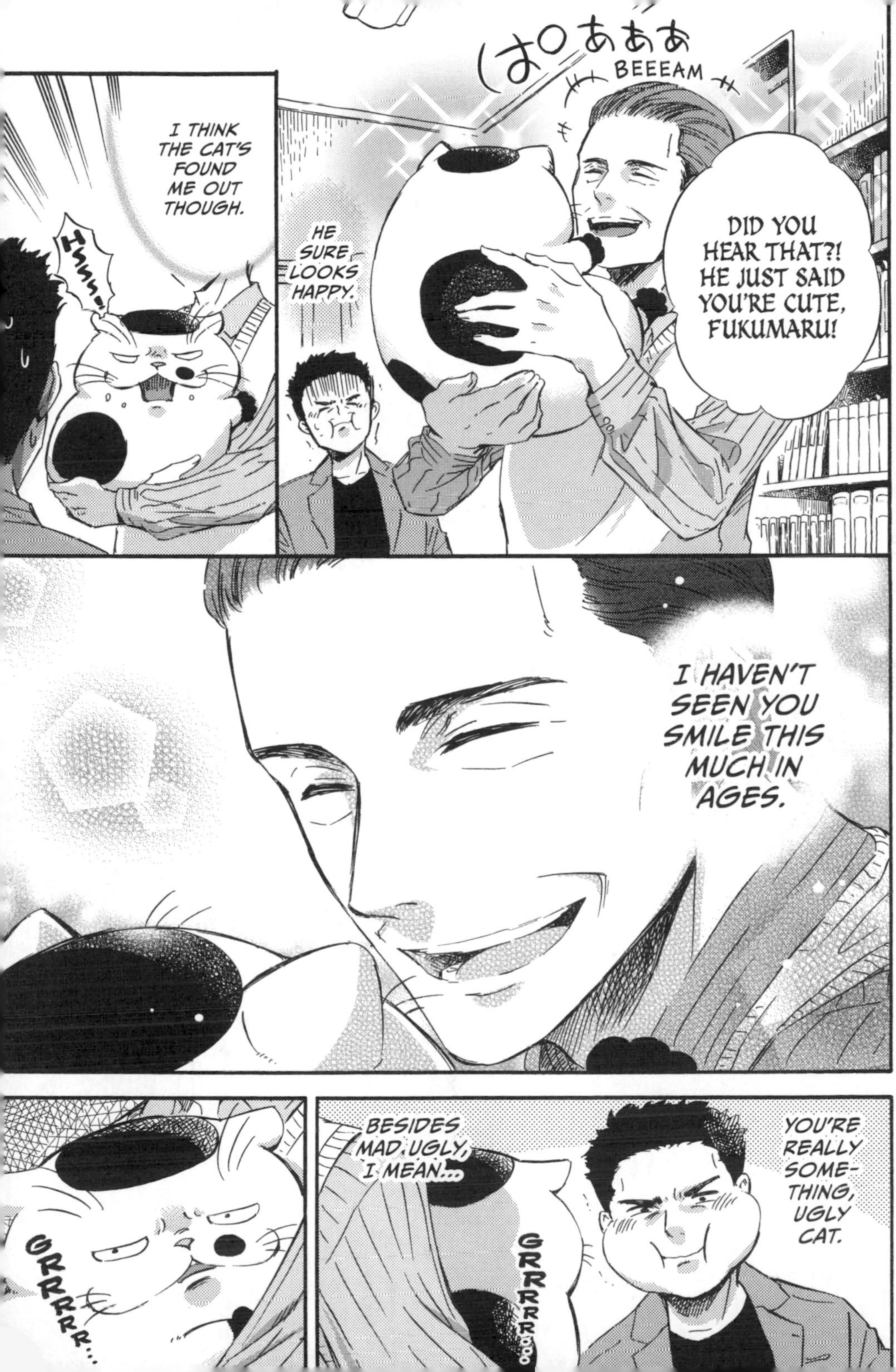
ぱあああ
BEEEAM
DID YOU HEAR THAT?! HE JUST SAID YOU'RE CUTE, FUKUMARU!
HE SURE LOOKS HAPPY.
I THINK THE CAT'S FOUND ME OUT THOUGH.
HSSS!!
I HAVEN'T SEEN YOU SMILE THIS MUCH IN AGES.
YOU'RE REALLY SOME-THING, UGLY CAT.
BESIDES MAD UGLY, I MEAN...
GRRRRR...
GRRRRR...

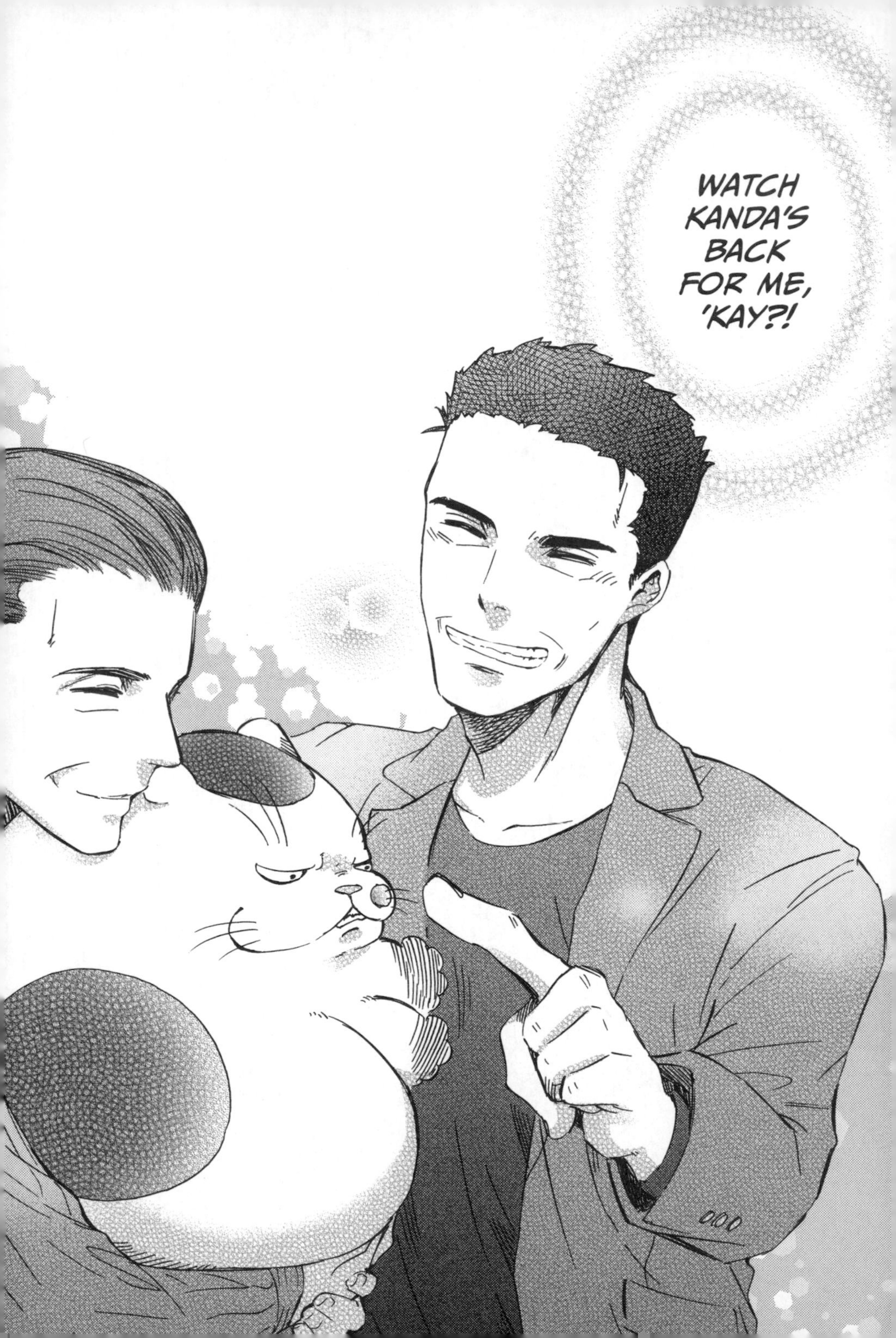
WATCH KANDA'S BACK FOR ME, 'KAY?!

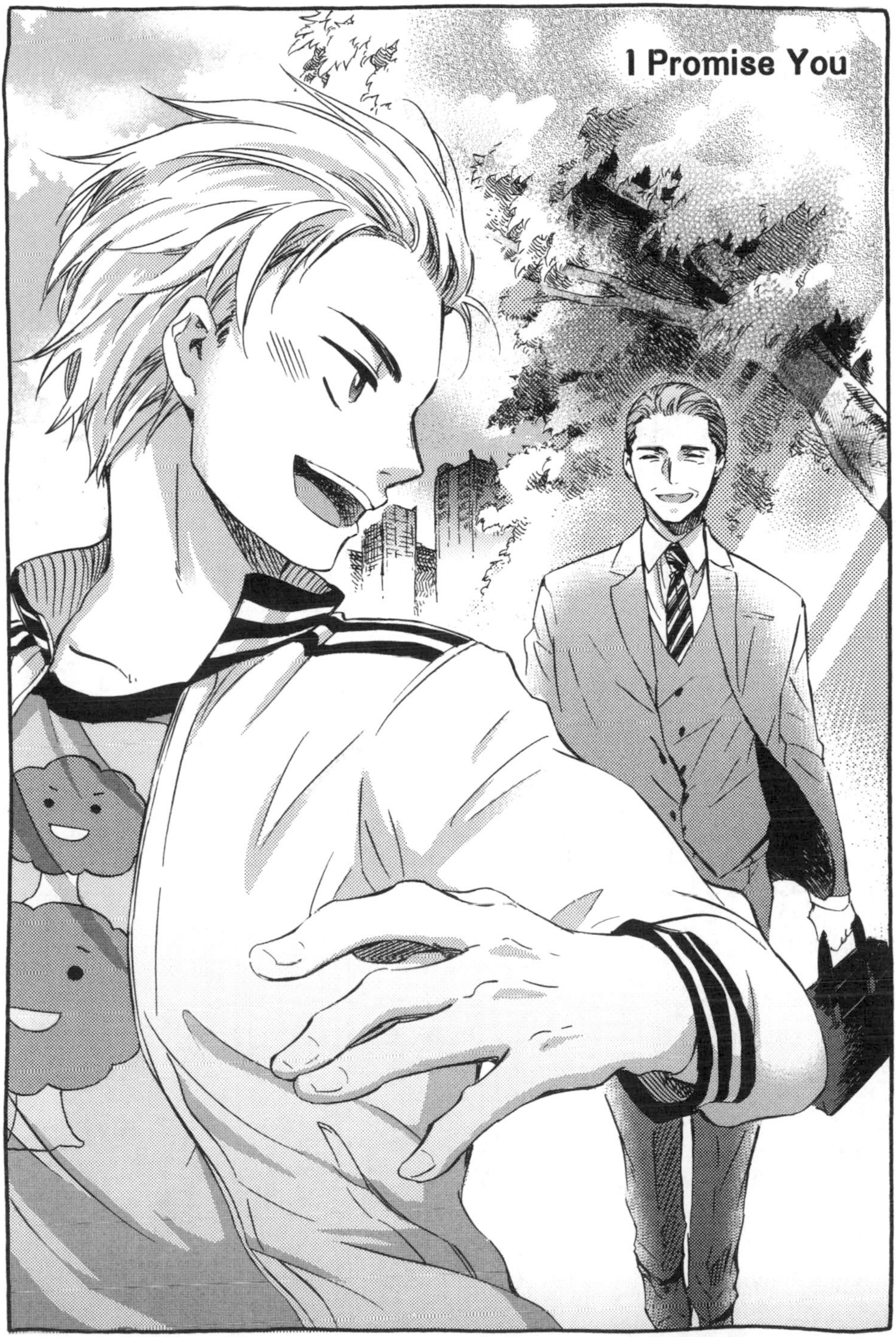
I Promise You

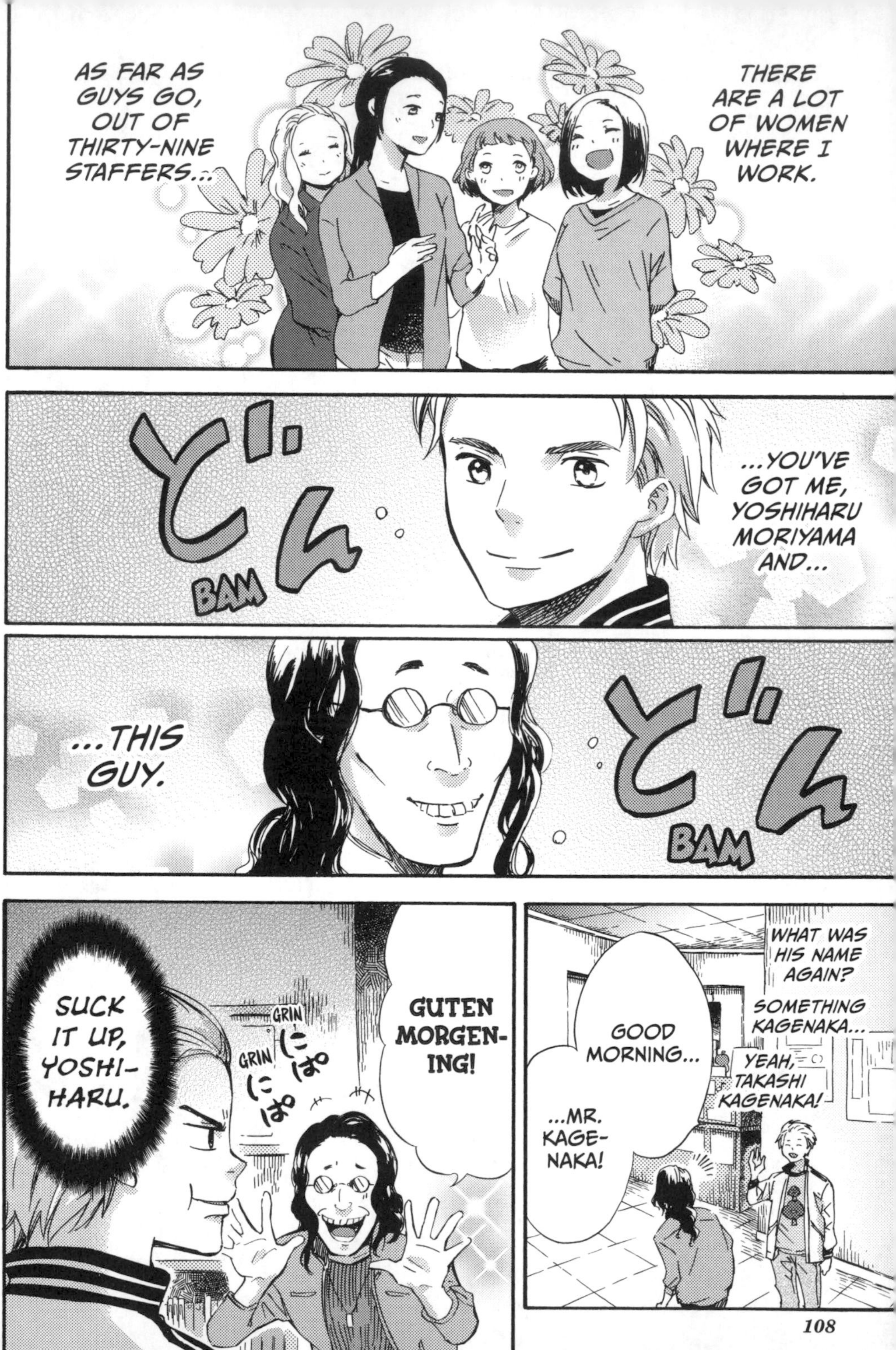
THERE ARE A LOT OF WOMEN WHERE I WORK.
AS FAR AS GUYS GO, OUT OF THIRTY-NINE STAFFERS...
...YOU'VE GOT ME, YOSHIHARU MORIYAMA AND...
どん
BAM
...THIS GUY.
どん
BAM
WHAT WAS HIS NAME AGAIN?
SOMETHING KAGENAKA...
YEAH, TAKASHI KAGENAKA!
GOOD MORNING...
...MR. KAGE-NAKA!
GUTEN MORGEN-ING!
GRIN にぱ
GRIN にぱ
SUCK IT UP, YOSHI-HARU.

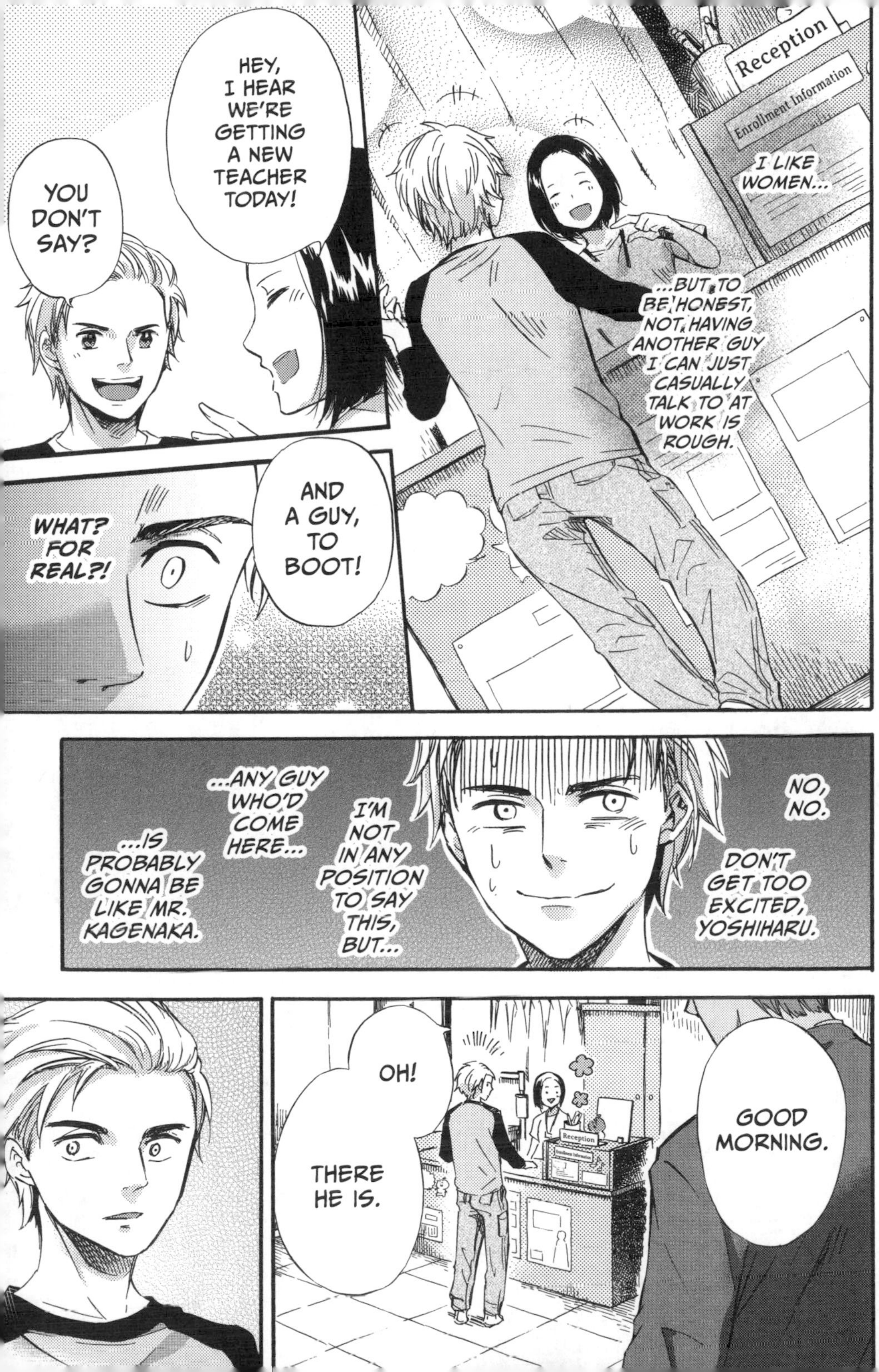
Reception
Enrollment Information
I LIKE WOMEN...
...BUT TO BE HONEST, NOT HAVING ANOTHER GUY I CAN JUST CASUALLY TALK TO AT WORK IS ROUGH.
HEY, I HEAR WE'RE GETTING A NEW TEACHER TODAY!
YOU DON'T SAY?
AND A GUY, TO BOOT!
WHAT? FOR REAL?!
NO, NO.
DON'T GET TOO EXCITED, YOSHIHARU.
I'M NOT IN ANY POSITION TO SAY THIS, BUT...
...ANY GUY WHO'D COME HERE...
...IS PROBABLY GONNA BE LIKE MR. KAGENAKA.
GOOD MORNING.
OH!
THERE HE IS.

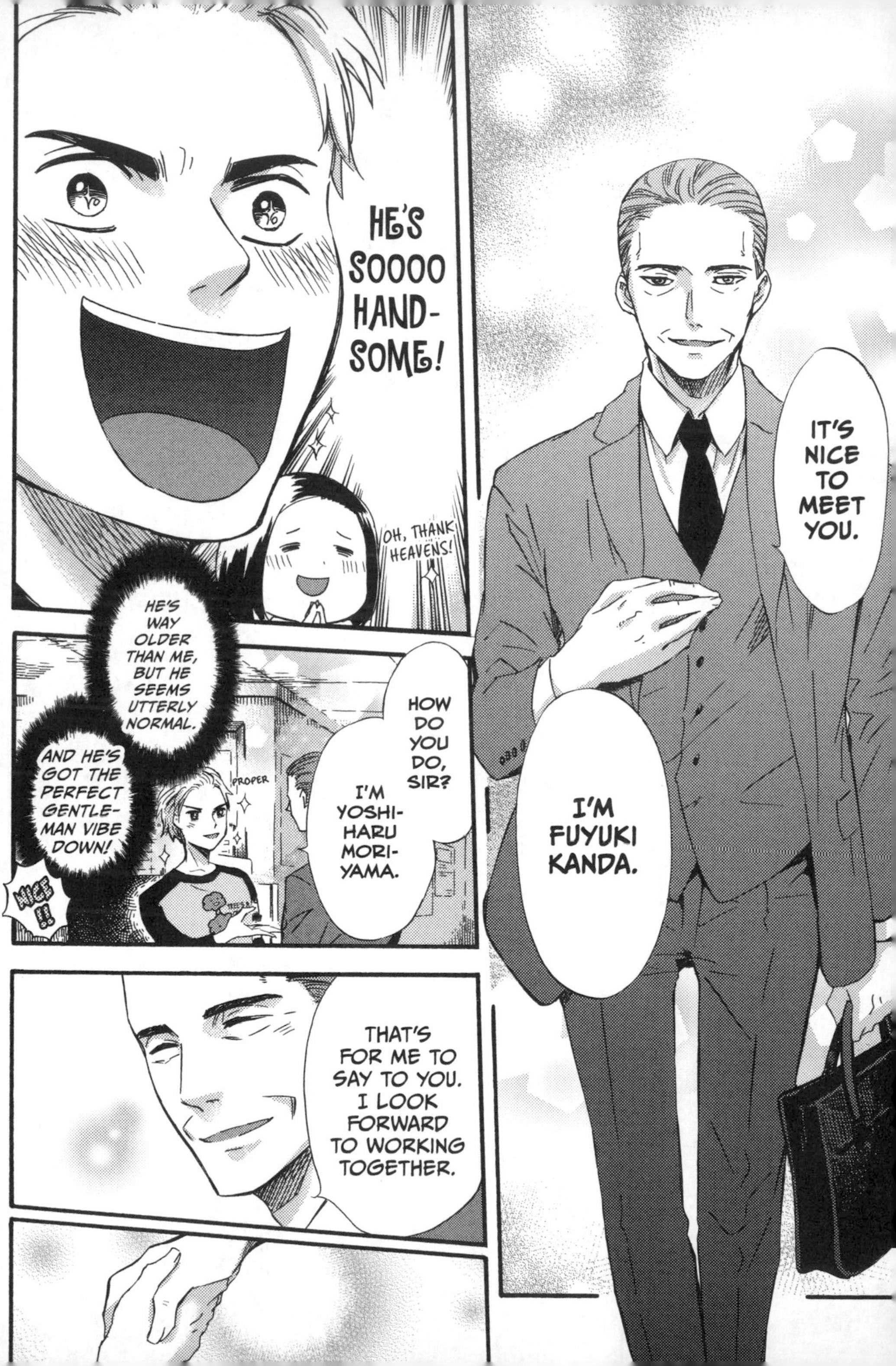
IT'S NICE TO MEET YOU.
I'M FUYUKI KANDA.
HE'S SOOOO HAND-SOME!
OH, THANK HEAVENS!
HE'S WAY OLDER THAN ME, BUT HE SEEMS UTTERLY NORMAL.
HOW DO YOU DO, SIR?
I'M YOSHI-HARU MORI-YAMA.
PROPER
AND HE'S GOT THE PERFECT GENTLE-MAN VIBE DOWN!
NICE!!
THAT'S FOR ME TO SAY TO YOU. I LOOK FORWARD TO WORKING TOGETHER.

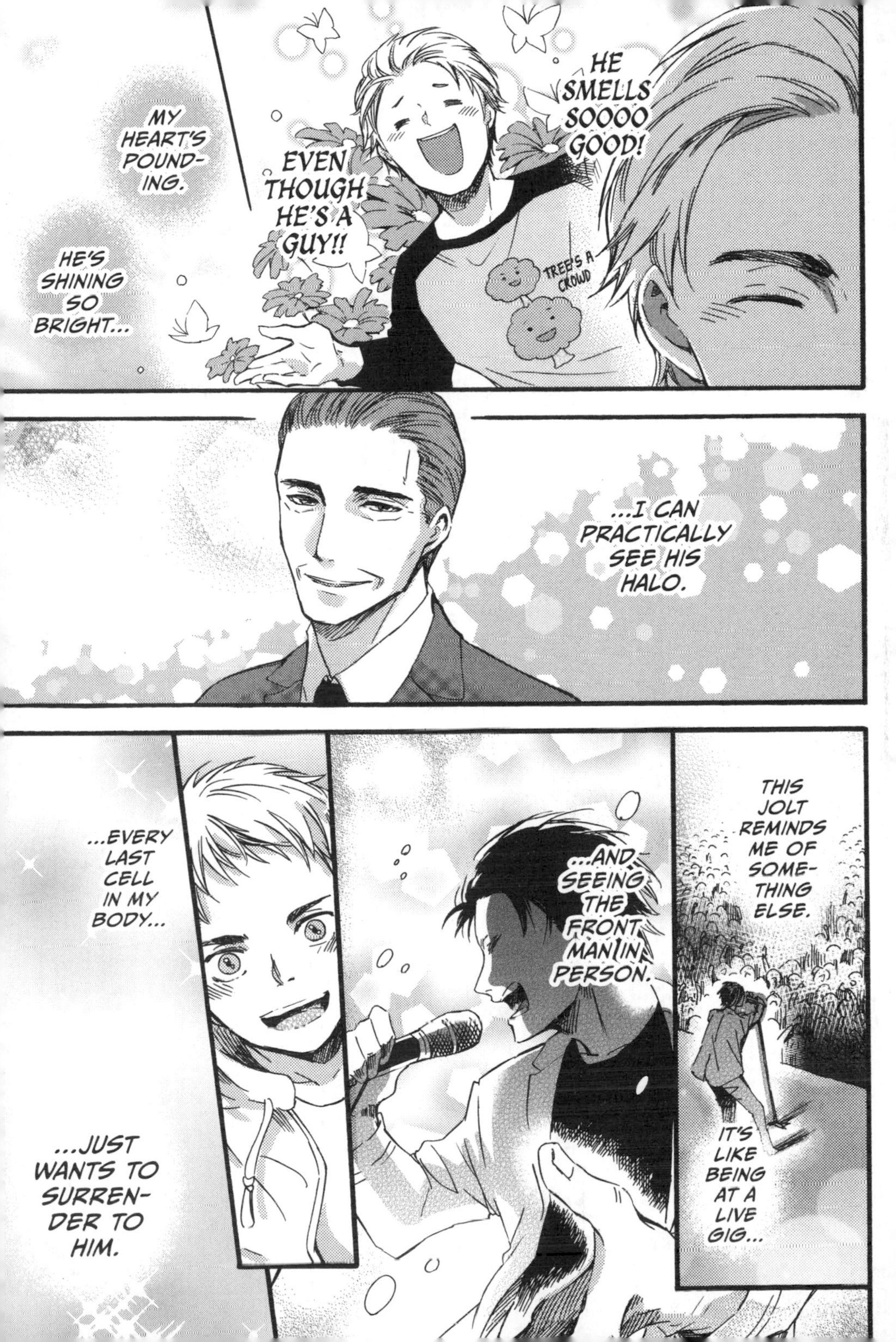
HE SMELLS SOOOO GOOD!
TREE'S A CROWD
EVEN THOUGH HE'S A GUY!!
MY HEART'S POUNDING.
HE'S SHINING SO BRIGHT...
...I CAN PRACTICALLY SEE HIS HALO.
THIS JOLT REMINDS ME OF SOMETHING ELSE.
IT'S LIKE BEING AT A LIVE GIG...
...AND SEEING THE FRONT MAN IN PERSON.
...EVERY LAST CELL IN MY BODY...
...JUST WANTS TO SURRENDER TO HIM.

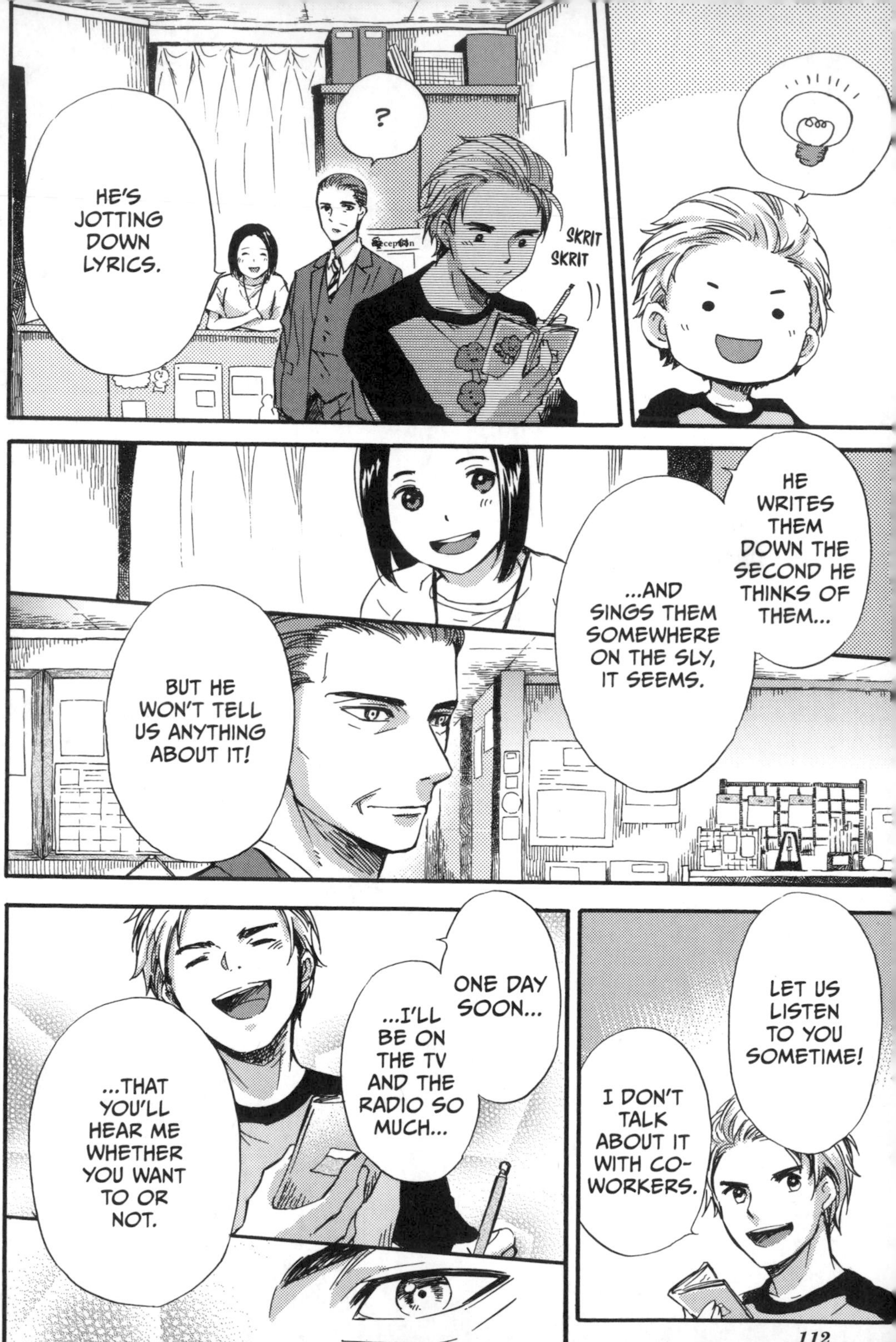
?
SKRIT SKRIT
HE'S JOTTING DOWN LYRICS.
HE WRITES THEM DOWN THE SECOND HE THINKS OF THEM...
...AND SINGS THEM SOMEWHERE ON THE SLY, IT SEEMS.
BUT HE WON'T TELL US ANYTHING ABOUT IT!
LET US LISTEN TO YOU SOMETIME!
I DON'T TALK ABOUT IT WITH CO-WORKERS.
ONE DAY SOON...
...I'LL BE ON THE TV AND THE RADIO SO MUCH...
...THAT YOU'LL HEAR ME WHETHER YOU WANT TO OR NOT.

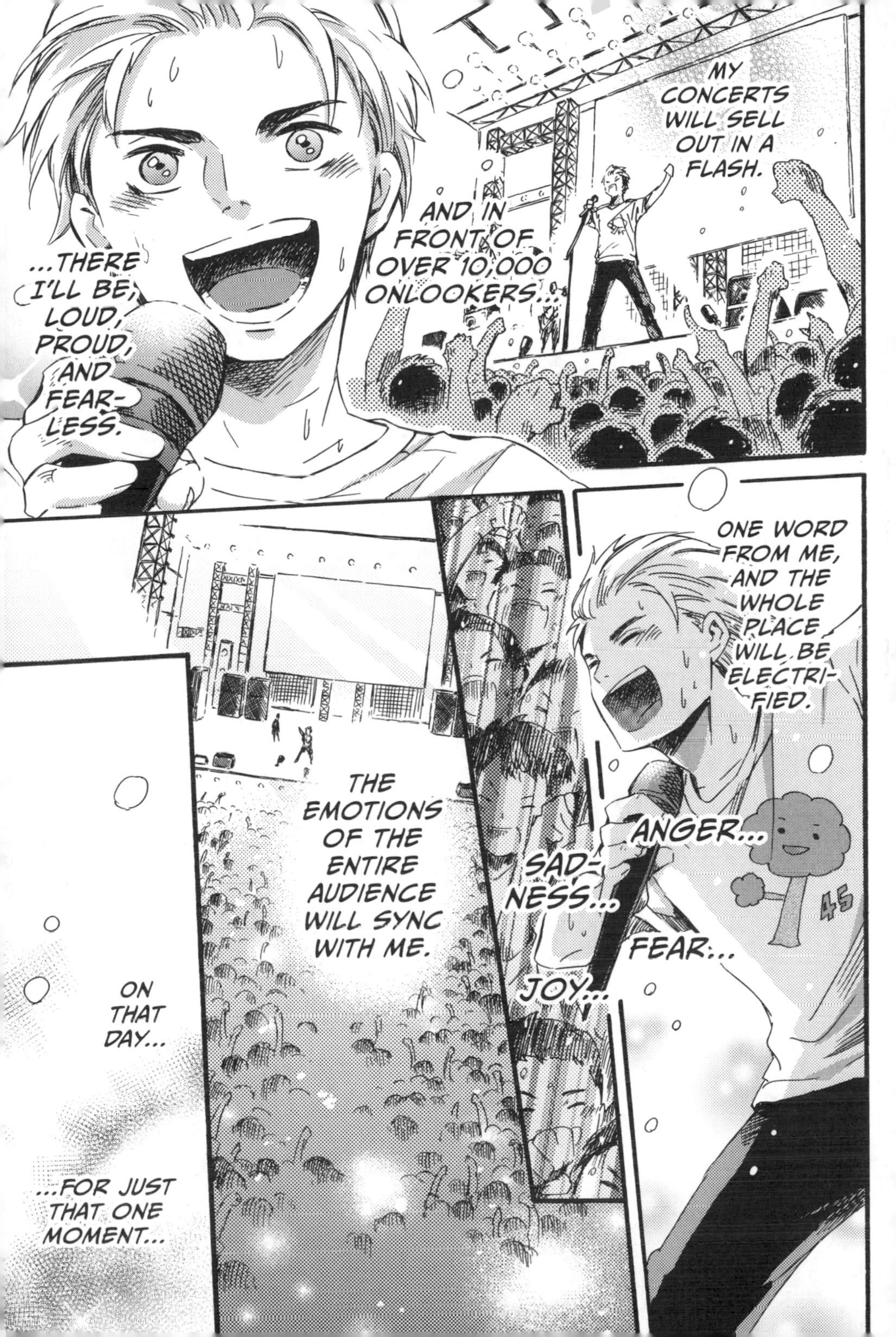
MY CONCERTS WILL SELL OUT IN A FLASH.
AND IN FRONT OF OVER 10,000 ONLOOKERS...
...THERE I'LL BE, LOUD, PROUD, AND FEARLESS.
ONE WORD FROM ME, AND THE WHOLE PLACE WILL BE ELECTRIFIED.
ANGER...
SADNESS...
FEAR...
JOY...
45
THE EMOTIONS OF THE ENTIRE AUDIENCE WILL SYNC WITH ME.
ON THAT DAY...
...FOR JUST THAT ONE MOMENT...

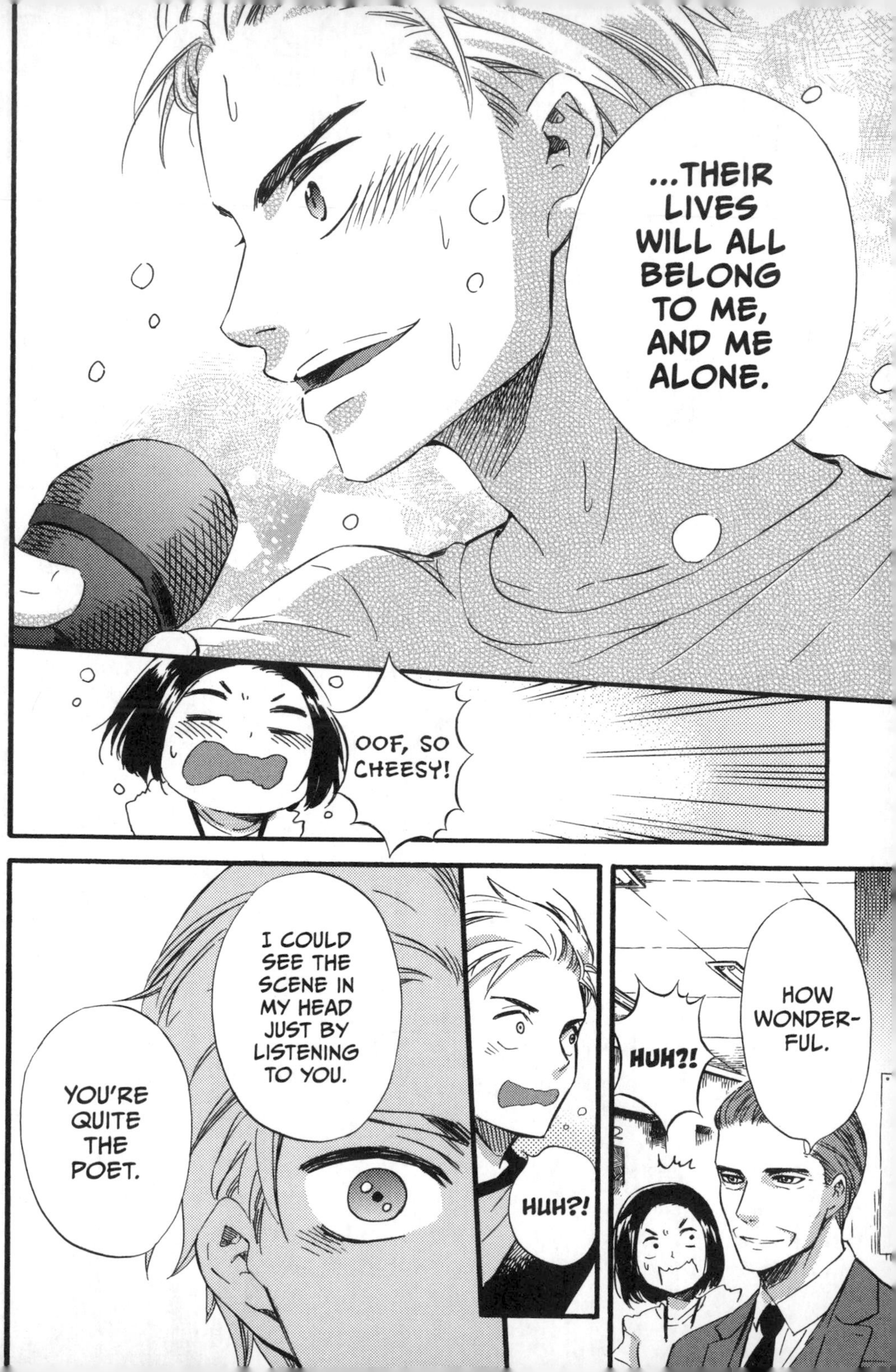
...THEIR LIVES WILL ALL BELONG TO ME, AND ME ALONE.
OOF, SO CHEESY!
HOW WONDER-FUL.
HUH?!
HUH?!
I COULD SEE THE SCENE IN MY HEAD JUST BY LISTENING TO YOU.
YOU'RE QUITE THE POET.

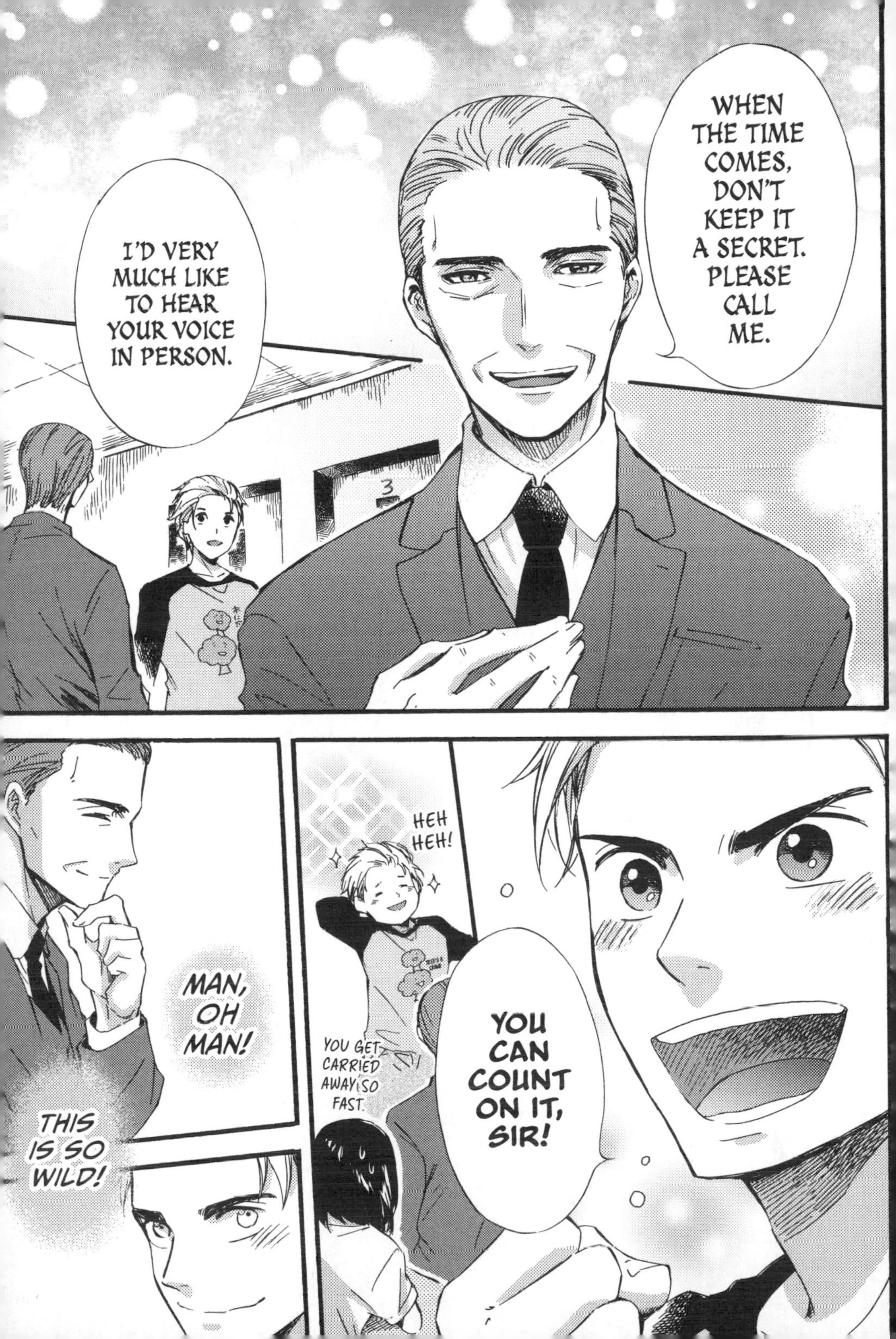
WHEN THE TIME COMES, DON'T KEEP IT A SECRET. PLEASE CALL ME.
I'D VERY MUCH LIKE TO HEAR YOUR VOICE IN PERSON.
HEH HEH!
YOU CAN COUNT ON IT, SIR!
YOU GET CARRIED AWAY SO FAST.
MAN, OH MAN!
THIS IS SO WILD!

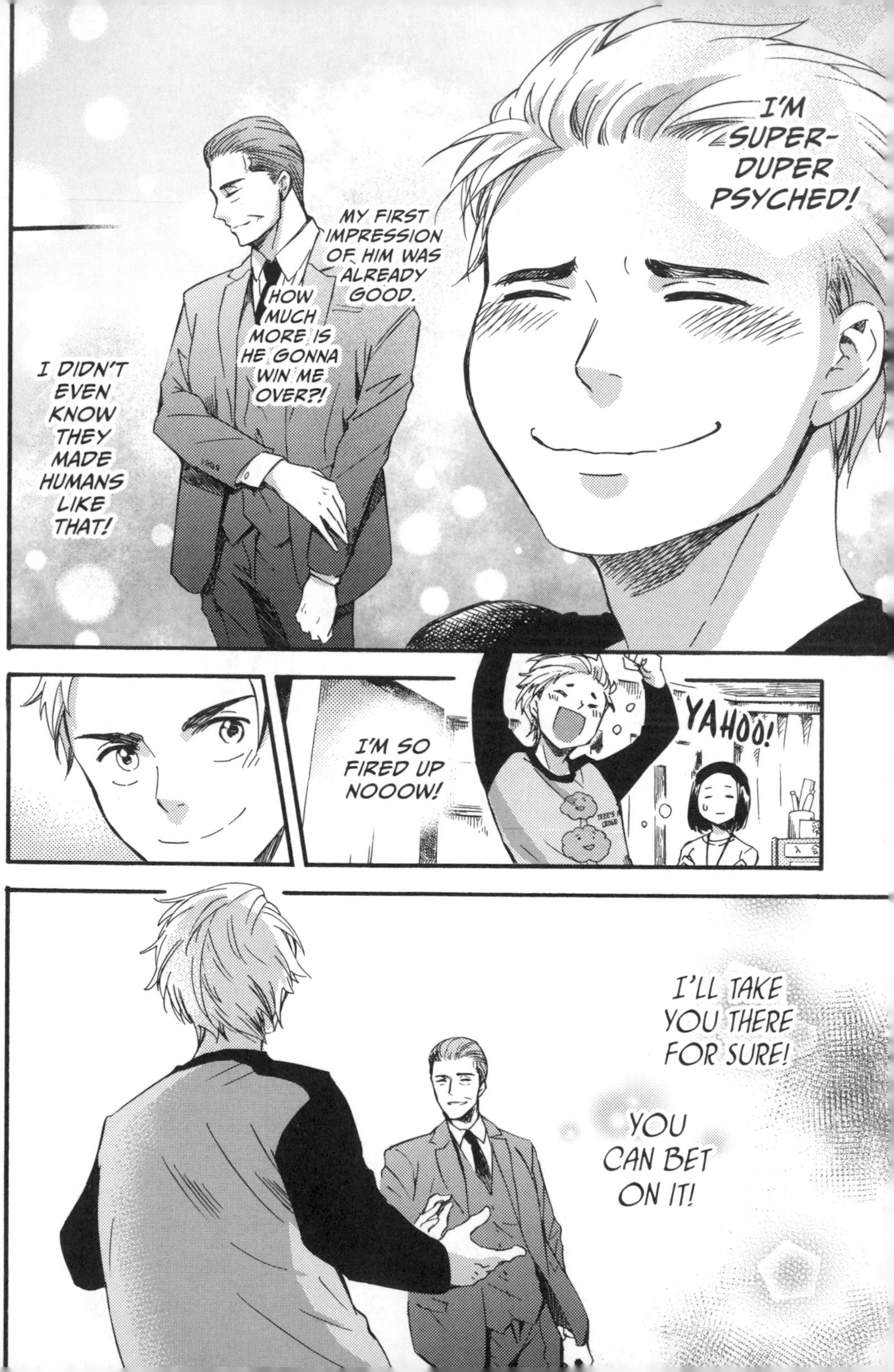
I'M SUPER-DUPER PSYCHED!
MY FIRST IMPRESSION OF HIM WAS ALREADY GOOD.
HOW MUCH MORE IS HE GONNA WIN ME OVER?!
I DIDN'T EVEN KNOW THEY MADE HUMANS LIKE THAT!
YAHOO!
I'M SO FIRED UP NOOOW!
I'LL TAKE YOU THERE FOR SURE!
YOU CAN BET ON IT!

## FUKUMARU GETS DISTRACTED

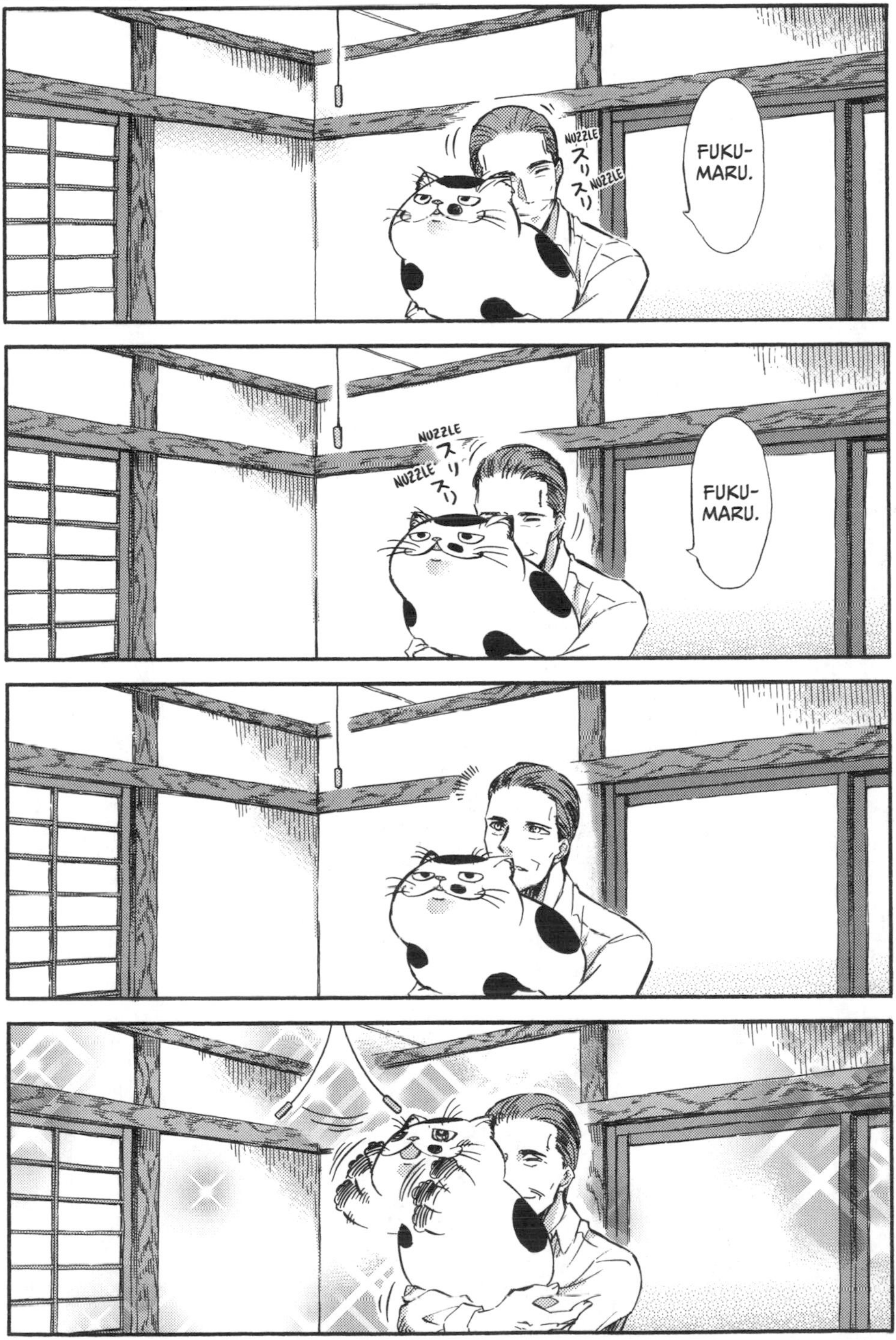
FUKU-MARU.
NUZZLE スリスリ NUZZLE
FUKU-MARU.
NUZZLE スリスリ NUZZLE

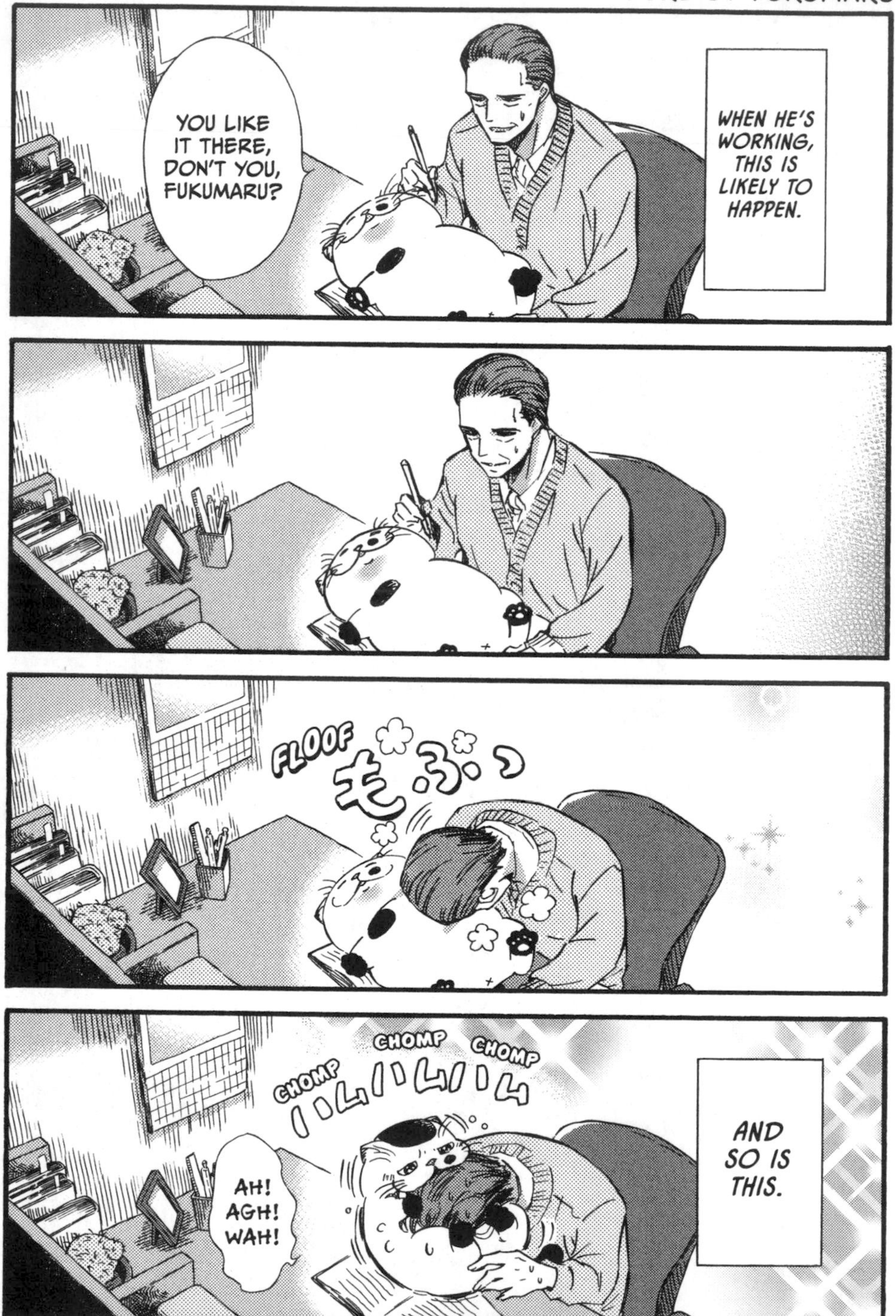
WHEN HE'S WORKING, THIS IS LIKELY TO HAPPEN.
YOU LIKE IT THERE, DON'T YOU, FUKUMARU?
FLOOF
もふっ
CHOMP
CHOMP
CHOMP
AND SO IS THIS.
AH! AGH! WAH!

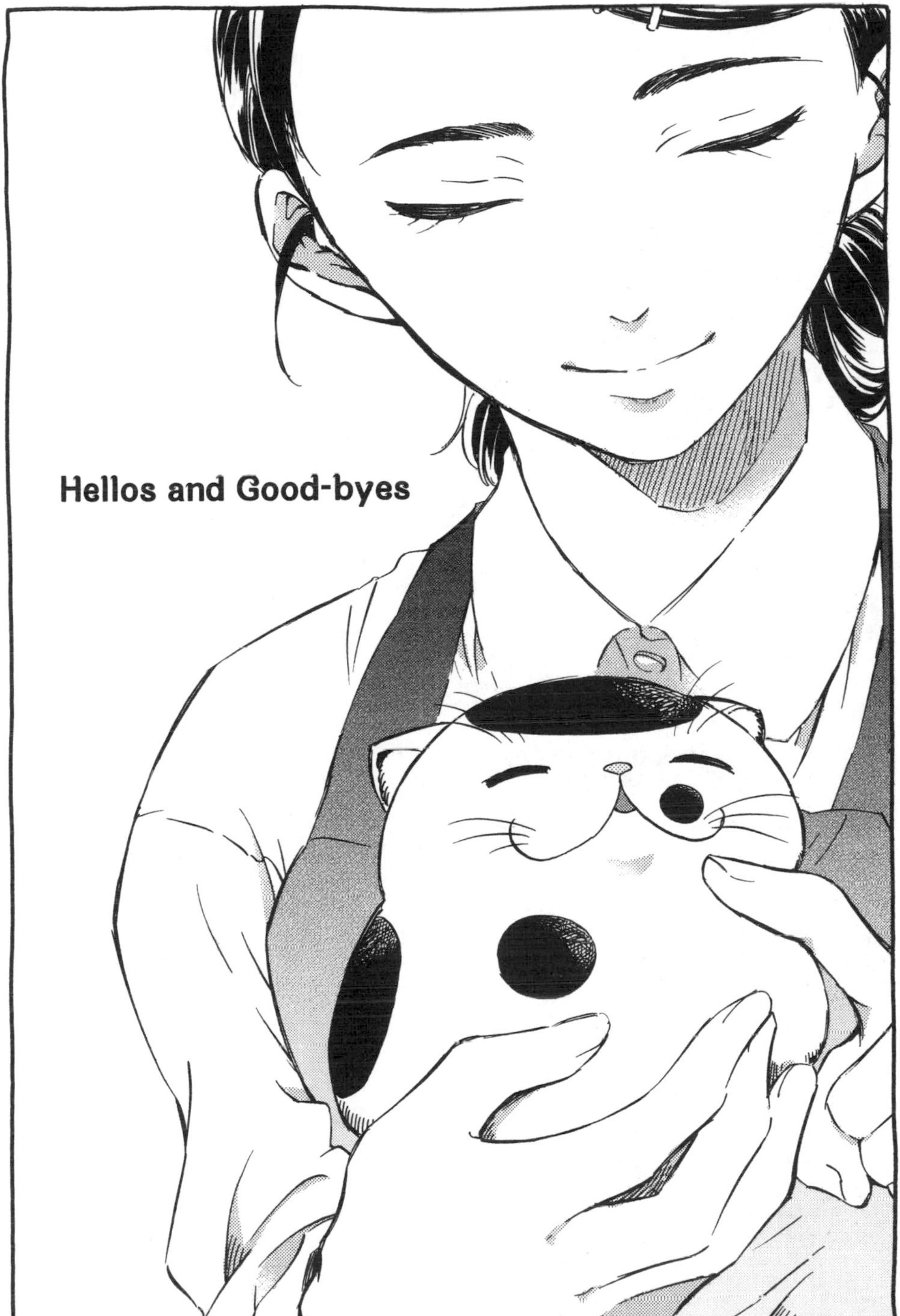
Hellos and Good-byes

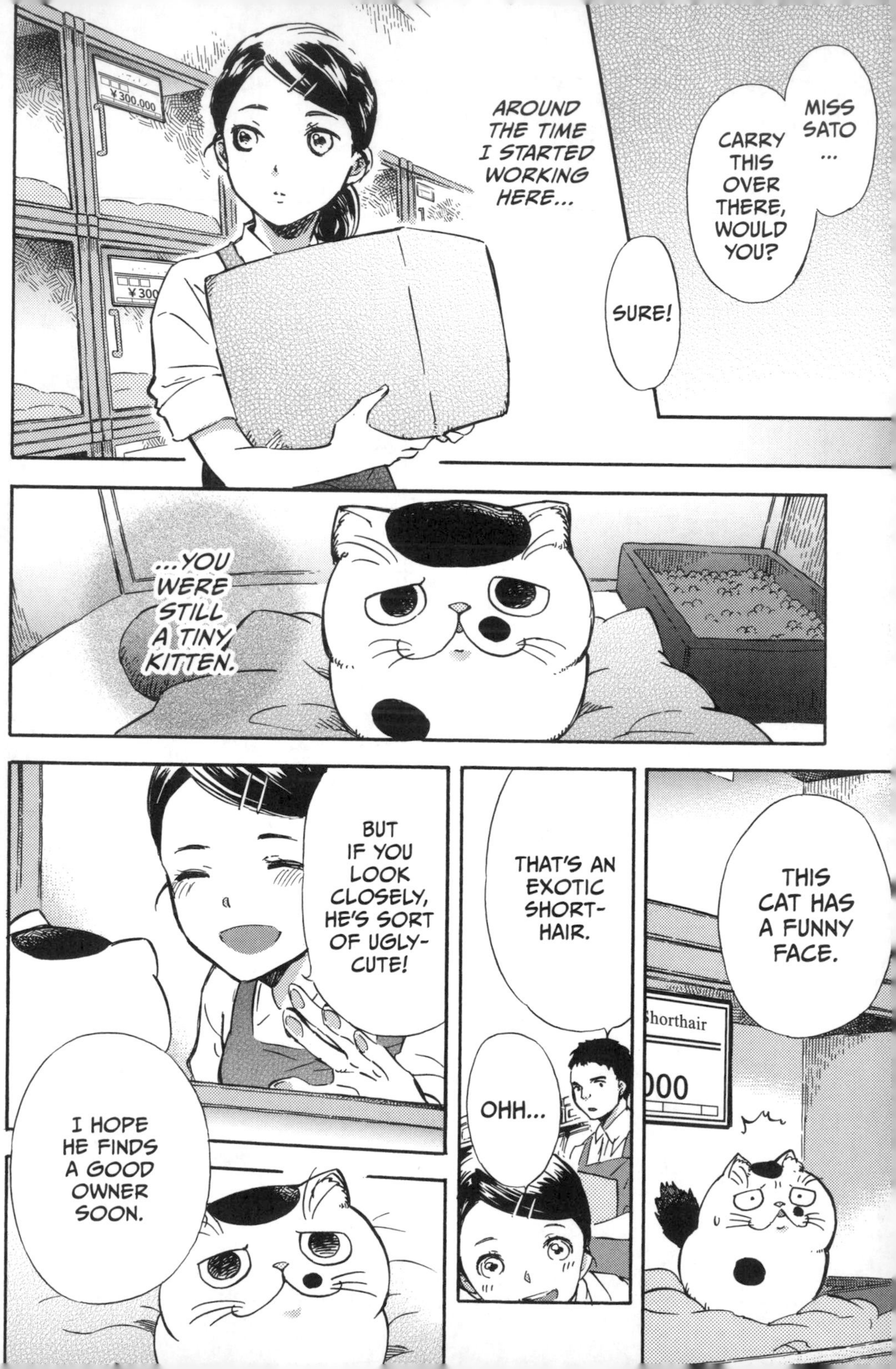
¥300,000
MISS SATO... CARRY THIS OVER THERE, WOULD YOU?
AROUND THE TIME I STARTED WORKING HERE...
SURE!
...YOU WERE STILL A TINY KITTEN.
THIS CAT HAS A FUNNY FACE.
Shorthair
THAT'S AN EXOTIC SHORT-HAIR.
OHH...
BUT IF YOU LOOK CLOSELY, HE'S SORT OF UGLY-CUTE!
I HOPE HE FINDS A GOOD OWNER SOON.

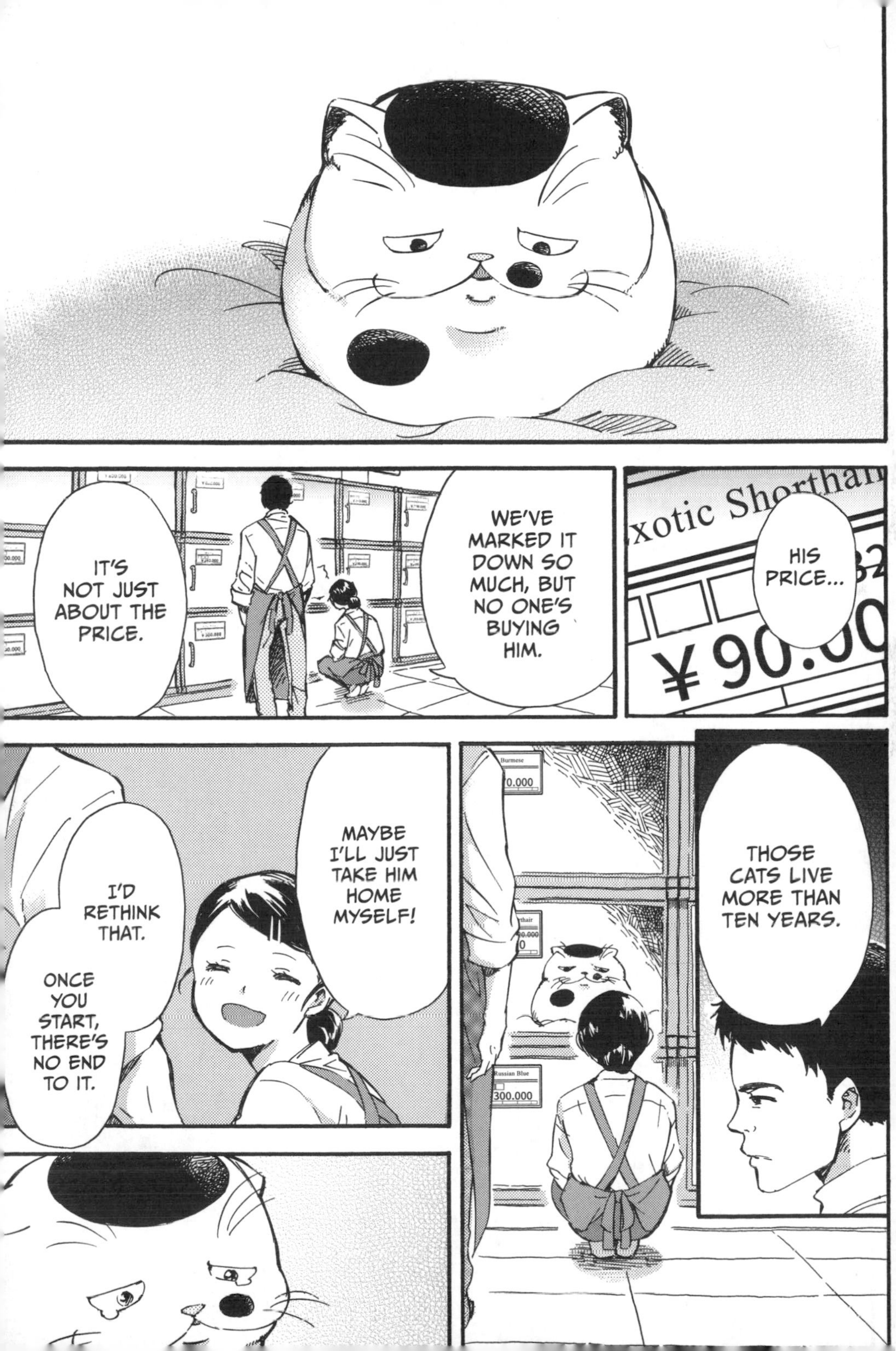
xotic Shortha
¥90.00
HIS PRICE...
WE'VE MARKED IT DOWN SO MUCH, BUT NO ONE'S BUYING HIM.
IT'S NOT JUST ABOUT THE PRICE.
THOSE CATS LIVE MORE THAN TEN YEARS.
Burmese
Russian Blue
300.000
MAYBE I'LL JUST TAKE HIM HOME MYSELF!
I'D RETHINK THAT.
ONCE YOU START, THERE'S NO END TO IT.

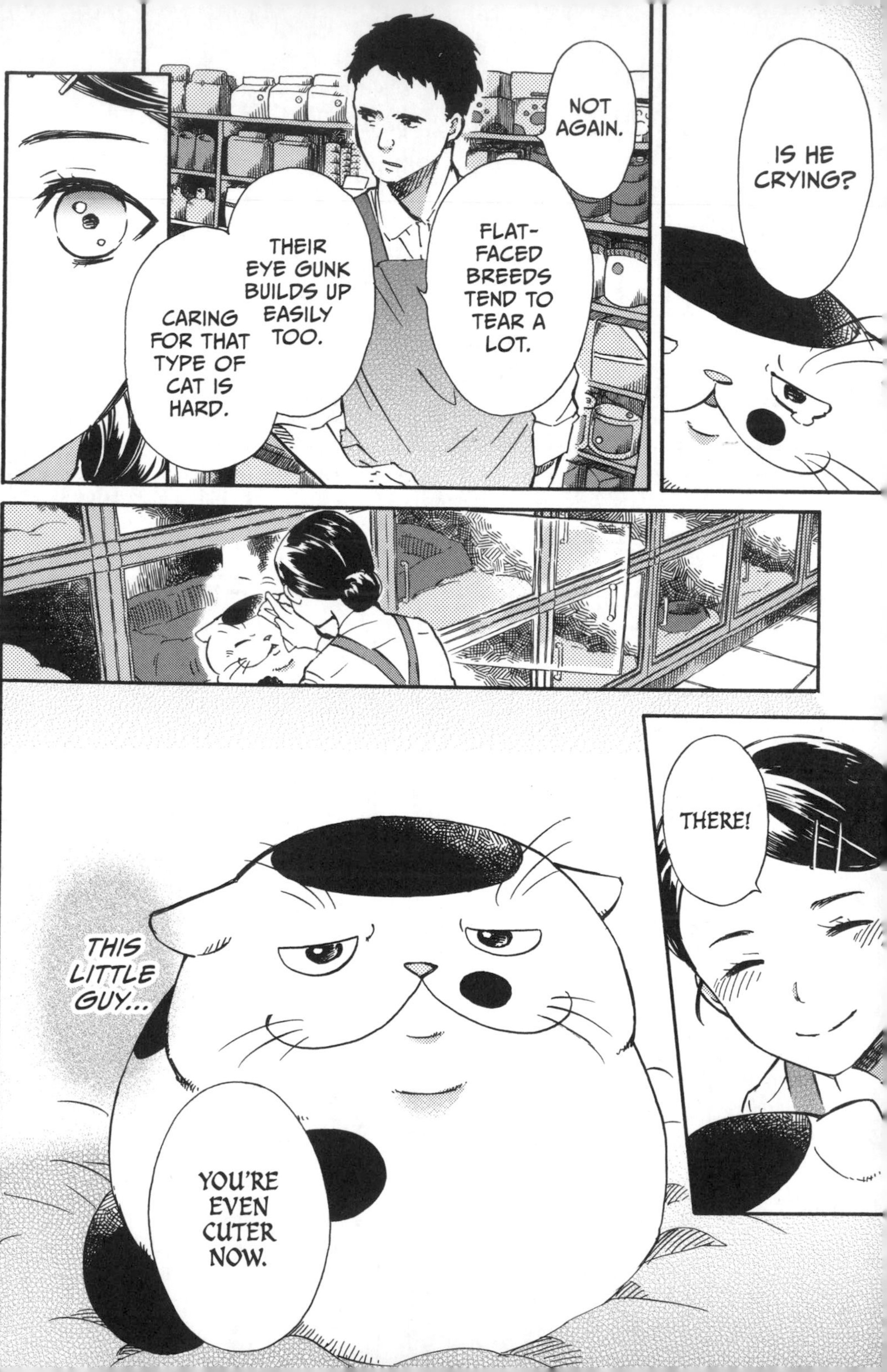
IS HE CRYING?
NOT AGAIN.
FLAT-FACED BREEDS TEND TO TEAR A LOT.
THEIR EYE GUNK BUILDS UP EASILY TOO.
CARING FOR THAT TYPE OF CAT IS HARD.
THERE!
THIS LITTLE GUY...
YOU'RE EVEN CUTER NOW.

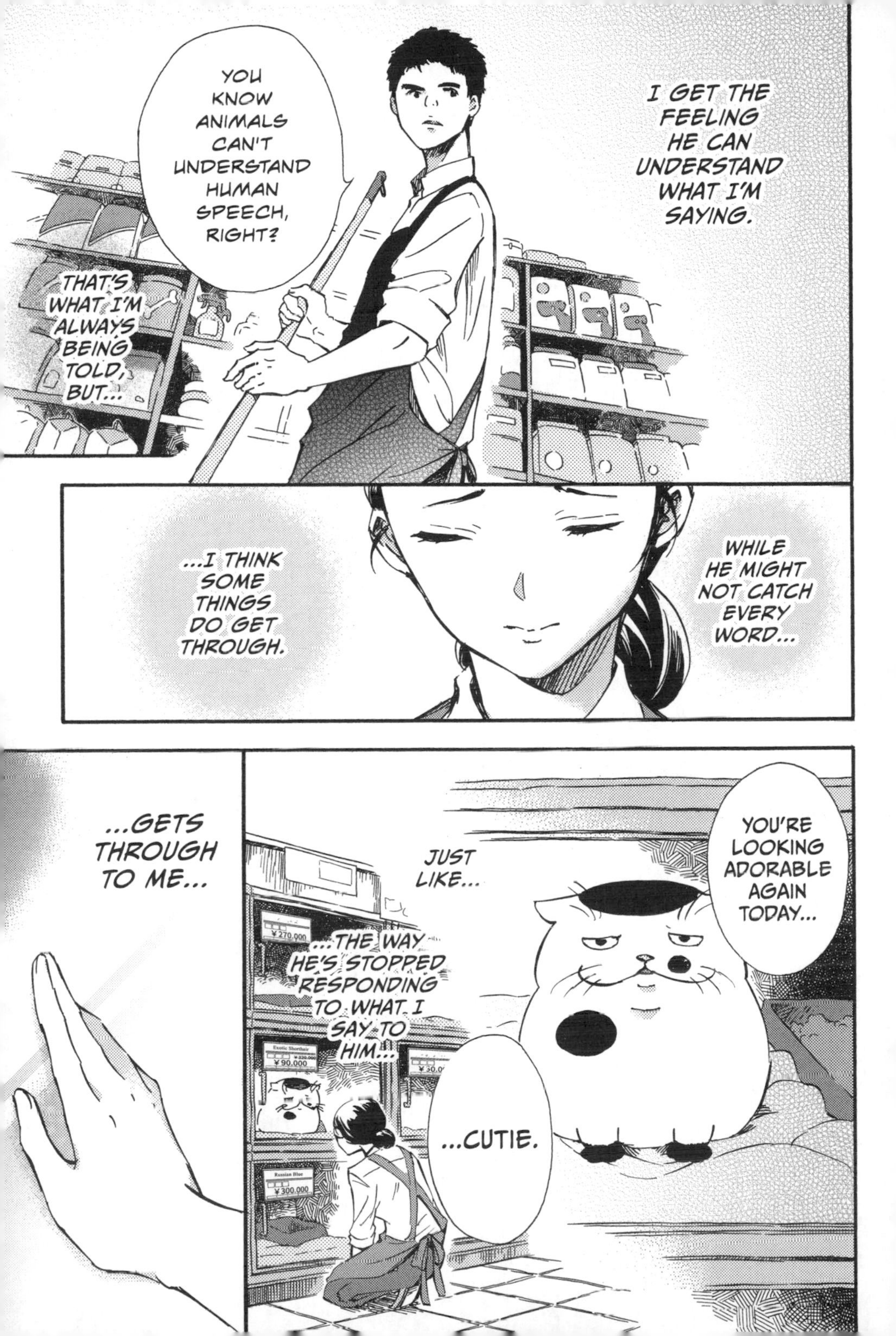
I GET THE FEELING HE CAN UNDERSTAND WHAT I'M SAYING.
YOU KNOW ANIMALS CAN'T UNDERSTAND HUMAN SPEECH, RIGHT?
THAT'S WHAT I'M ALWAYS BEING TOLD, BUT...
WHILE HE MIGHT NOT CATCH EVERY WORD...
...I THINK SOME THINGS DO GET THROUGH.
YOU'RE LOOKING ADORABLE AGAIN TODAY...
JUST LIKE...
¥270,000
...THE WAY HE'S STOPPED RESPONDING TO WHAT I SAY TO HIM...
Exotic Shorthair
¥90,000
Russian Blue
¥300,000
...CUTIE.
...GETS THROUGH TO ME...

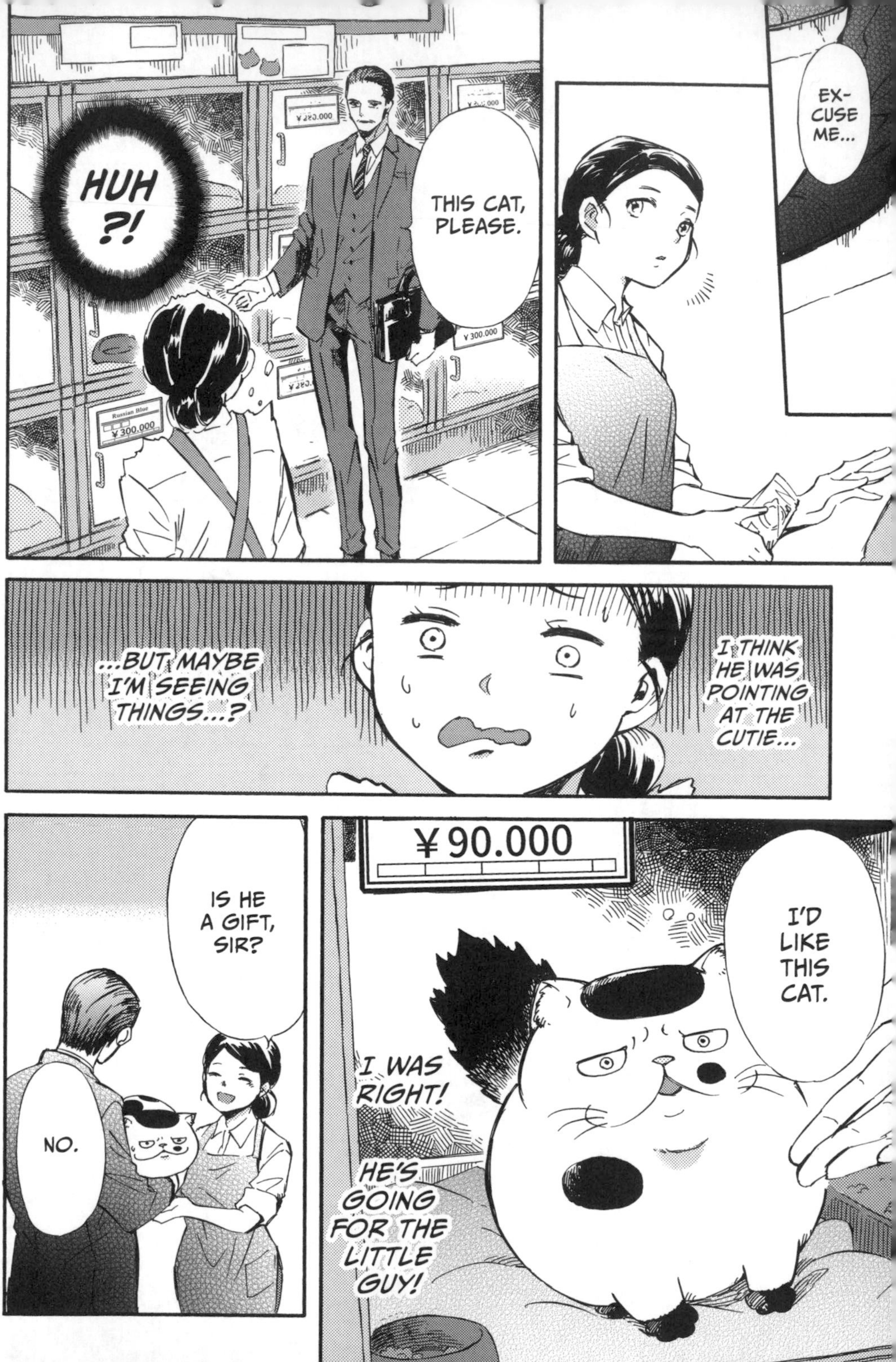
EX-CUSE ME...
THIS CAT, PLEASE.
HUH ?!
I THINK HE WAS POINTING AT THE CUTIE...
...BUT MAYBE I'M SEEING THINGS...?
¥90.000
I'D LIKE THIS CAT.
I WAS RIGHT!
HE'S GOING FOR THE LITTLE GUY!
IS HE A GIFT, SIR?
NO.

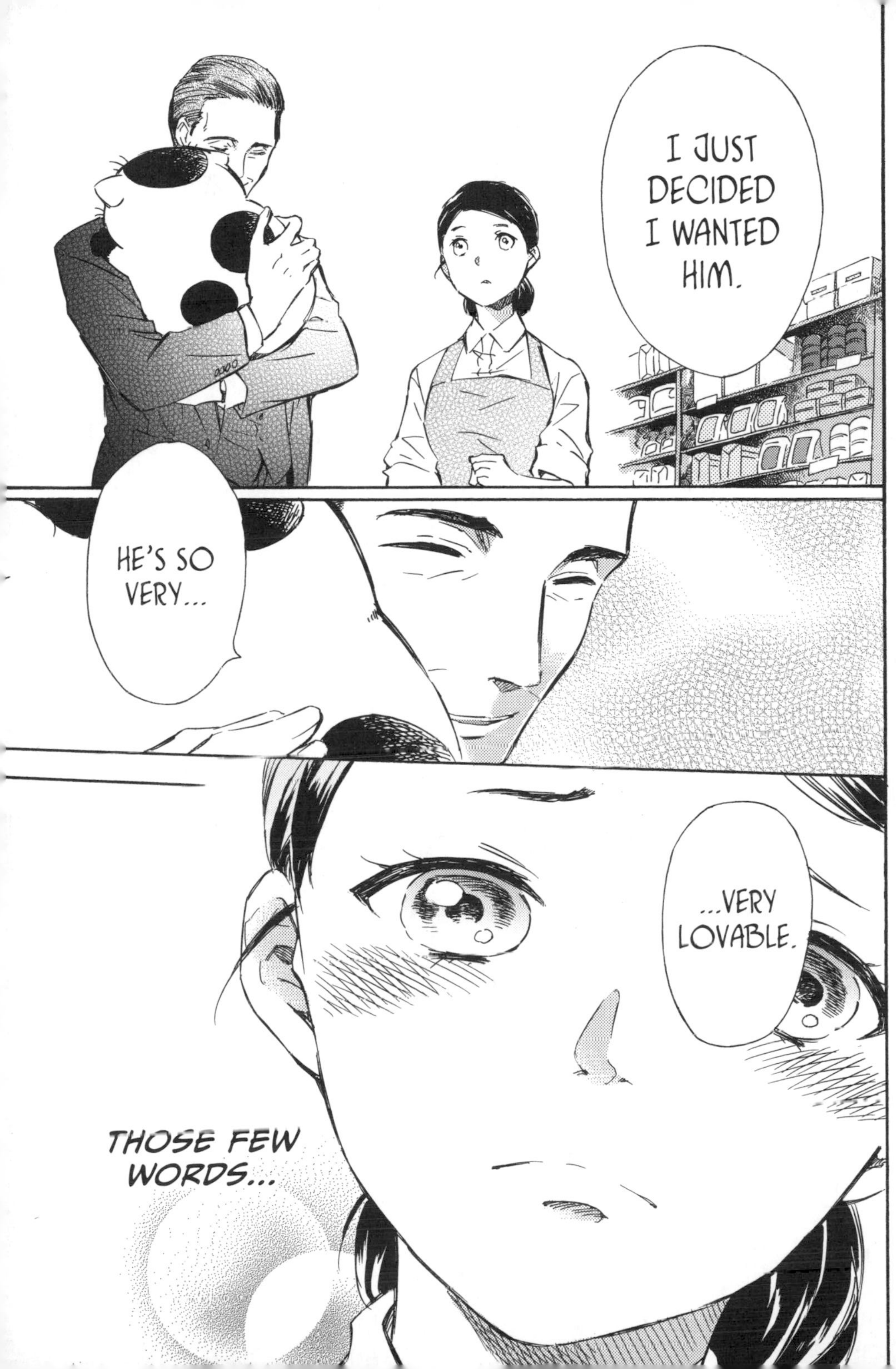
I JUST DECIDED I WANTED HIM.
HE'S SO VERY...
...VERY LOVABLE.
THOSE FEW WORDS...

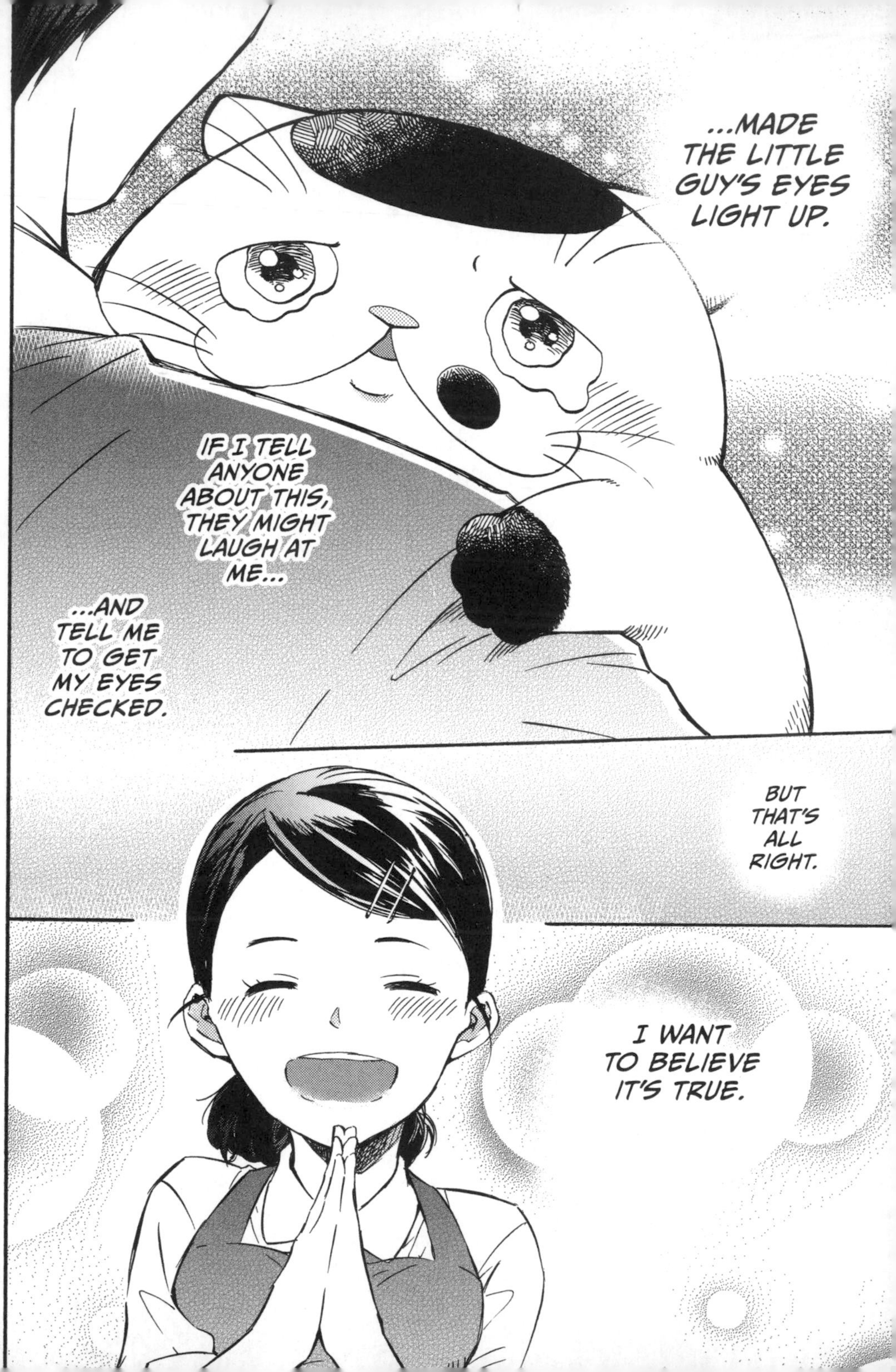
...MADE THE LITTLE GUY'S EYES LIGHT UP.
IF I TELL ANYONE ABOUT THIS, THEY MIGHT LAUGH AT ME...
...AND TELL ME TO GET MY EYES CHECKED.
BUT THAT'S ALL RIGHT.
I WANT TO BELIEVE IT'S TRUE.

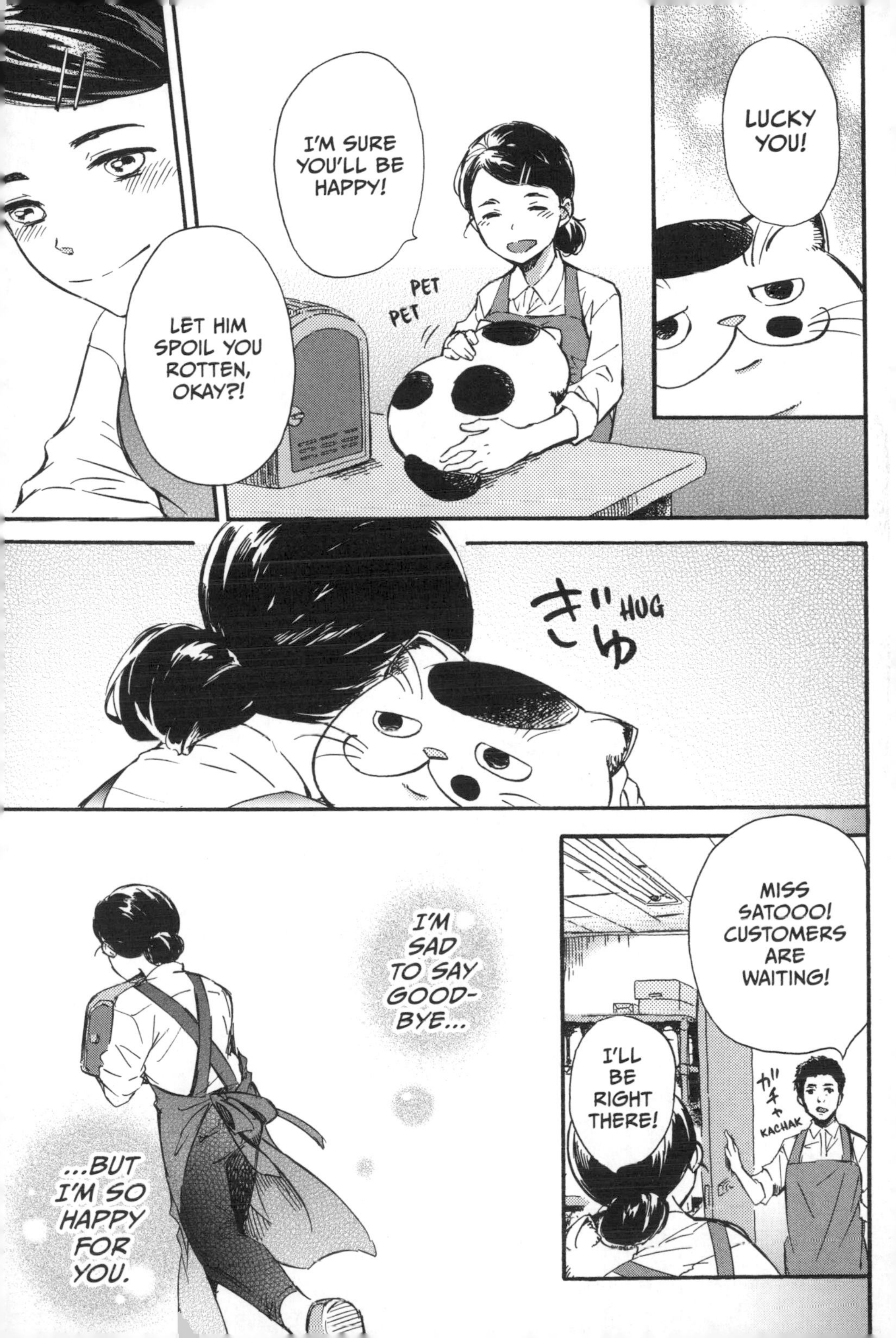
LUCKY YOU!
I'M SURE YOU'LL BE HAPPY!
PET PET
LET HIM SPOIL YOU ROTTEN, OKAY?!
ぎゅ HUG
MISS SATOOO! CUSTOMERS ARE WAITING!
ガチャ KACHAK
I'LL BE RIGHT THERE!
I'M SAD TO SAY GOOD-BYE...
...BUT I'M SO HAPPY FOR YOU.

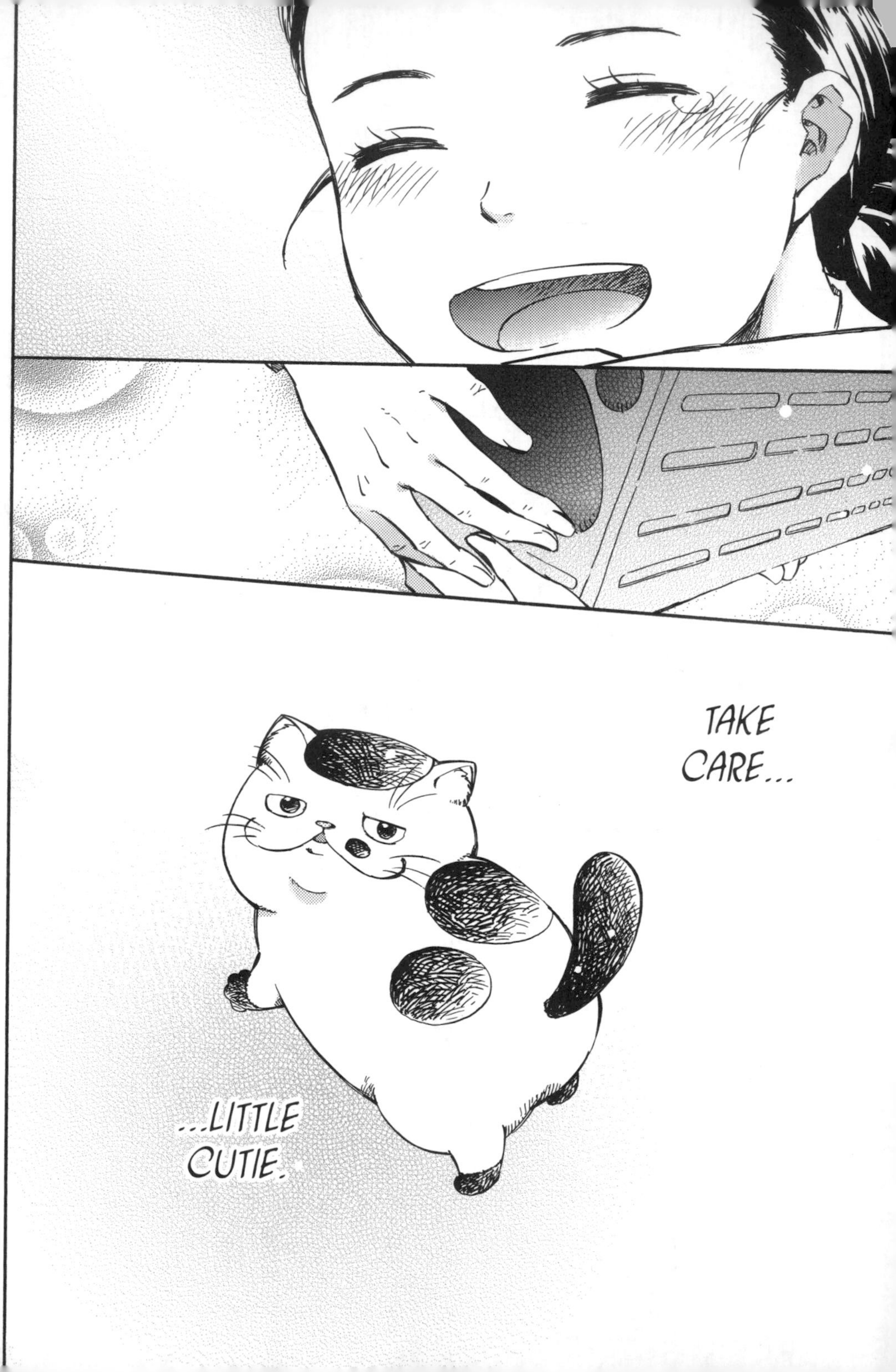
TAKE CARE...
...LITTLE CUTIE.

# With Fukumaru

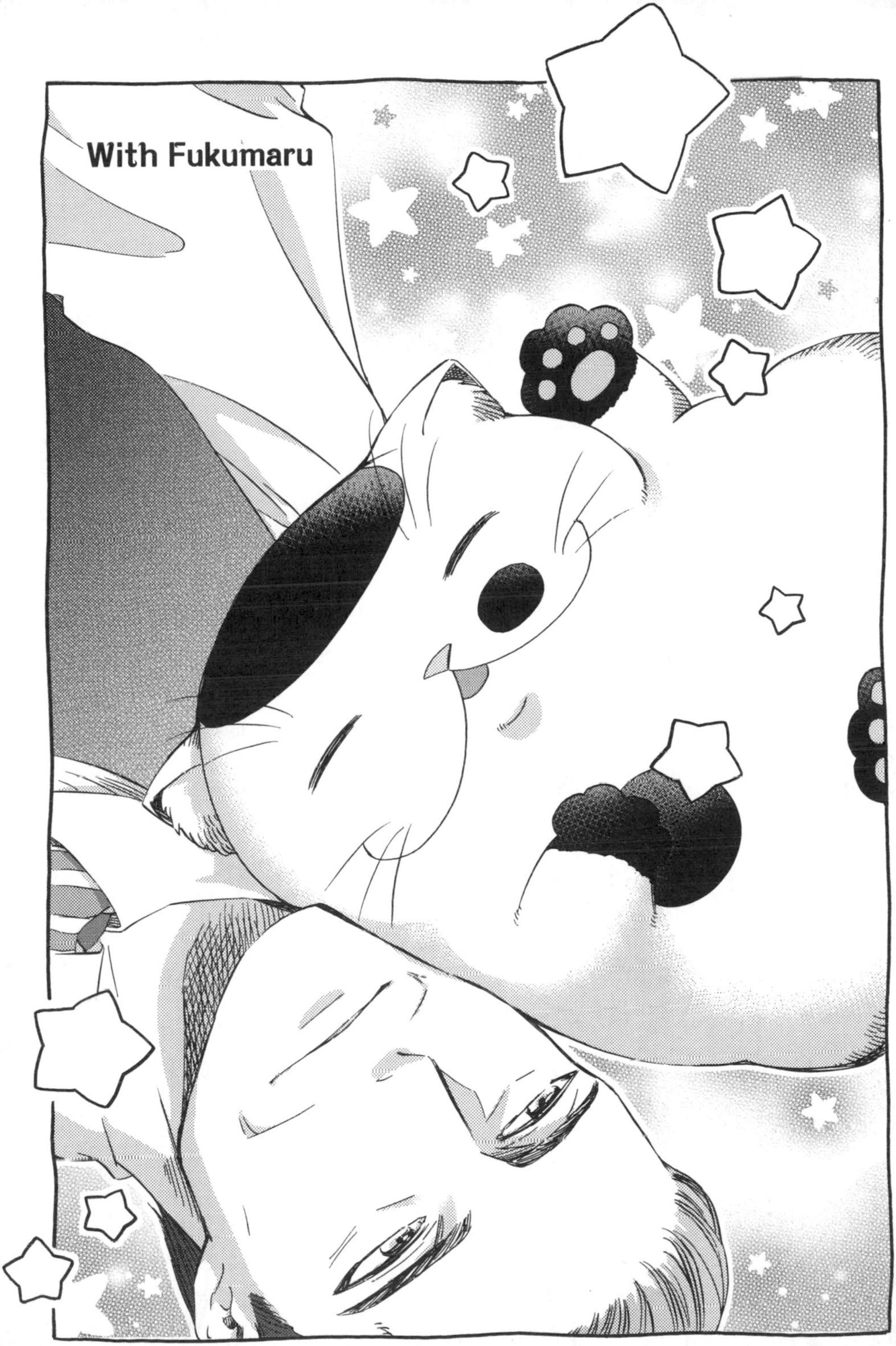

I THOUGHT THE FUNERAL CURTAIN RESEMBLED A KEYBOARD.
AS IF I WAS A MERE SPECTATOR LOOKING ON...
...THAT OBSERVATION POPPED INTO MY DAZED MIND.
THAT SIGHT...
...IS ALL I REMEMBER FROM THAT DAY.

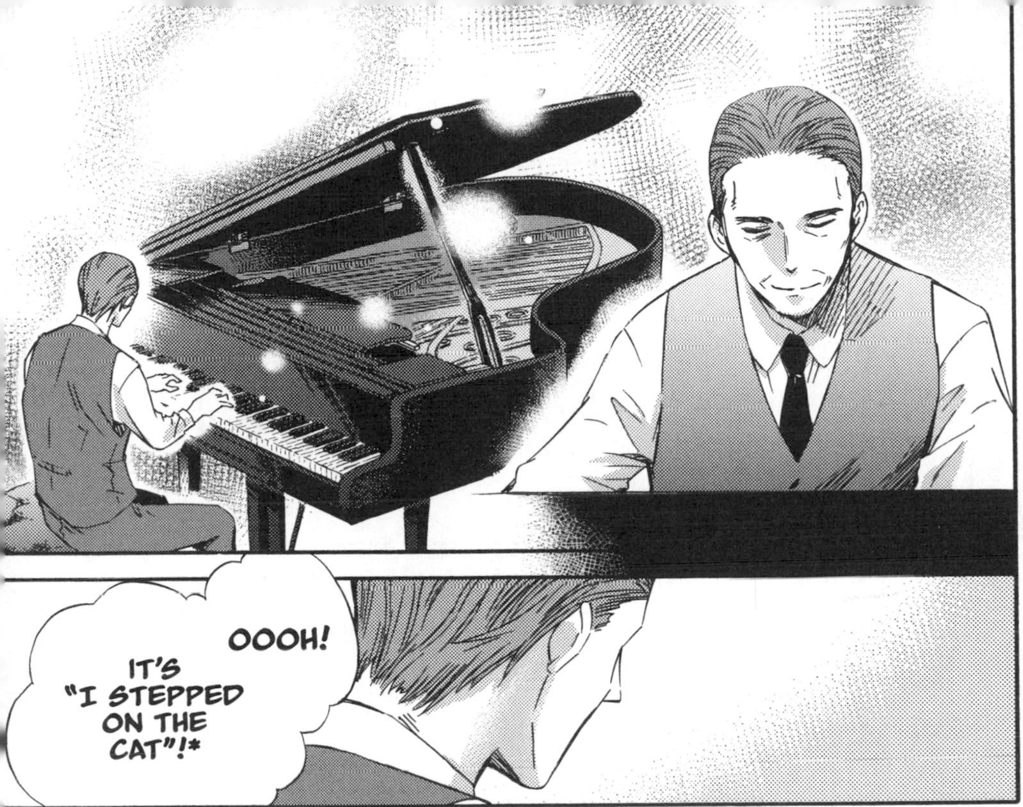
OOOH!
IT'S "I STEPPED ON THE CAT"!*
*THIS IS THE JAPANESE TITLE OF THE GERMAN PIANO PIECE "FLOHWALZER," OR "FLEA WALTZ."
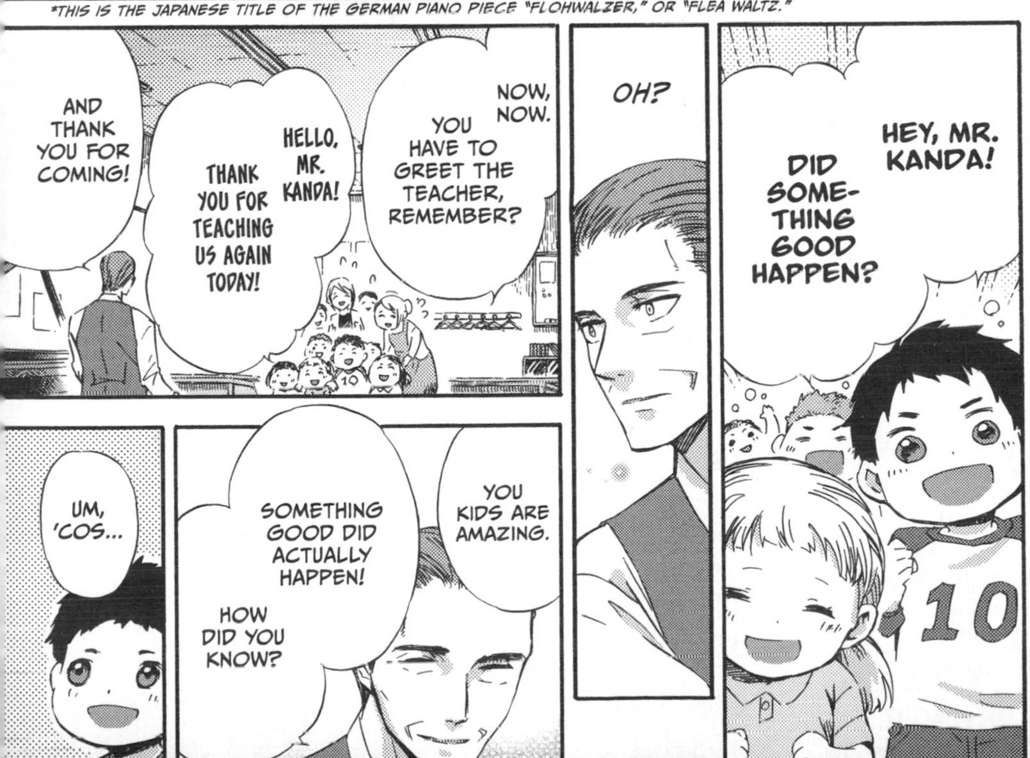
HEY, MR. KANDA!
DID SOMETHING GOOD HAPPEN?
OH?
NOW, NOW.
YOU HAVE TO GREET THE TEACHER, REMEMBER?
HELLO, MR. KANDA!
THANK YOU FOR TEACHING US AGAIN TODAY!
AND THANK YOU FOR COMING!
YOU KIDS ARE AMAZING.
SOMETHING GOOD DID ACTUALLY HAPPEN!
HOW DID YOU KNOW?
UM, 'COS...

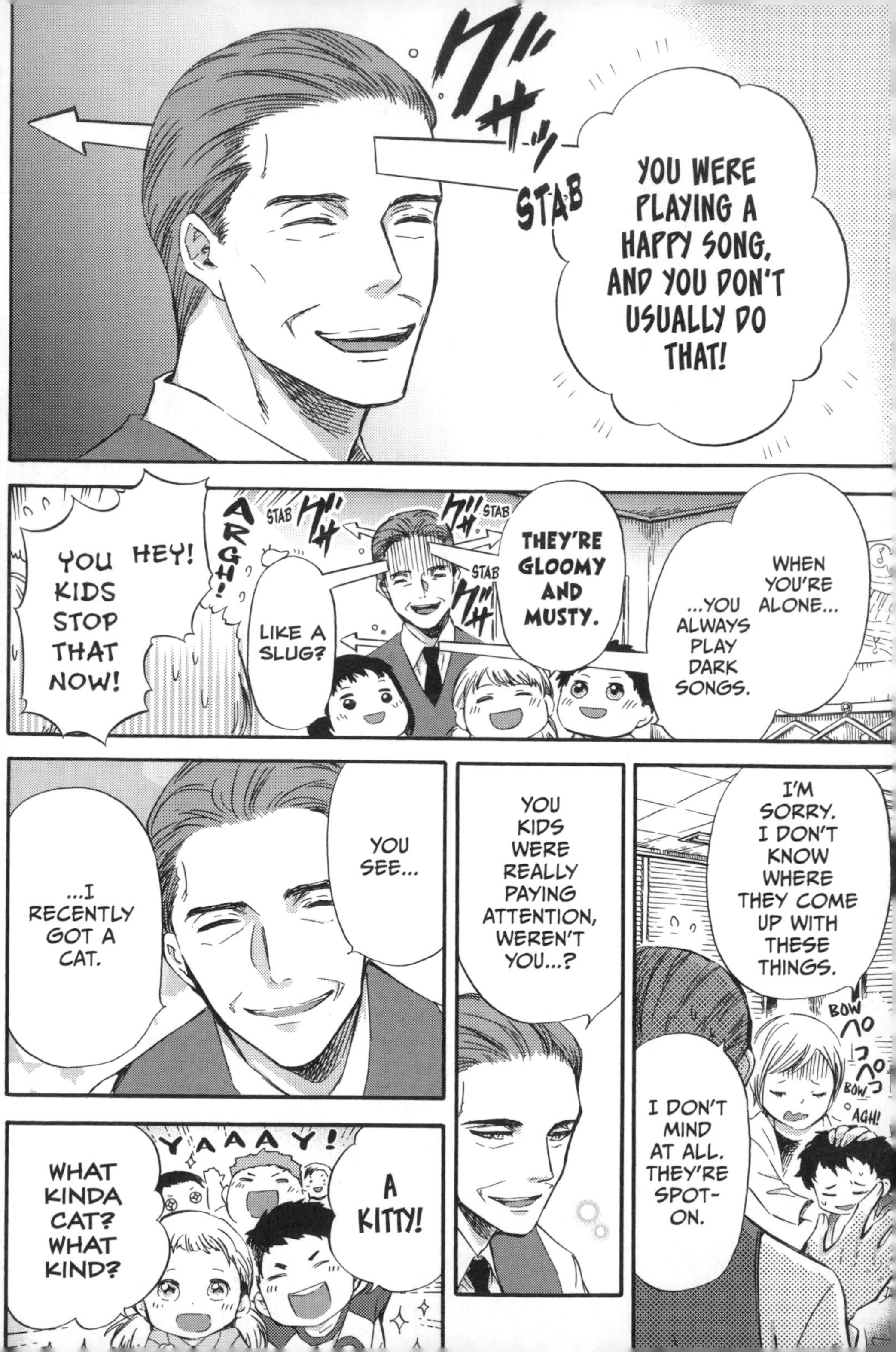
STAB
YOU WERE PLAYING A HAPPY SONG, AND YOU DON'T USUALLY DO THAT!
WHEN YOU'RE ALONE...
...YOU ALWAYS PLAY DARK SONGS.
THEY'RE GLOOMY AND MUSTY.
STAB
STAB
STAB
LIKE A SLUG?
ARGH!
HEY!
YOU KIDS STOP THAT NOW!
I'M SORRY. I DON'T KNOW WHERE THEY COME UP WITH THESE THINGS.
BOW
BOW
AGH!
I DON'T MIND AT ALL. THEY'RE SPOT-ON.
YOU KIDS WERE REALLY PAYING ATTENTION, WEREN'T YOU...?
YOU SEE...
...I RECENTLY GOT A CAT.
YAAAY!
A KITTY!
WHAT KINDA CAT? WHAT KIND?

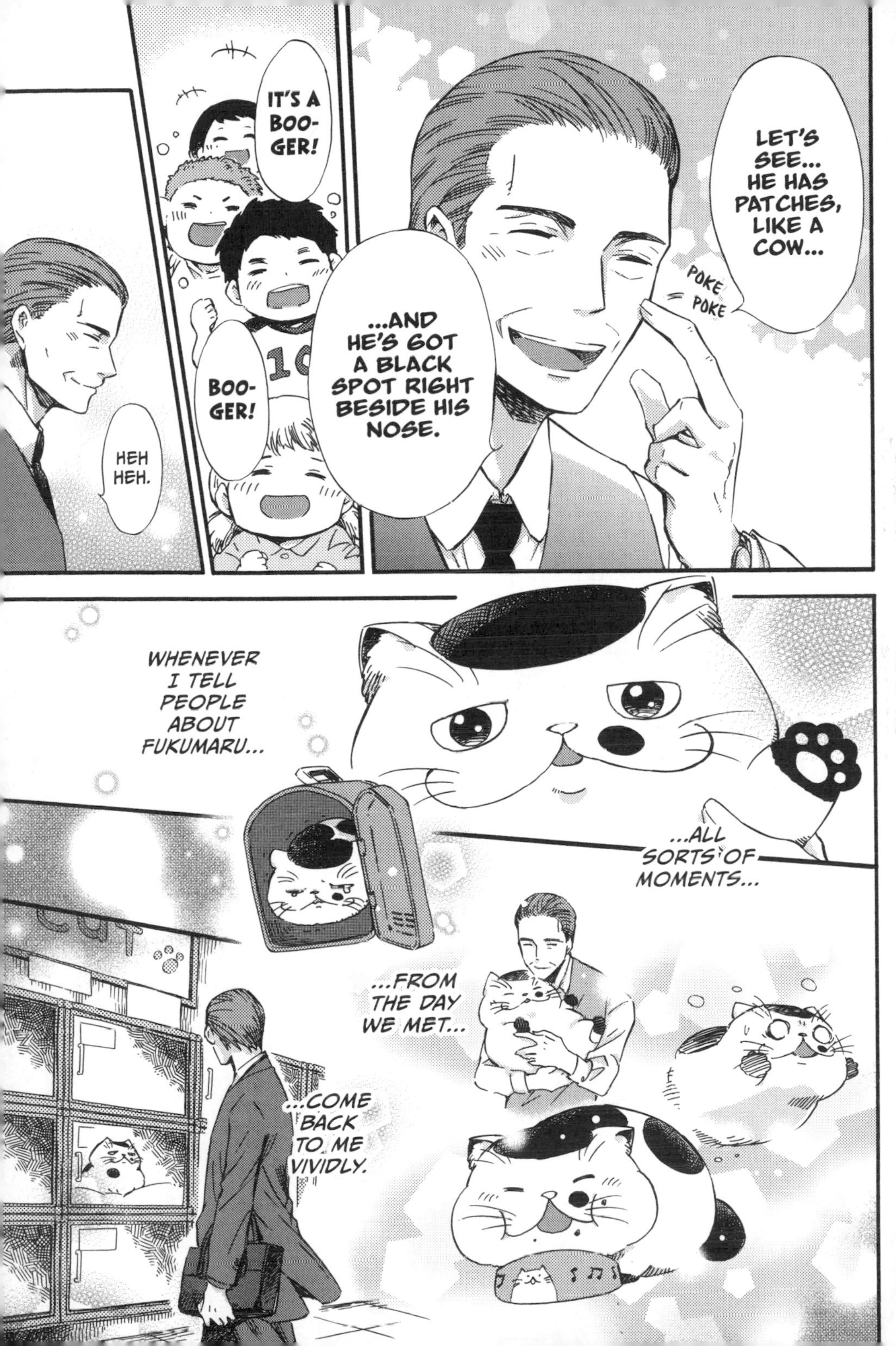
LET'S SEE... HE HAS PATCHES, LIKE A COW...
POKE POKE
...AND HE'S GOT A BLACK SPOT RIGHT BESIDE HIS NOSE.
IT'S A BOOGER!
BOO-GER!
HEH HEH.
WHENEVER I TELL PEOPLE ABOUT FUKUMARU...
...ALL SORTS OF MOMENTS...
...FROM THE DAY WE MET...
...COME BACK TO ME VIVIDLY.

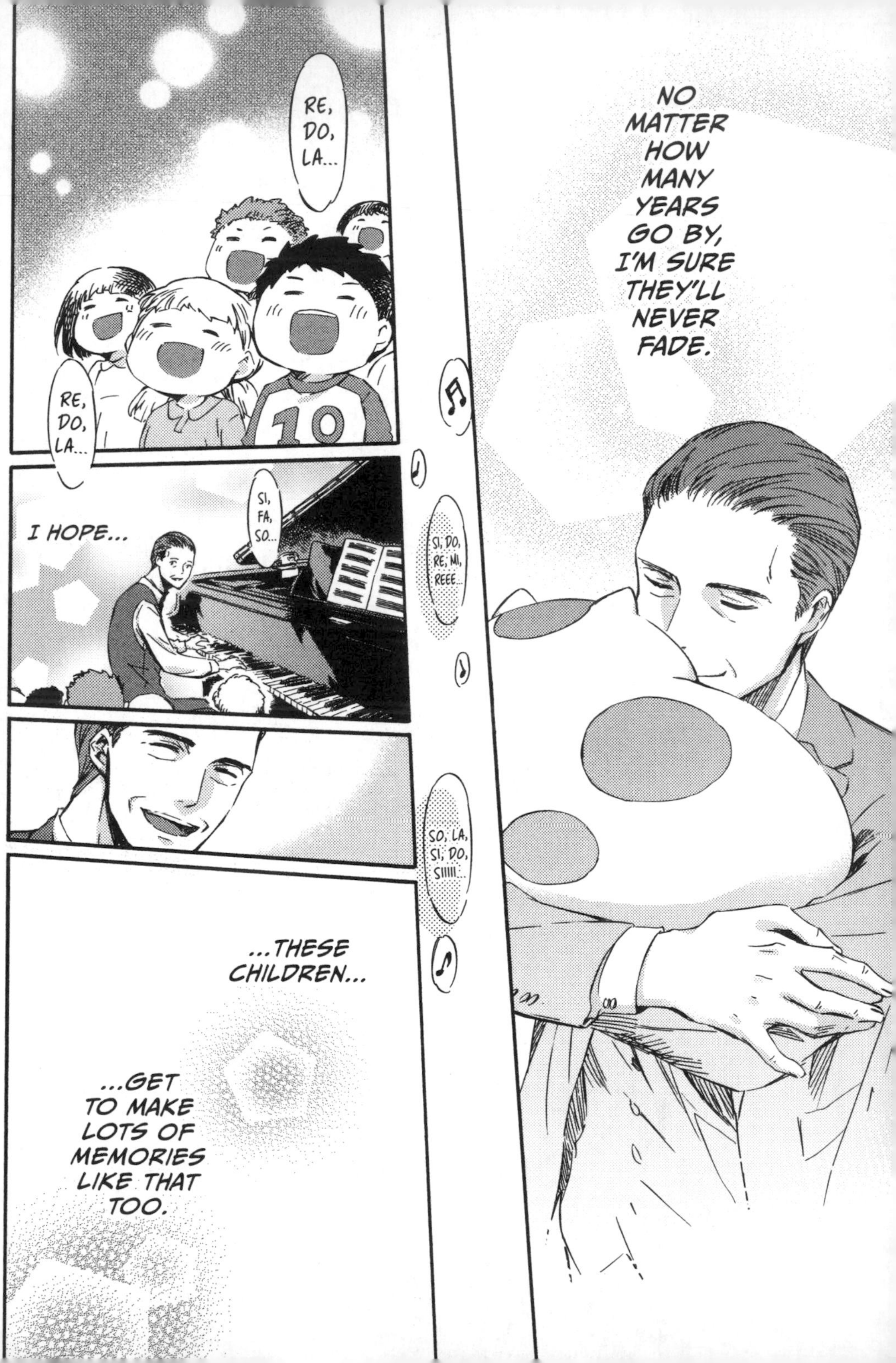
NO MATTER HOW MANY YEARS GO BY, I'M SURE THEY'LL NEVER FADE.
RE, DO, LA...
RE, DO, LA...
SI, DO, RE, MI, REEE...
SI, FA, SO...
I HOPE...
SO, LA, SI, DO, SIIIII...
...THESE CHILDREN...
...GET TO MAKE LOTS OF MEMORIES LIKE THAT TOO.

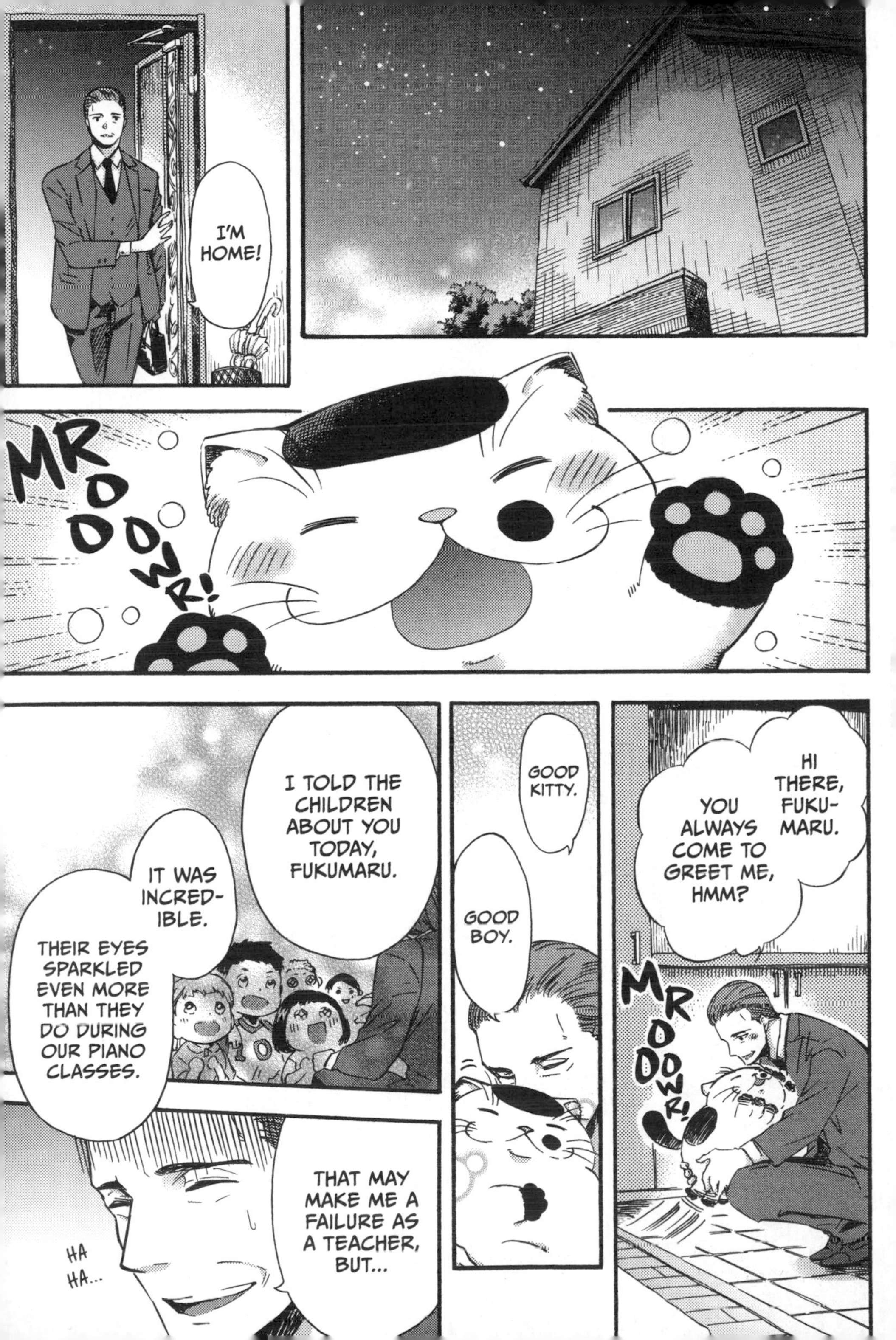
I'M HOME!
MROOOWR!
HI THERE, FUKUMARU.
YOU ALWAYS COME TO GREET ME, HMM?
MROOOWR!
GOOD KITTY.
GOOD BOY.
I TOLD THE CHILDREN ABOUT YOU TODAY, FUKUMARU.
IT WAS INCREDIBLE.
THEIR EYES SPARKLED EVEN MORE THAN THEY DO DURING OUR PIANO CLASSES.
THAT MAY MAKE ME A FAILURE AS A TEACHER, BUT...
HA HA...

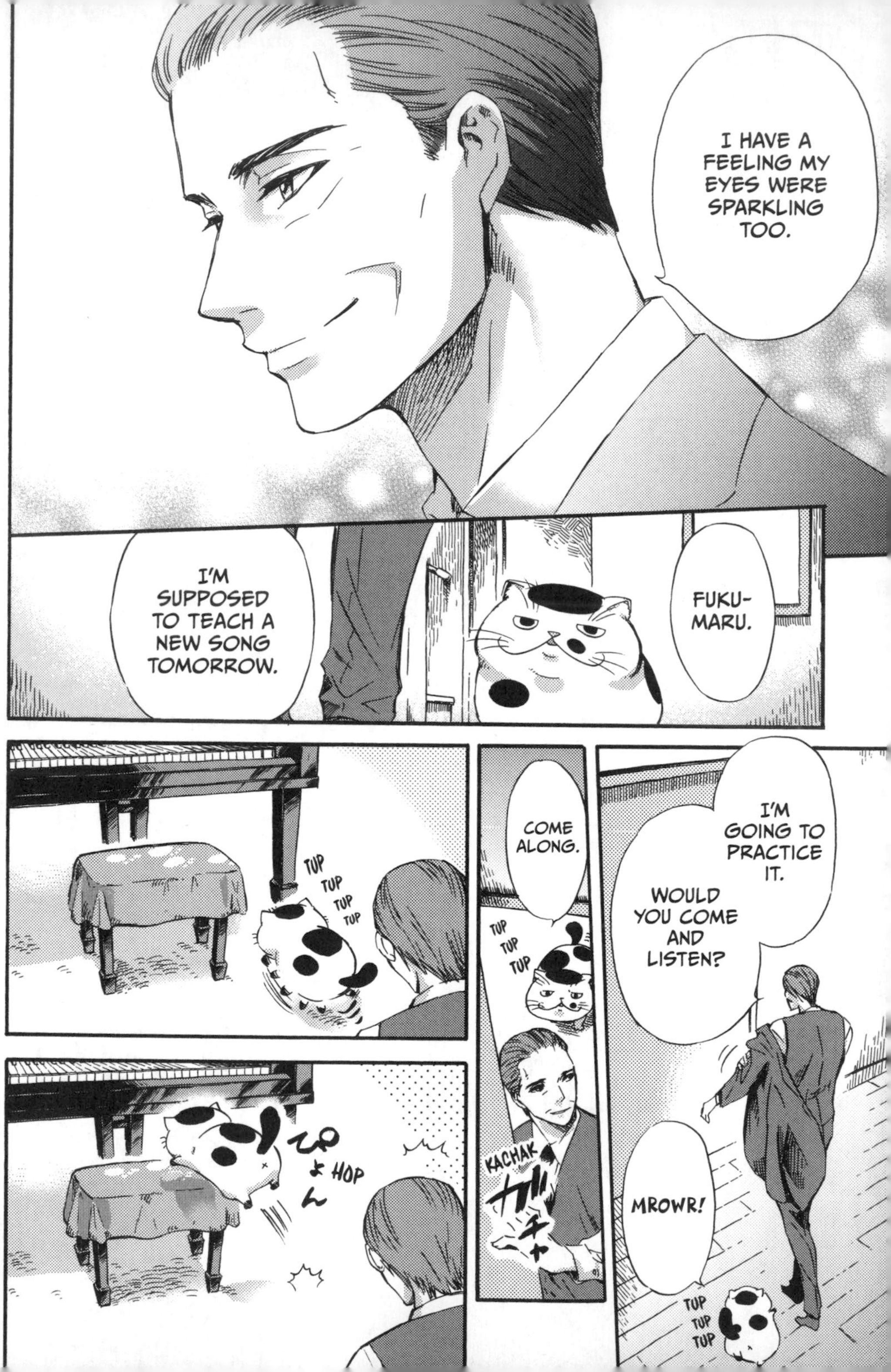
I HAVE A FEELING MY EYES WERE SPARKLING TOO.
FUKU-MARU.
I'M SUPPOSED TO TEACH A NEW SONG TOMORROW.
I'M GOING TO PRACTICE IT.
WOULD YOU COME AND LISTEN?
MROWR!
TUP TUP TUP
COME ALONG.
TUP TUP TUP
KACHAK
カチャ
TUP TUP TUP TUP
ぴょん
HOP

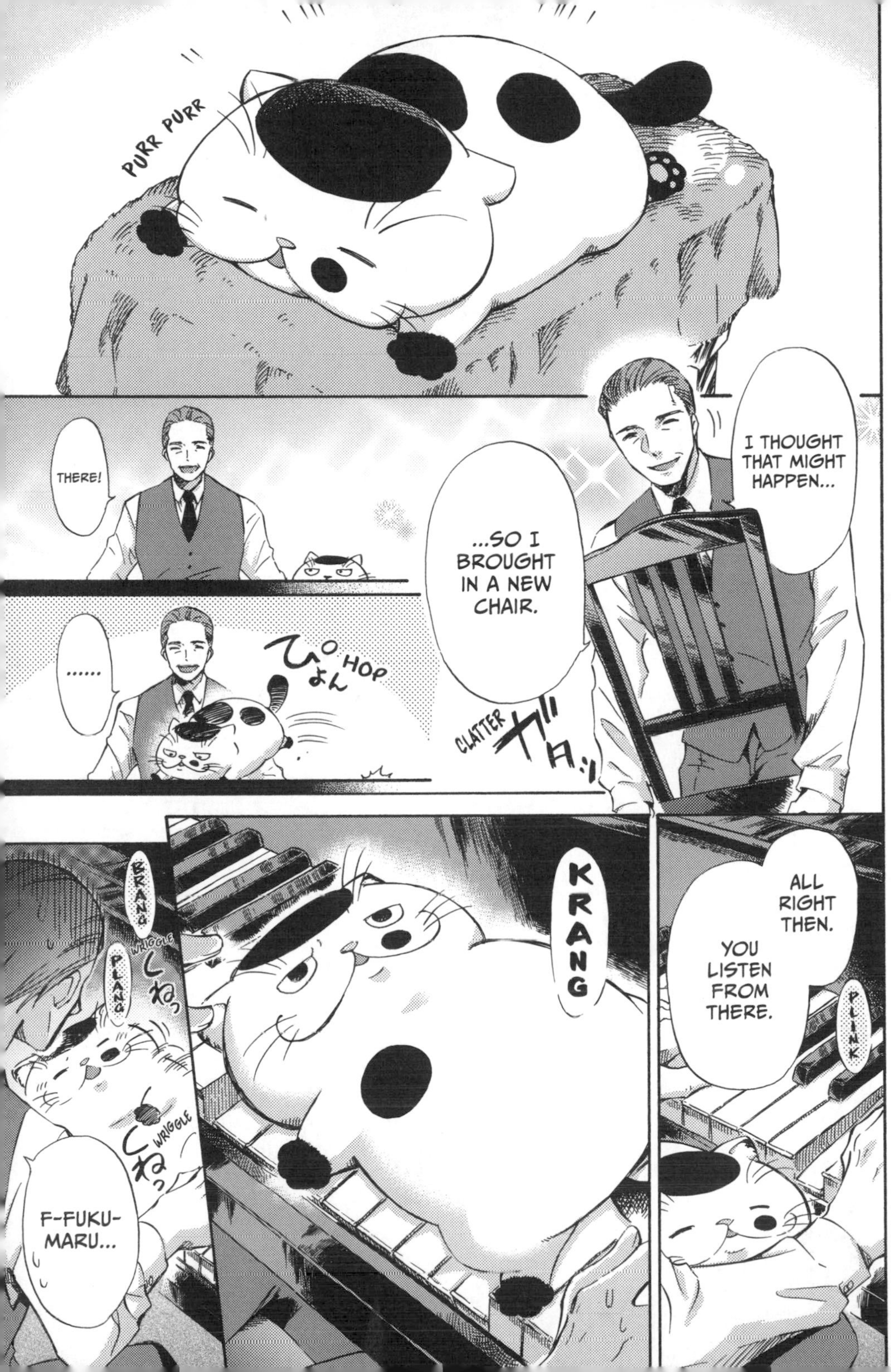
PURR PURR
I THOUGHT THAT MIGHT HAPPEN...
...SO I BROUGHT IN A NEW CHAIR.
CLATTER
ガタッ
THERE!
......
ぴょん HOP
ALL RIGHT THEN.
YOU LISTEN FROM THERE.
PLINK
KRANG
BRANG
PLANG
くねっ WRIGGLE
くねっ WRIGGLE
F-FUKU-MARU...

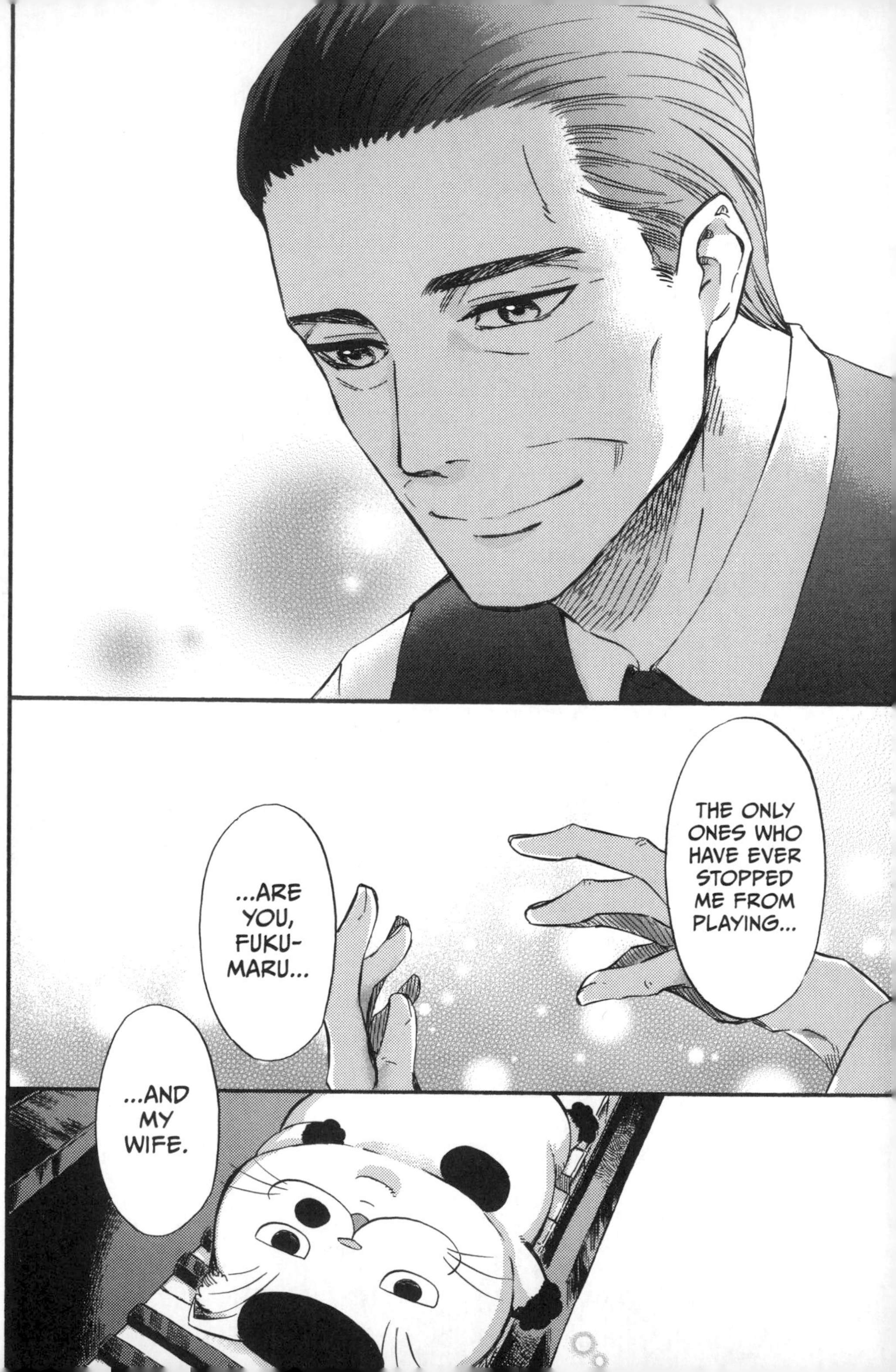
THE ONLY ONES WHO HAVE EVER STOPPED ME FROM PLAYING...
...ARE YOU, FUKU-MARU...
...AND MY WIFE.

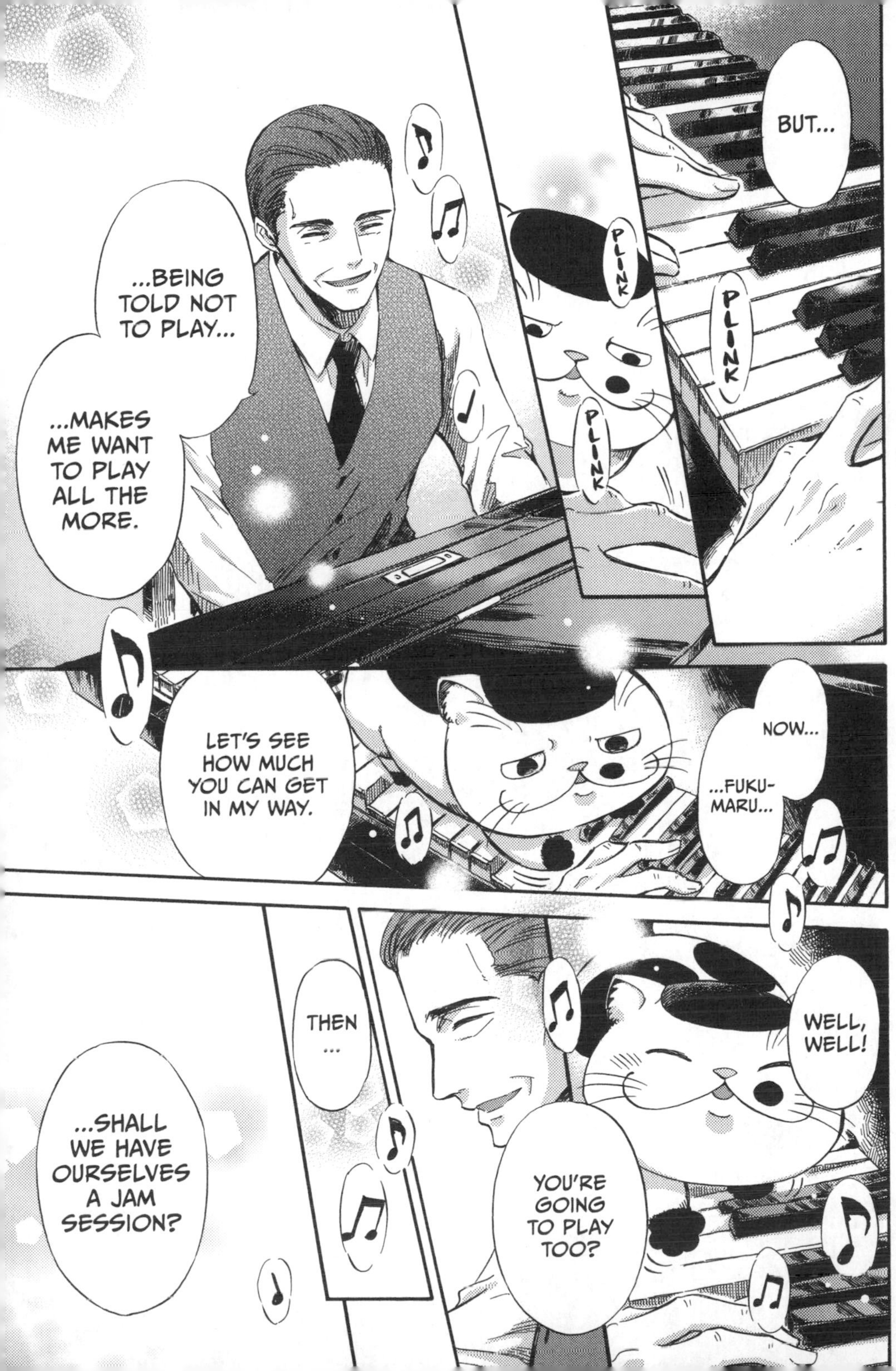
BUT...
PLINK
PLINK
PLINK
...BEING TOLD NOT TO PLAY...
...MAKES ME WANT TO PLAY ALL THE MORE.
NOW...
...FUKU-MARU...
LET'S SEE HOW MUCH YOU CAN GET IN MY WAY.
WELL, WELL!
YOU'RE GOING TO PLAY TOO?
THEN ...
...SHALL WE HAVE OURSELVES A JAM SESSION?

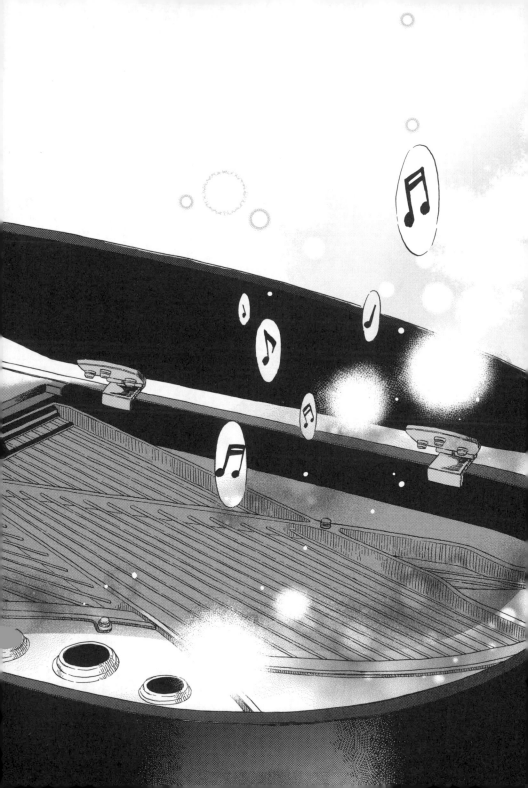

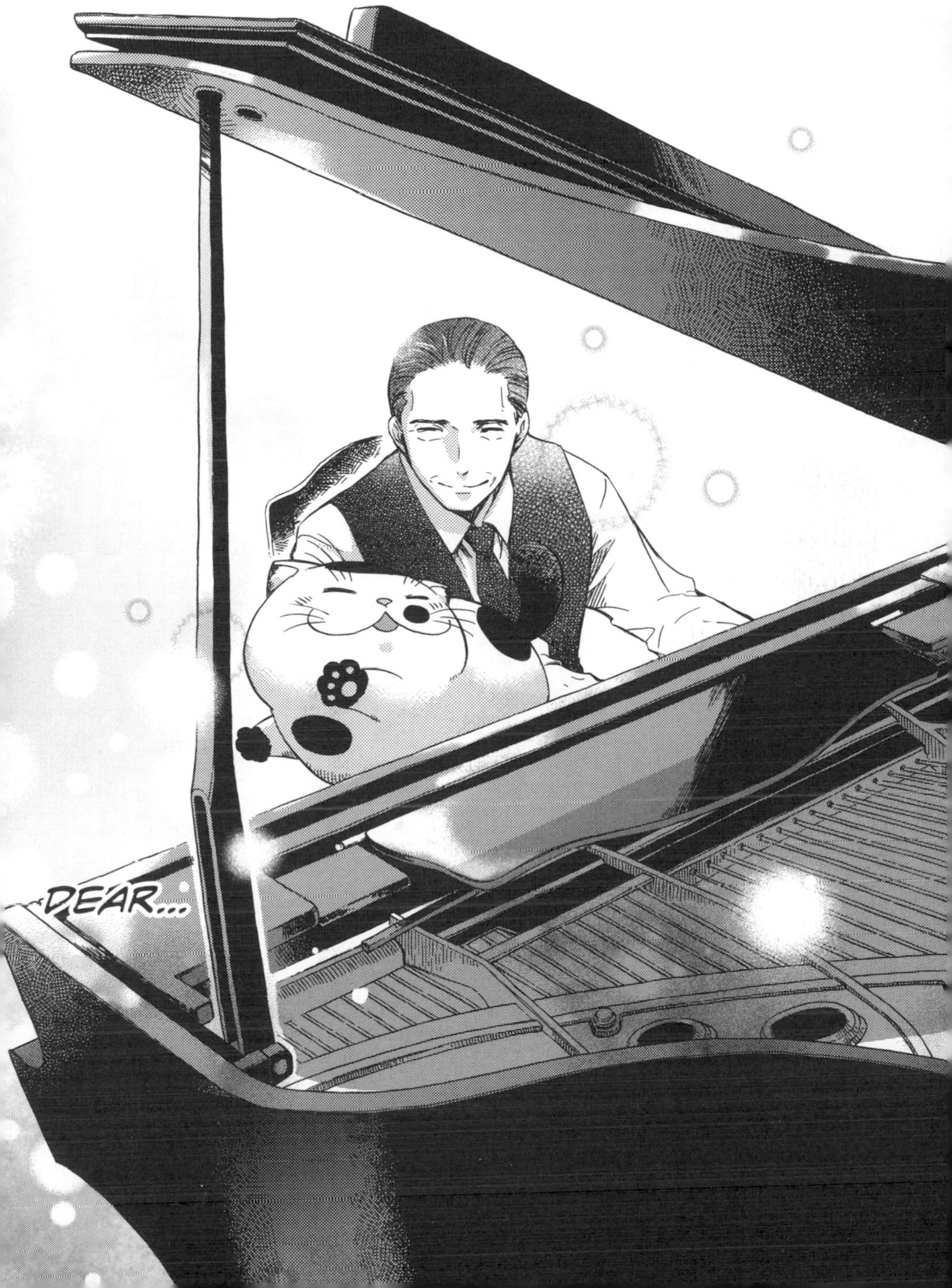
DEAR...

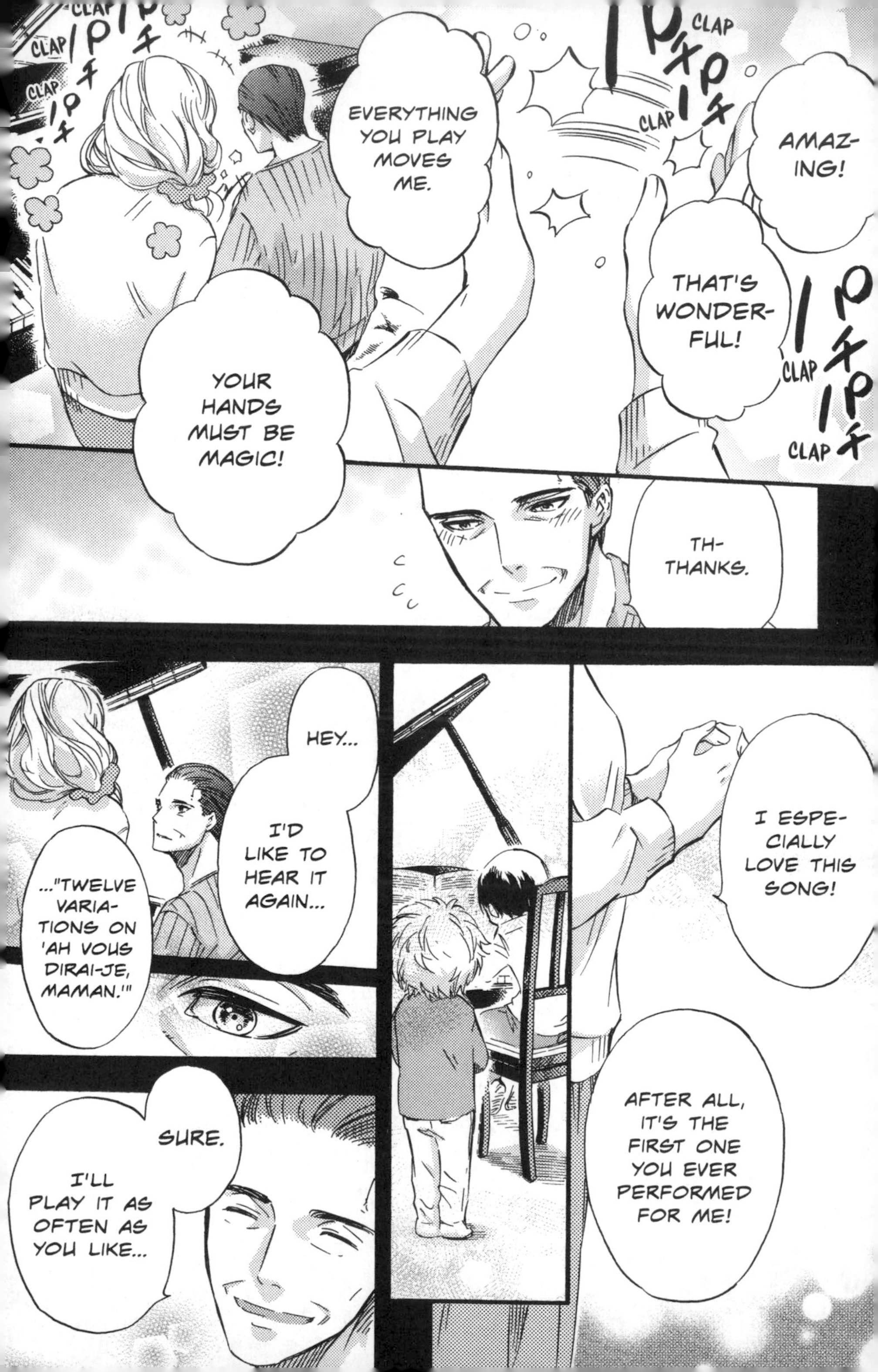
CLAP
CLAP
AMAZ-ING!
THAT'S WONDER-FUL!
CLAP
CLAP
EVERYTHING YOU PLAY MOVES ME.
CLAP
CLAP
CLAP
YOUR HANDS MUST BE MAGIC!
TH-THANKS.
I ESPE-CIALLY LOVE THIS SONG!
AFTER ALL, IT'S THE FIRST ONE YOU EVER PERFORMED FOR ME!
HEY...
I'D LIKE TO HEAR IT AGAIN...
..."TWELVE VARIA-TIONS ON 'AH VOUS DIRAI-JE, MAMAN.'"
SURE.
I'LL PLAY IT AS OFTEN AS YOU LIKE...

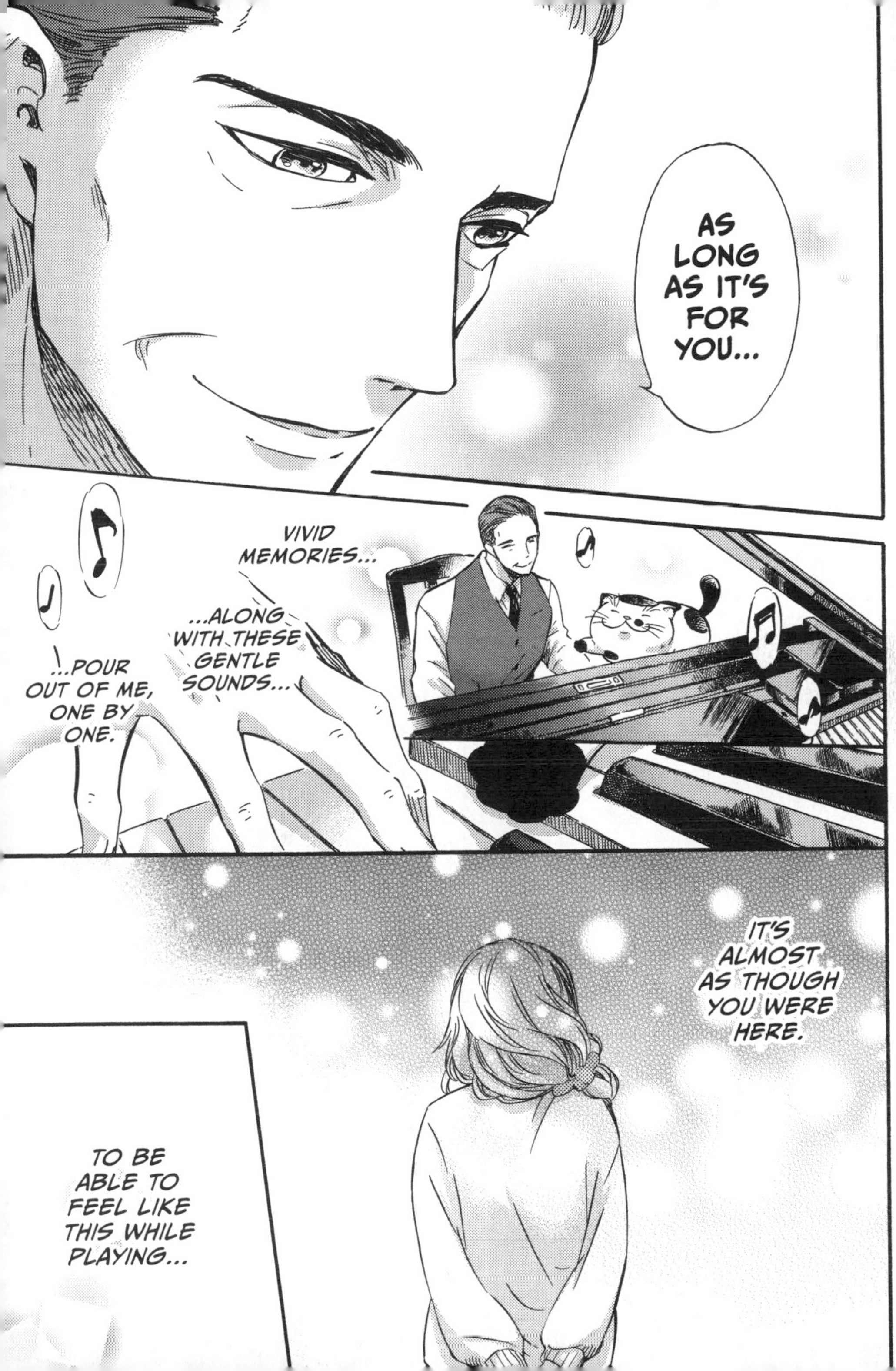
AS LONG AS IT'S FOR YOU...
VIVID MEMORIES...
...ALONG WITH THESE GENTLE SOUNDS...
...POUR OUT OF ME, ONE BY ONE.
IT'S ALMOST AS THOUGH YOU WERE HERE.
TO BE ABLE TO FEEL LIKE THIS WHILE PLAYING...

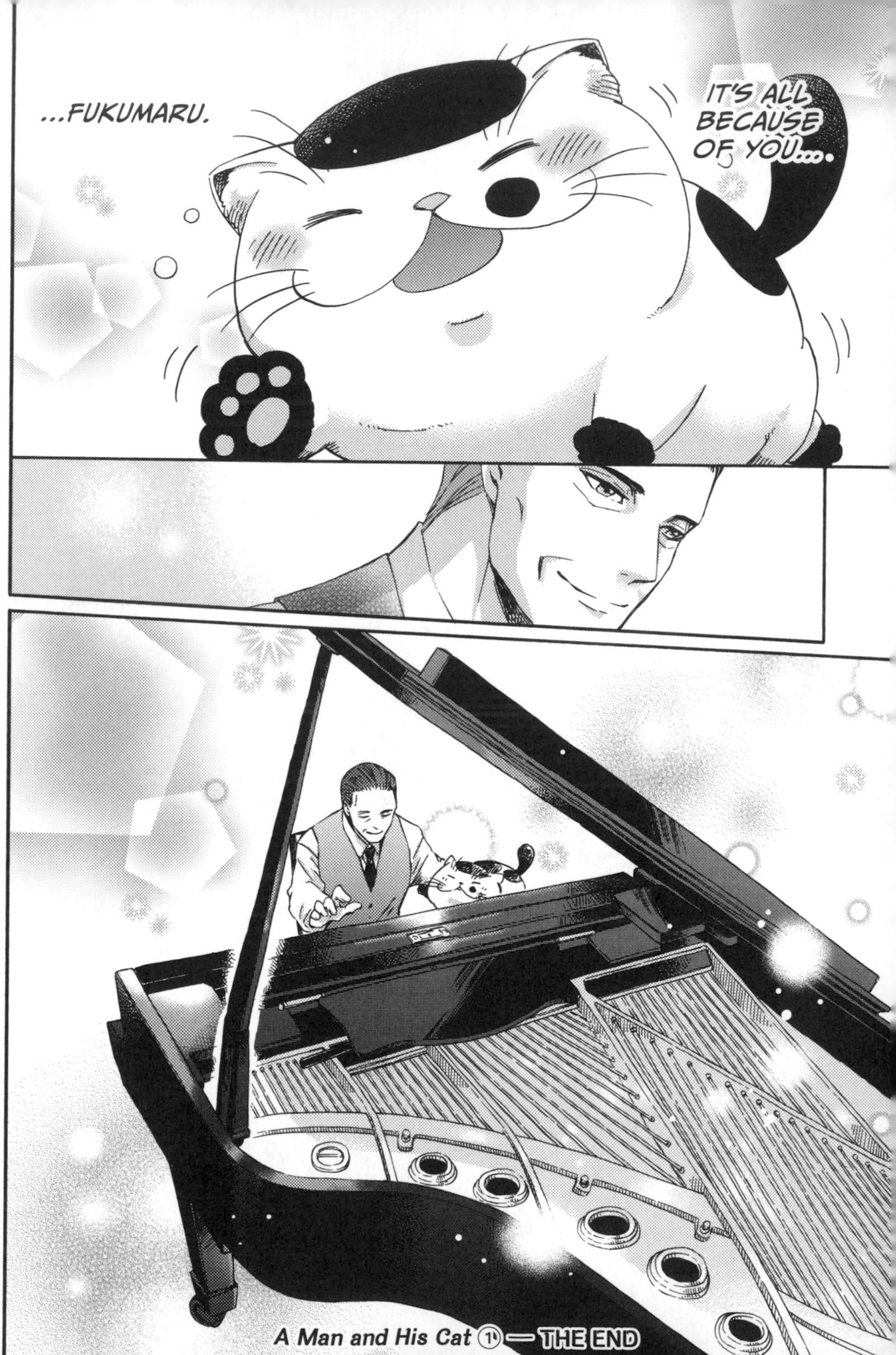
IT'S ALL BECAUSE OF YOU...
...FUKUMARU.
A Man and His Cat ① — THE END

AFTERWORD TIME

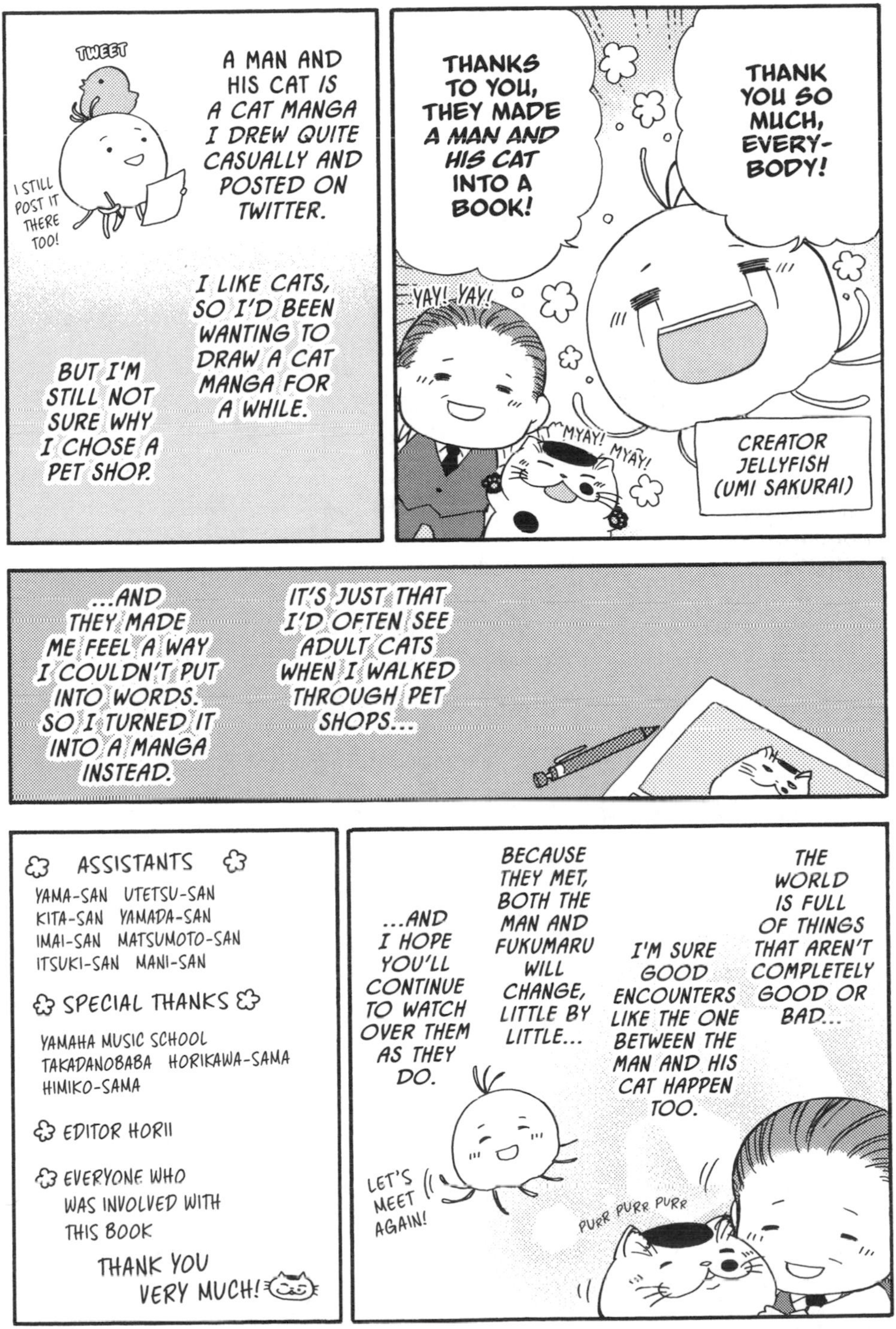
THANK YOU SO MUCH, EVERYBODY!
THANKS TO YOU, THEY MADE A MAN AND HIS CAT INTO A BOOK!
YAY! YAY!
MYAY! MYAY!
CREATOR JELLYFISH (UMI SAKURAI)
A MAN AND HIS CAT IS A CAT MANGA I DREW QUITE CASUALLY AND POSTED ON TWITTER.
TWEET
I STILL POST IT THERE TOO!
I LIKE CATS, SO I'D BEEN WANTING TO DRAW A CAT MANGA FOR A WHILE.
BUT I'M STILL NOT SURE WHY I CHOSE A PET SHOP.
IT'S JUST THAT I'D OFTEN SEE ADULT CATS WHEN I WALKED THROUGH PET SHOPS...
...AND THEY MADE ME FEEL A WAY I COULDN'T PUT INTO WORDS. SO I TURNED IT INTO A MANGA INSTEAD.
THE WORLD IS FULL OF THINGS THAT AREN'T COMPLETELY GOOD OR BAD...
I'M SURE GOOD ENCOUNTERS LIKE THE ONE BETWEEN THE MAN AND HIS CAT HAPPEN TOO.
BECAUSE THEY MET, BOTH THE MAN AND FUKUMARU WILL CHANGE, LITTLE BY LITTLE...
...AND I HOPE YOU'LL CONTINUE TO WATCH OVER THEM AS THEY DO.
LET'S MEET AGAIN!
PURR PURR PURR
ASSISTANTS
YAMA-SAN UTETSU-SAN
KITA-SAN YAMADA-SAN
IMAI-SAN MATSUMOTO-SAN
ITSUKI-SAN MANI-SAN
SPECIAL THANKS
YAMAHA MUSIC SCHOOL
TAKADANOBABA HORIKAWA-SAMA
HIMIKO-SAMA
EDITOR HORII
EVERYONE WHO WAS INVOLVED WITH THIS BOOK
THANK YOU VERY MUCH!

# A Man & His Cat

1

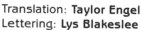

**Story and Art by**
**Umi Sakurai**

Translation: **Taylor Engel**
Lettering: **Lys Blakeslee**
Cover Design: **Tania Biswas, Patrick Crotty**
Editor: **Tania Biswas**

A MAN AND HIS CAT Volume 1
© 2018 Umi Sakurai/SQUARE ENIX CO., LTD.
First published in Japan in 2018 by SQUARE ENIX CO., LTD.
English translation rights arranged with SQUARE ENIX CO., LTD.
and SQUARE ENIX, INC.
English translation © 2020 by SQUARE ENIX CO., LTD.

ISBN: 978-1-64609-026-6

Library of Congress Cataloging-in-Publication data
is on file with the publisher.

Printed in the U.S.A.

10 9 8 7 6 5 4

**SQUARE ENIX**
MANGA & BOOKS

www.square-enix-books.com